CHARTERS OF
SHAFTESBURY ABBEY

ANGLO-SAXON CHARTERS

I CHARTERS OF ROCHESTER, edited by A. Campbell (1973)

II CHARTERS OF BURTON ABBEY, edited by P. H. Sawyer (1979)

III CHARTERS OF SHERBORNE, edited by M. A. O'Donovan (1988)

IV CHARTERS OF ST AUGUSTINE'S ABBEY, CANTERBURY, AND MINSTER-IN-THANET, edited by S. E. Kelly (1995)

V CHARTERS OF SHAFTESBURY ABBEY, edited by S. E. Kelly (1996)

SUPPLEMENTARY VOLUMES

I FACSIMILES OF ANGLO-SAXON CHARTERS, edited by Simon Keynes (1991)

ANGLO-SAXON CHARTERS · V

CHARTERS OF SHAFTESBURY ABBEY

EDITED BY

S. E. KELLY

Published for THE BRITISH ACADEMY
by OXFORD UNIVERSITY PRESS

Oxford University Press, Walton Street, Oxford OX2 6DP

Oxford New York
Athens Auckland Bangkok Bombay
Calcutta Cape Town Dar es Salaam Delhi
Florence Hong Kong Istanbul Karachi
Kuala Lumpur Madras Madrid Melbourne
Mexico City Nairobi Paris Singapore
Taipei Tokyo Toronto

and associated companies in
Berlin Ibadan

British Library Cataloguing in Publication Data
Data available
ISBN 0-19-726151-5

Typeset by Latimer Trend & Company Ltd.
Printed in Great Britain
on acid-free paper by
The Cromwell Press Limited
Melksham, Wiltshire

To My Parents

FOREWORD

The joint committee of the British Academy and the Royal Historical Society, set up in 1966 to organize the publication of a new critical edition of the entire corpus of Anglo-Saxon charters, is pleased to announce a significant step on the road towards the realisation of the project. Coming so shortly after the appearance of the *Charters of St Augustine's Canterbury*, this volume is a witness to the new momentum achieved as a result of the generous support of the Newton Trust and of the Leverhulme Trust. They have made it possible for the committee to employ Dr Susan Kelly full-time in editing charters, a very practical help when the increasing pressures upon academics make large-scale interdisciplinary research projects ever more difficult to achieve.

The nunnery of Shaftesbury was founded by King Alfred for his daughter as abbess. Continuing links with the English royal dynasty ensured that the house prospered for much of the Anglo-Saxon period. The thirty charters edited here are therefore evidence both of an important chapter in English women's religious history and of the formation of a major lordship in northern Dorset and southern Wiltshire. They are preserved in a single fifteenth-century cartulary, written apparently by a Shaftesbury nun who was working from a very defective exemplar. Scholars will therefore welcome an edition which clarifies many of the copyists' corruptions, provides both authoritative texts and essential critical guidance and locates the boundaries of the estates in terms of modern maps. I am proud to introduce another volume in which Dr Kelly, with assistance from several members of the committee, is setting new standards in the editing of Anglo-Saxon charters.

NICHOLAS BROOKS

CONTENTS

ACKNOWLEDGEMENTS   xi

INTRODUCTION
  1. The History of the Abbey   xiii
  2. The Archive and its History   xvi
  3. The Manuscript   xviii
  4. The Authenticity of the Charters   xx
  5. The Estates of Shaftesbury Abbey   xxii

ABBREVIATIONS   xxviii

LIST OF CHARTERS   xxxv

CONCORDANCE   xxxvii

NOTE ON THE METHOD OF EDITING   xxxviii

THE CHARTERS   3

INDEXES
  1. Index of Personal Names   129
  2. Index of Place-Names   133
  3. Words and Personal Names used in Boundary Marks   136
  4. Latin Glossary   146
  5. Diplomatic Index   149

LIST OF PLATES

(between page 122 and page 123)

I. BL Harley 61, 1ʳ (**29**)
II. BL Harley 61, 15ʳ (**9**)

ACKNOWLEDGEMENTS

My heartfelt thanks are due to the members of the Anglo-Saxon Charters committee who have helped me in the preparation of this edition. I am particularly grateful to Margaret Gelling, Simon Keynes and Patrick Wormald for their comments, and I should also like to thank Michael Lapidge, Eric Stanley, Richard Sharpe, Neil Wright, Peter Kitson and Laurence Keen. During the period that I have been working on this volume I have received generous funding from the British Academy, the Leverhulme Trust and the Newton Trust, for which I am most grateful. I also owe a great deal to the support of the fellows of St Catherine's College in Oxford and Newnham College in Cambridge.

The photographs of BL Harley 61 are reproduced by permission of the British Library.

INTRODUCTION

I. THE HISTORY OF THE ABBEY

The nunnery at Shaftesbury was founded and endowed by King Alfred, who appointed his daughter, Æthelgifu, as its first abbess and devoted to it one-sixteenth of his royal revenues.[1] The exact date of the foundation is unknown, but the community was certainly in existence by 893, when Asser was writing.[2] Shaftesbury was one of the new Alfredian burhs, established, perhaps in 880, on a highly defensible upland site.[3] The nunnery was built 'by the eastern gate' of the burh (*iuxta orientalem portam*), according to Asser; it is not clear whether it stood inside or outside the fortifications.[4] Shaftesbury prospered during the tenth and eleventh centuries, so that by the time of the Conquest it was one of the wealthier houses in the kingdom.[5] It continued to have strong links with the West Saxon dynasty. Eadgifu, the third wife of King Edward the Elder, may have become a lay associate of Shaftesbury after her husband's death (see **17**). Her daughter-in-law, Ælfgifu, the first wife of King Eadmund, was buried there, probably in 944, and

---

[1] *Asser*, pp. 85, 88; Keynes and Lapidge, *Alfred the Great*, pp. 105, 107.

[2] Keynes and Lapidge, *Alfred the Great*, p. 272 n. 237; E. Murphy, 'The Nunnery that Alfred Built at Shaftesbury', *The Hatcher Review*, iv. 38 (Autumn, 1994), pp. 40–53. Suggestions that there may have been an earlier minster on the site (see, for example, *RCHM Dorset*, iv. 58; Keen 1984, p. 213) are based largely on the fact of the preservation of **1** in the Shaftesbury archive; but this charter is likely to have come into the abbey's possession in the tenth century, as an earlier title-deed for its estate at Fontmell Magna (see pp. 9–10; and Murphy 1992, pp. 28–9). Alfred's foundation is sometimes attributed to 871 × 877, the apparent date of his 'foundation charter' (**7**); but this is a late forgery.

[3] The date depends on an inscription seen and described by William of Malmesbury: see *RCHM Dorset*, iv. 57.

[4] It is generally assumed that the burh defences lay to the west of the abbey, and thus excluded it: see C.A.R. Radford, 'The Later Pre-Conquest Boroughs and their Defences', *Medieval Archaeology* xiv (1970), pp. 83–103 at 87; *RCHM Dorset*, iv. 56, 137. For the alternative view, see Keen 1984, pp. 232–3, with map on p. 223; Murphy 1992, pp. 29–30. See also the comments of K.J. Penn, *Historic Towns in Dorset*, Dorset Natural History and Archaeological Society, Monograph ser. i (Dorchester, 1980), p. 89.

[5] D. Knowles, *The Monastic Order in England*, 2nd edn (Cambridge, 1963), p. 702 (note that the thirteenth entry on the list, just above Shaftesbury, should read Wilton; Shaftesbury was thus the second wealthiest nunnery in England).

later venerated as a saint; Ælfgifu's mother, Wynflæd, also appears to have had some connection with the community.[6] The alleged remains of King Edward the Martyr were removed from Wareham to Shaftesbury in 979 by Ealdorman Ælfhere, and seem rapidly to have become the focus of a royally-sponsored cult; on 20 June 1001 Edward's relics were ceremonially translated into the abbey on the command of King Æthelred.[7] Later in the same year the king gave to the nuns the minster of Bradford-on-Avon with its appurtenant lands, specifically to provide a refuge for them and their relics at a time of increased Viking activity on the south coast.[8] Since Bradford is strategically far less defensible than Shaftesbury, this grant may indicate that the abbey and perhaps the burh had become temporarily uninhabitable at this time; Æthelred's charter clearly assumes that the community would take up residence at Bradford, specifying that, in the event of a return to Shaftesbury, some of the nuns were to remain at Bradford to ensure continuity of worship (see further discussion on pp. 119–20). There is no other evidence apart from this charter that communal life at Shaftesbury was disrupted in the early eleventh century; if the nuns did move temporarily, they would appear to have been back in residence soon afterwards. Æthelred's decree in 1008 that his brother's feastday was to be celebrated throughout England is likely to have increased Shaftesbury's reputation.[9] The abbey church was originally dedicated to the Virgin, but by the time of the Conquest Shaftesbury was becoming more closely associated with St Edward; in Domesday Book it is referred to in different

---

[6] For Ælfgifu's cult, see Ridyard, *Royal Saints*, pp. 170, 175n; for the date of her death, see *Æthelweard*, p. 54; and for Wynflæd see **13** and **26**. Ælfgifu bequeathed an estate at Tisbury to the community (see **28**). William of Malmesbury (*GP*, pp. 186–7) appears to have thought that Ælfgifu was the founder of Shaftesbury, and this has been seen as evidence for a refoundation of the minster (see *VCH Dorset* II, p. 73); but it is likely that William simply confused Ælfgifu with Alfred's daughter, Æthelgifu. The two charters of King Æthelstan (**8**, **9**) show that the Shaftesbury community was flourishing in the 930s.

[7] *Edward King and Martyr*, ed. C.E. Fell, Leeds Texts and Monographs, n.s. (Leeds, 1971), pp. 12–13.

[8] For Æthelred's role in fostering Edward's cult, see Keynes, *Diplomas*, pp. 169–71; Ridyard, *Royal Saints*, pp. 154–75. It may have been Æthelred who granted to Shaftesbury the land at Corfe which was supposed to have been the site of Edward's murder (see **16**).

[9] V Æthelred 16; Liebermann, *Gesetze*, i. 240–1. It has been suggested that this clause may be an interpolation: see K. Sisam, 'The Relationship of Æthelred's Codes V and VI', *Studies in the History of Old English Literature* (Oxford, 1953), pp. 280–1; P. Wormald, 'Æthelred the Lawmaker', *Ethelred the Unready: Papers from the Millenary Conference*, ed. D. Hill, British Archaeological Reports, Brit. ser. 59 (1978), pp. 47–80 at 53–4. For an alternative view, see *Councils and Synods with other Documents relating to the English Church I: A.D. 871–1204*, ed. D. Whitelock, M. Brett and C.N.L. Brooke, 2 parts (Oxford, 1981), i. 353–4.

places as both St Mary's and St Edward's.[10] The will of Æthelred's son
Æthelstan includes a bequest of six pounds to the 'Holy Cross and St
Edward at Shaftesbury'.[11] Under the Confessor, the community may have
run into difficulties; Earl Harold was apparently able to seize several
Shaftesbury estates, and to retain them despite a writ of King Edward
ordering their restoration.[12]

Shaftesbury Abbey seems to have weathered the Conquest reasonably
well, with minimal loss of property. A list of donations made to the nunnery
between c. 1086 and c. 1121 by the families of girls entering the house
shows that Shaftesbury was already enjoying the support of local Norman
landowners.[13] Shaftesbury Abbey became immensely (indeed notoriously)
wealthy in the later medieval period.[14] It was surrendered to the king's
commissioners by the last abbess, Elizabeth Zouche, on 23 March 1539.
Many of the abbey's estates passed between 1540 and 1547 into the possession
of Sir Thomas Arundell, who played an active role in the suppression of
the monasteries; when he was attainted in 1552 the property passed to the
Crown and later to the Earls of Pembroke.[15] Part of the Shaftesbury
muniments seem to have remained in the hands of the Arundell family until
the Civil War (see below p. xvii).

[10] In the surveys of Dorset and Wiltshire, the nunnery's lands appear under the heading *Ecclesia
sancte Marie Sceptesberiensis* (GDB 67v, 78v); since the nunnery itself and the greater part of
the endowment were located in this area, this was probably still the official dedication of the
community. Records of Shaftesbury's two outlying manors in Somerset and Sussex are by
contrast headed *Terra sancti Edwardi* (GDB 17v, 91r), no doubt reflecting popular association
of Shaftesbury with the cult of the murdered king.

[11] S 1503, probably A.D. 1014. There is no other reference to a dedication to the Holy Cross
(see Whitelock, *Wills*, pp. 169–70). Shaftesbury is also mentioned as a beneficiary in earlier
wills of Wynflæd (S 1539) and Æthelmær (S 1498); from the latter the community received a
gift of two pounds, from the former an estate at Chinnock in Somerset. For Wynflæd and
S 1539, see below, p. xvi n. 17 and p. 56.

[12] S 1868 and GDB 78v (see pp. xxiii, 27, 104).

[13] BL Harley 61, 54r; *Mon. Angl.* (rev. edn), ii. 482–3. See discussion by K. Cooke, 'Donors
and Daughters: Shaftesbury Abbey's Benefactors, Endowments and Nuns c. 1086–1130',
Anglo-Norman Studies xii (1989), pp. 29–45. See also Cooke 1982 for a more detailed discussion
of the abbey's immediate post-Conquest history.

[14] For general discussion of the history of the abbey in the later medieval period, see *VCH
Dorset* II, pp. 73–9; L. Sydenham, *Shaftesbury and its Abbey* (Lingfield, 1959). The history of
the fabric and the fate of the abbey site are considered in *RCHM Dorset*, iv. 57–61, which
includes references to excavation reports.

[15] See J.H. Bettey, 'The Suppression of the Benedictine Nunnery of Shaftesbury in 1539', *The
Hatcher Review*, iv. 34 (Autumn, 1992), pp. 3–11. For Arundell's career, see Hoare, *Wilts.*, Vale
of Noddre and Hundred of Dunworth, pp. 176–7; *Dictionary of National Biography*, i. 620. He
acquired the manors of Tisbury, Dinton, Cheselbourne, Donhead, Compton Abbas, Melbury
Abbas, Fontmell Magna, Sixpenny Handley, Encombe (in Kingston) and Barton in Shaftesbury.

2. THE ARCHIVE AND ITS HISTORY

The pre-Conquest archive of Shaftesbury Abbey consists of thirty documents. Twenty-nine of these are royal diplomas granting or confirming land; the exception is **1**, which was drawn up in its present form by a bishop of Winchester on the occasion of a dispute-settlement, and consists of an edited version of a seventh-century land-charter with an explanatory addition by the bishop. The six earliest charters in the archive date from the period before the nunnery was founded and would appear to be the title-deeds of estates which later came into the community's possession. King Alfred's foundation charter (**7**) is a late forgery. Twenty-one of the remaining twenty-three diplomas are from the tenth century; the latest document in the archive is a charter of Cnut dated 1019. There are only two vernacular texts; the forged foundation charter (**7**), which survives in both Latin and English versions, and **6**, which appears to be based on a free translation of **5**, perhaps made before the Conquest. Originally the archive would have included a wide range of vernacular documents, in the form of sealed royal writs, wills, leases and miscellaneous agreements, but these did not survive the winnowing of later copyists.[16] A lost writ of the Confessor restoring to the abbey land at Cheselbourne, Stour and Melcombe Horsey is mentioned in Domesday Book.[17]

All the documents here edited are preserved only as copies in BL Harley 61, a Shaftesbury cartulary of the early fifteenth century (see further, pp. xviii–xx). The texts of the pre-Conquest charters in this manuscript appear to have been copied from an earlier cartulary or cartularies, and not from the originals. BL Egerton 3135, produced at around the same time as BL Harley 61, is a register containing deeds relating to property which was given to Shaftesbury at the turn of the fourteenth century for the endowment of a chantry; none of the documents is pre-Conquest. In 1784 BL Egerton 3135 belonged to a member of the Wild family of Marchwood, Hampshire;

---

[16] For the types of vernacular documentation produced to supplement Anglo-Saxon royal diplomas, see Kelly 1990, pp. 46–51.

[17] S 1868; GDB 78v (see pp. 27, 104). There is a possibility that S 1539 was at one stage part of the Shaftesbury archive. It is the will of a woman named Wynflæd, who appears to have been a lay associate of a religious community, most probably Shaftesbury (see p. 56; and Whitelock, *Wills*, p. 109). S 1539 survives as a single-sheet original (BL Cotton Ch. viii. 3); its provenance is unknown, and there is no significant endorsement which might link it with Shaftesbury or any other centre. S 1539 will be edited in a separate volume, with other charters of uncertain provenance.

it was purchased by Sir Thomas Phillipps from Payne the bookseller in 1845.[18]

Sir Thomas Arundell appears to have come into possession of part of the Shaftesbury muniments when he acquired the abbey site and many of the Shaftesbury manors in the 1540s. At least some portion of these muniments remained in the possession of his family after his execution in 1552. The first sixty-four folios of BL Add. 29976 are a series of miscellaneous letters and memoranda relating to the manor of Kingston on the Isle of Purbeck, apparently dating from just before the Civil War.[19] This collection includes two pages of notes taken from manuscripts in Wardour Castle, the seat of the Arundell family.[20] Fol. 13 has the heading: 'In the Register booke of the Abbey of Shafton (which?) remaines at th' evidence house in Warder Castle'. Fol. 17 is headed: 'From a kalendar of all the Liberties and Evidences of the Abbey of Shafton made 1500, and in the third year of Margery Twyneyne of Shafton'. At its foot comes an even more intriguing note: 'The Lord Arundell of Wardour hath the legier booke and divers auntiente writings'. It is a great pity that the notes themselves are very brief and of absolutely no pre-Conquest interest. However, it can be deduced that the register mentioned on fol. 13 must have been very substantial, since the notes are said to have been taken from fol. 482. The calendar of muniments made at the instance of Margery Twynyho was evidently the original of which BL Egerton 3098 is a contemporary copy, apparently made for the abbess's brother; the latter remained in the possession of the Twynyho family until this century.[21] The calendar does not mention any pre-Conquest charters. The Shaftesbury muniments at Wardour Castle have since disappeared, and may have been destroyed or dispersed during the sack of Wardour Castle in 1643 or shortly afterwards.[22]

The 'Legier Book' belonging to Lord Arundell may have come into the

[18] Davis, *Cartularies*, no. 886; A.J. Collins, 'A Cartulary of Shaftesbury Abbey', *British Museum Quarterly* x (1936), pp. 66–8.

[19] *Catalogue of Additions to the Manuscripts in the British Museum 1876–1881* (London, 1882), p. 13.

[20] Wardour Manor and Castle were bought by Sir Thomas Arundell in 1547. They passed to the Crown after his attainder in 1552, but were regained by his son, Matthew, in 1570. Matthew's son, Thomas, was created first Baron Wardour in 1605. See *VCH Wilts.* XIII, pp. 208, 221.

[21] Davis, *Cartularies*, no. 887; H.I. Bell, 'A Register of Deeds from Shaftesbury Abbey', *British Museum Quarterly* viii (1934), pp. 18–20. There are long extracts in Hutchins, *Dorset*, ii. 511–22.

[22] There were no Shaftesbury documents in the Wardour archive when it was inspected in the nineteenth century: *Second Report of the Royal Commission on Historical Manuscripts* (London, 1874), Appendix, pp. 33–6. For the siege and capture of Wardour, see *Dictionary of National Biography*, i. 615; *VCH Wilts.* XIII, p. 222.

hands of a certain John Lowe in the middle of the seventeenth century. In a series of notes on the location of medieval cartularies, the antiquary John Aubrey observes: 'Sir John Lowe of Shaftesbury hath the Legier Book – a copie of it – of the Abbey of Shaftesbury'.[23] In 1680 it was in the hands of Sir John's trustees, but it had vanished by the later eighteenth century.[24] In a list of cartularies published in 1834–5, there is reference to a Shaftesbury cartulary owned by one Thomas Schutz of Shotover in Oxfordshire;[25] this may have been the same manuscript that had belonged to John Lowe, but nothing more is known of it.

3. THE MANUSCRIPT

The pre-Conquest charters from Shaftesbury are preserved in a single manuscript, BL Harley 61, a cartulary written in the abbey in the early fifteenth century. It later formed part of the library of Sir Simonds D'Ewes, who provided the present foliation.[26] The initials 'W. P.' on fol. 1 are those of a previous owner (s. xvi/xvii); the same mark is found on BL Harley MSS 42 (from Syon Abbey), 59 (from Waltham Abbey), 261 (from Rochester) and 636 (from Christ Church, Canterbury), all of which passed to D'Ewes and then into the Harley collection.[27] The first eight documents were transcribed by Dodsworth in 1642–3 (Bodleian, Dodsworth 38, 1r-8v). A transcription of **29**, also from BL Harley 61, appears among the papers of Henry Spelman (now Lawrence, Kansas, University of Kansas, Kenneth Spencer Research Library, Department of Special Collections, MS E. 107, pp. 13–14).

The cartulary appears to be a unified production, written by a single scribe or by a number of co-operating scribes with very similar hands. It is a tidy and well-produced volume, with rubrics in red ink and red initials.

---

[23] *Wiltshire: the Topographical Collections of John Aubrey F.R.S.* A.D. *1659–70*, ed. J.E. Jackson (Devizes, 1862), p. 2. See also T. Tanner, *Notitia Monastica* (Oxford, 1695): 'Cartular. de Shafton penes D. Joh. Low de Shafton.' (and in the 1744 edition: 'Cartularium de Shafton penes dom. Joannem Law de eadem'). For a Shaftesbury house associated with the Low family, see Hutchins, *Dorset*, ii. 23.

[24] T. Tanner, *Notitia Monastica*, repr. with additions by J. Nasmith (Cambridge, 1787), Dorsetshire XIII, Shaftesbury (citing Hutchins, *Dorset*, preface; but apparently incorrectly).

[25] [T.] P[hillipps] and [F.] M[adden], 'List of Monastic Cartularies at present existing, or known to have existed since the Dissolution of Religious Houses', *Collectanea Topographica et Genealogica* i (1834), pp. 73–9, 197–208, 399–404; and ii (1835), pp. 102–14, 400, at ii. 106.

[26] A.G. Watson, *The Library of Sir Simonds D'Ewes* (London, 1966), p. 123 (art. 214).

[27] C.E. Wright, *Fontes Harleiani: a Study of the Sources of the Harleian Collection of Manuscripts preserved in the Department of Manuscripts in the British Museum* (London, 1972), p. 264.

The organisation is to a certain extent chronological; the cartulary begins with the ' pre-Conquest diplomas, followed by some charters and writs of the Anglo-Norman kings. But thereafter the documents copied are of a very mixed character: private charters and final concords, records of inquisitions, a list of abbey tenants in the thirteenth century, and various miscellaneous agreements. The cartulary appears to have been intended as a record of rights and privileges, rather than a register of title-deeds.[28]

The pre-Conquest documents are grouped together at the beginning of the manuscript (1–22r). The first two chapters are both directly in favour of Shaftesbury itself, and provide title to two of the most important Domesday manors, Bradford-on-Avon (29) and Tisbury (28). Thereafter the arrangement of the charters follows no obvious pattern: charters relating to the same property are widely separated; charters in favour of the abbey mingle with grants to individuals; there is no organisation on a chronological or topographical basis. The last two documents to be copied were Eadwig's grant of eighty or ninety hides to the abbey (21), of dubious authenticity but clearly of the first importance for Shaftesbury, and Alfred's spurious foundation-charter (7), both of which would seem to have merited a more prominent position; it is possible that these texts were added to an existing collection.

The charter-texts are in a generally poor state, consistent with repeated copying. The Latin sections require a great deal of emendation; words have fallen out, and the more difficult passages are now sometimes in-comprehensible. The language and orthography of the vernacular bounds have been modernised to a considerable extent, and certain passages are now corrupt or defective. The Old English personal names are also much distorted. Some responsibility for this can be laid at the door of the fifteenth-century scribe of BL Harley 61, who would here have been dealing with ancient and unfamiliar material, but it is clear that her exemplar was already at least one remove from the original charters. This is most clearly signalled in the vernacular boundary clauses, where the Anglo-Saxon letter-forms cause predictable confusion. The scribe of BL Harley 61 does not distinguish between *wyn* (ƿ) and *thorn* (þ), and uses the same modified letter for each; she may not have recognised that there was a difference. Yet most instances of *wyn* have been accurately converted into *w*, presumably by an earlier copyist who did have some knowledge of Old English. Moreover, there are several instances where *wyn* has been transformed into *d*, which indicates a stage when it was mistaken for *thorn* by a scribe familiar

---

[28] Davis, *Cartularies*, no. 885. For a list of the contents, see *Mon. Angl.* (rev. edn), ii. 474–5.

with Anglo-Saxon letter-forms, and subsequently transformed into *eth* (ð); elsewhere *d* appears as þ, indicating a reverse process.[29] The implication is that the pre-Conquest texts in BL Harley 61 were taken from an earlier cartulary.

The copies available to the scribe of BL Harley 61 seem to have been remarkably full and she has reproduced them with diligence; in **2** she has copied out in two places the early Insular abbreviation for *autem*, which would have been incomprehensible to a fifteenth-century reader. She includes the boundary clauses, which are in some places very long, and reproduces in full the lengthy witness-lists of the first eight charters; in most of the remaining texts, the witness-lists have been abbreviated, either by the scribe or in her exemplar, the only exceptions being **21** and **7** (which may be additions to an existing collection; see above).

4. THE AUTHENTICITY OF THE CHARTERS

The Shaftesbury archive has a high proportion of authentic charters. The majority of the thirty diplomas appear to be generally acceptable on their own terms and can be used with some confidence (**1**, **3**, **4**, **8**, **9**, **10**, **11**, **12**, **13**, **14**, **15**, **16**, **17**, **18**, **19**, **22**, **23**, **24**, **25**, **26**, **27**, **28**, **29**, **30**). Some are marred by mechanical errors, which do not detract from the general reliability of the texts; thus in **23** the king's name has been transformed from Eadwig to *Adric* and *Adwid*, while **3** and **4**, which are related, have the same incorrect indiction (probably added by a later copyist). Two apparently authentic charters include passages which may be the result of early interpolation (**10**, **13**). **18** is an otherwise acceptable charter in the name of Eadred with the unexpected date of 956; this is not due to a copying error by a Shaftesbury scribe, for a charter in favour of the same beneficiary preserved in the archive of Winchester cathedral has the same impossible incarnation year (S 571). There is no simple explanation for the problems raised by these two documents, but it does seem likely that both are fundamentally authentic.

It is probable that **2** has also suffered some tampering with the aim of making it more relevant to the later endowment. The present boundary clause is probably a substitution or insertion of the tenth or eleventh century, and it seems possible that a narrative passage concerning divisions of the estate is an interpolation; the details may have been taken from supplementary documentation (see pp. 11–14).

---

[29] See, for instance, *wiscan/discan* (**16**, **19**, **20**); *hiþe* for *hide* (**28**).

The two earliest Cheselbourne charters (**5, 6**) present considerable difficulty. **5** appears to be based on a genuine diploma of *c*. 870, but it seems to have been revised at some stage in order to make it more relevant as an earlier title-deed to Cheselbourne, which was disputed in the eleventh century; the boundary clause is almost certainly a substitution, the date is corrupt, and a doubt hangs over the details of the original transaction it recorded. **6** is best regarded as a free vernacular translation of the revised version of **5**. At some stage the hidage in **6** appears to have been altered so as to produce a document complementary to **5**, apparently with the intention of strengthening the abbey's title to Cheselbourne (see pp. 24–7).

21 is of dubious authenticity. The present text is clearly based on a genuine diploma of 956, apparently one in favour of Shaftesbury itself, but the details of the transaction and certain anomalous features suggest that it may have been considerably rewritten or reworked.

Two diplomas in the archive are certainly spurious: the foundation-charter in the name of King Alfred (**7**), and a curious charter concerning the abbey's manor of Kingston (**20**), which was created by the conflation of two genuine diplomas each giving title to part of the estate (**16, 19**). It is possible that **20** was fabricated immediately after the Conquest (see p. 82); **7** probably belongs to a rather later period.

*　　*　　*

The Shaftesbury archive includes representatives of most of the different types of diploma which were issued in the tenth century. It has one example of the elaborate standardized texts which were produced between 928 and 935 and which are known by their name of the conjectural common scribe, 'Æthelstan A' (**8**).[30] From 935 the characteristic 'Æthelstan A' texts were superseded by a much simpler model, which we know from surviving originals to have had a standardized layout (see **9, 10, 11, 13, 15, 16**). This new charter-type was popular and influential until the end of the century, but in accordance with characteristic Anglo-Saxon practice it was altered and adapted; one early variant involved the transfer of the dating-clause to a position after the superscription, apparently under the influence of ninth-century charters (see **14**). The standard charter-type co-existed with some radically different models, including the so-called 'alliterative charters', which were produced in the 940s and 950s, and seem to have had a special

---

[30] For these, see Drögereit 1935, pp. 345–8; Chaplais 1965, p. 60 [p. 41]; Keynes, *Diplomas*, pp. 43–4; *BAFacs.*, p. 9.

connection with the West Midland area.[31] Another aberration was the
'Dunstan B' model, which was in common use between 951 and 955 and
again in Edgar's reign, and which appears to be associated with Glastonbury;
it is characterized by its extreme brevity and the conciseness of its constituent
formulas, by the position of the dating clause at the very beginning of the
document, and (in Eadred's reign) by the omission of a royal subscription
from the witness-list (see **17, 18**).[32] In 956, for reasons that are still a matter
of debate, there was an enormous expansion of charter-production;[33] the
Shaftesbury archive includes two of the sixty-odd diplomas surviving from
that year (**19, 21**). Edgar's reign saw a new drive towards standardization,
especially in the earliest years, when we find a version of the post-935
charter-type with a very limited range of standard formulas, associated with
a scribe known as 'Edgar A' (see **24**, and also **26, 27**).[34] From the time of
Æthelred royal diplomas tended to be more literary and elaborate, and there
was less repetition of standard formulas; **28, 29** and **30** illustrate this trend.
28 is also an example of another development of Æthelred's reign, the
occasional practice of incorporating detail about the previous history of the
estate covered by the charter.[35]

5. THE ESTATES OF SHAFTESBURY ABBEY

a. *The endowment at the time of the Conquest*

In 1066 the Shaftesbury estates were concentrated in northern and central
Dorset and in southern Wiltshire, with single outlying manors in Sussex
(Felpham) and Somerset (Abbas Combe). There was a total assessment
TRE of 161 hides in Dorset (along with rights in Shaftesbury itself) and
172 hides in Wiltshire, together with twenty-one hides in Sussex and five in
Somerset.[36] Most of the nuns' property was to be found within a radius of

---

[31] *Charters of Burton Abbey*, ed. P.H. Sawyer, Anglo-Saxon Charters ii (London, 1979),
pp. xlvii–ix; Keynes 1985, pp. 156–9; *BAFacs.*, p. 12 and no. 43; C.R. Hart, *The Danelaw*,
(London, 1992), pp. 431–5.
[32] C.R. Hart, *The Early Charters of Northern England and the North Midlands* (Leicester, 1975),
pp. 19–22; Keynes, *Diplomas*, pp. 46–8; Keynes 1994b. S 563, which survives as an original, is
a guide to the physical appearance of charters of this type.
[33] Keynes, *Diplomas*, pp. 48–69.
[34] Drögereit 1935, p. 416; Chaplais 1965, p. 60 [p. 42]; Keynes, *Diplomas*, pp. 70–9.
[35] Keynes, *Diplomas*, pp. 95–7; F.M. Stenton, *The Latin Charters of the Anglo-Saxon Period*
(Oxford, 1955), pp. 74–82.
[36] *VCH Dorset* III, pp. 42–3; see GDB 17v, 67v, 75r, 78v, 83v, 91r.

fifteen miles of Shaftesbury itself. To the north-east were three large manors grouped around the Nadder valley: Donhead (40 hides), Tisbury (20 hides) and Dinton (40 hides). The community owned most of Sixpenny hundred; this comprised the manors of Fontmell Magna, Compton Abbas, Melbury Abbas and Iwerne Minster, together with Shaftesbury itself. Elsewhere in Dorset most of Shaftesbury's holdings lay scattered in the fertile lands of the Vale of Blackmoor, to the south-west of the burh, but the abbey also owned land in the chalk downs and a large manor on the Isle of Purbeck (Kingston, 16 hides TRE). The major outliers were the large estates at Bradford-on-Avon and Liddington in north Wiltshire (with respective assessments of 42 (plus 7) and 38 hides in 1066), the manor of (Sixpenny) Handley, sandwiched between the borders of Wiltshire and Hampshire (20 hides TRE, probably including Gussage St Andrew), and the Sussex manor of Felpham (21 hides TRE).

According to Domesday Book (GDB 78v, and see 75v), Earl Harold seized four of Shaftesbury's Dorset estates before 1066: Cheselbourne, *Sture* (East and West Stour), Melcombe Horsey and *Pidele*. Cheselbourne and Stour were returned to the nunnery by King William, after the opportune discovery of a writ of the Confessor ordering their restoration (S 1868). The writ also covered Melcombe Horsey, but this was still in the king's hands in 1086, with an assessment of 10 hides; the Domesday entry mentions Harold's illegal confiscation, and also says that Countess Goda had held Melcombe in 1066 (GDB 75v). The estate at *Pidele* was also not recovered, and is said to have been held by the Count of Mortain at the time of the survey. Identification of this property proves difficult. In 966 King Edgar confirmed Shaftesbury's possession of ten hides at *Uppidele*, which were apparently located in the northern part of Piddletrenthide (**26**). By 1086 the whole of Piddletrenthide seems to have been in the possession of the New Minster, Winchester (GDB 77v); it appears that the land covered in **26** was not that confiscated by Harold. Among the Domesday lands of the Count of Mortain were three estates called 'Piddle', two of them very tiny and probably located between Piddlehinton and Puddletown (GDB 79v); the third was a ten-hide manor at Piddlehinton, held by two thegns as two manors TRE. It is possible that one or more of these manors had at some stage belonged to Shaftesbury (see further, pp. 104-5).

b. *The accumulation of the endowment*

Asser states that Alfred made generous grants of land to his new foundation, but there is no evidence which would permit the identification of the estates which formed the initial endowment. The forged 'foundation charter'

(7) mentions seven places with a total assessment of 100 hides: forty hides at Donhead and Compton (Abbas), twenty at (Sixpenny) Handley and Gussage (St Andrew), ten at Tarrant (Hinton), fifteen at Iwerne (Minster) and fifteen at Fontmell (Magna). All these places lie within a few miles of Shaftesbury, a likely area for early endowment, but the assessments generally correspond precisely with the Domesday reckonings (often a suspicious feature in an early document) and the list includes two properties which were given to the community by King Æthelstan (Tarrant Hinton and Fontmell Magna: see **9**, **8**) and a third which may still have been in the king's hands in 963 (Iwerne Minster: see **21**, **24**); it seem unwise to take the details in the 'foundation charter' as in any way a reflection of valid information about the initial endowment of the nunnery. The list of properties in **7** is probably an elaboration of the similar list in **21**, in the name of Eadwig; this purports to cover an area of eighty (or ninety) hides, apparently consisting of fifty hides at Donhead, with Easton Bassett (in Berwick St John) and Compton Abbas, and of unspecified areas at Sixpenny Handley and Iwerne Minster. **21** itself is unlikely to be authentic, at least in its

GDB	Shire	Manor	Hides	Charter
17v	Sussex	Felpham	21 TRE	**17**
67v	Wiltshire	Beechingstoke	5	**12**
		Tisbury	20	**28**
		Donhead	40	**21**
		Bradford-on-Avon	42	**29**
		Liddington	38	**11**
		Dinton	20	**3, 4, 25**
78v	Dorset	Sixpenny Handley	20	**21**
		Hinton St Mary	8	**15, 23**
		(East and West) Stour	17	
		Fontmell Magna	15	**1, 8**
		Compton Abbas	10	**21**
		Melbury Abbas	10	
		Iwerne Minster	18	**21**
		Tarrant Hinton	10	**9**
		Fifehead St Quinton	5	
		Kingston	16	**16, 19, 20**
		Stoke Wake	5	**2**
		Mapperton	11	**14**
		Cheselbourne	16	**5, 6, 13, 30**
		Farnham	1	
91r	Somerset	Abbas Combe	5	**18**

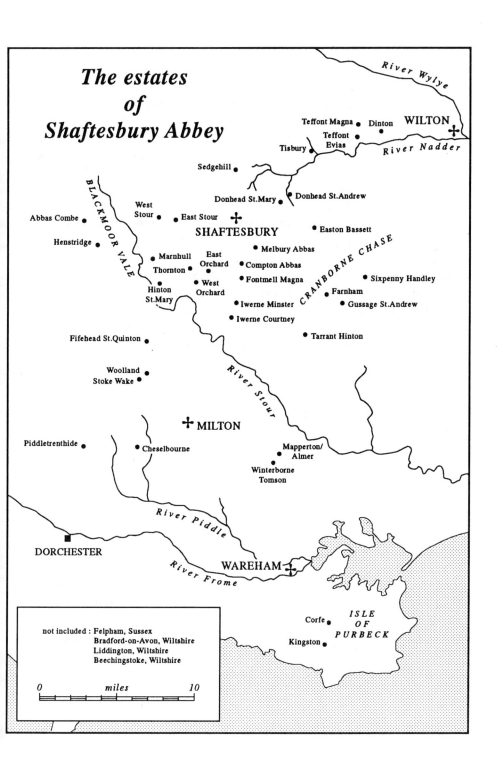

The estates
of
Shaftesbury Abbey

River Wylye

Teffont Magna • Dinton • WILTON
Teffont Evias •
Tisbury • River Nadder

Sedgehill •

Donhead St.Mary • • Donhead St.Andrew

West Stour • • East Stour ✝
Abbas Combe • SHAFTESBURY
BLACKMOOR VALE
Henstridge • • Easton Bassett

• Melbury Abbas
• Marnhull East Orchard • Compton Abbas CRANBORNE CHASE
Thornton • • Fontmell Magna • Sixpenny Handley
• West Orchard • Farnham
Hinton St.Mary • Iwerne Minster • Gussage St.Andrew
• Iwerne Courtney

Fifehead St.Quinton • • Tarrant Hinton

Woolland •
Stoke Wake •

River Stour

✝ MILTON

Piddletrenthide • • Cheselbourne Mapperton/ Almer •
Winterborne Tomson

River Piddle

■ DORCHESTER
River Frome WAREHAM ✝

ISLE OF PURBECK
Corfe •
Kingston •

not included : Felpham, Sussex
Bradford-on-Avon, Wiltshire
Liddington, Wiltshire
Beechingstoke, Wiltshire

0   miles   10

received form; but the fact that the grant of these estates could at some stage have been ascribed to Eadwig highlights the weakness of the tradition that these were part of Alfred's endowment.

Discussion of the major acquisitions in the first half of the tenth century can be more confident. In 932 King Æthelstan granted the community eleven and a half hides at Fontmell Magna, located just south of Shaftesbury on the edge of the Vale of Blackmoor (**8**), and three years later he followed this by a further grant of twelve hides at Tarrant Hinton, which lies on the far side of Cranborne Chase, eight miles from Shaftesbury (**9**). Both places still belonged to Shaftesbury at the Conquest, with slightly different assessments. We also know that Shaftesbury had acquired a major estate at Tisbury in Wiltshire by the time of King Eadmund, for it figured in an exchange made with that king for another property at an unidentified *Butticanlea*; in the region of Eadwig Shaftesbury received back Tisbury, in accordance with the wishes of Eadmund's queen, but at the same time gave up *Butticanlea* to the king (see **28**). Tisbury had been the site of an ancient minster (see **1**), which had probably been dissolved by the end of the ninth century; land there belonging to a thegn was forfeited to King Edward the Elder, and it is possible that it was he or Æthelstan who passed it on to Shaftesbury (see further, pp. 111–12).

The Shaftesbury community is mentioned in the mid-tenth-century will of Wynflæd, as the beneficiary of a bequest of an estate at Chinnock in Somerset (S 1539; see p. xvi n. 17, p. 56). Chinnock was not among Shaftesbury's Domesday possessions, and it is possible that the bequest never came into effect or that the estate was alienated for some reason, perhaps because it was so far removed from other Shaftesbury estates.[37] A more certain gift or bequest was made by King Edgar's grandmother, also called Wynflæd and conceivably the same woman; at some point before 966 she granted the community ten hides in the northern part of the parish of Piddletrenthide in Dorset, which is located in the downland about fifteen miles south-west of Shaftesbury (see **26**). By 1086 Piddletrenthide belonged to New Minster, Winchester (GDB 77v); the Domesday entry does not refer to any Shaftesbury claim, although it does indicate that another estate at *Pidele* had been seized by Earl Harold (GDB 78v; see pp. xxiii, 104–5). The Piddletrenthide property was perhaps lost or alienated at an earlier date. Wynflæd also owned an estate of fifteen hides at Cheselbourne, just to the east of Piddletrenthide (**13**), but she does not appear to have bequeathed

---

[37] In 1086 Chinnock was in the hands of the Count of Mortain; before the Conquest it had belonged to Eadmer Ator, with an assessment of nine hides (GDB 92v).

this to Shaftesbury, since King Cnut was subsequently in a position to grant sixteen hides there to one of his Danish followers (**30**); these sixteen hides must have passed to Shaftesbury at some point between 1019 and 1066 (GDB 78v). Cheselbourne was another of the manors seized by Harold, but in this instance it was restored by King William.

In 1001 Shaftesbury acquired from King Æthelred the minster of Bradford-on-Avon and its lands, to serve as a refuge for the nuns and their relics at a time of intensified Viking activity (**29**). The charter does not include an assessment, but the land-grant probably corresponded to the nuns' Domesday manor there, assessed at forty-two hides in 1066, with a separate area of seven hides at an unidentified placed called *Alvestone* (GDB 67v). Bradford-on-Avon lies in northern Wiltshire, some twenty-four miles north of Shaftesbury.

It is not usually possible to determine at what point Shaftesbury acquired the remaining estates which it held in 1066. Almost all of the charters in the archive appear to relate to land which was in the community's possession at the Conquest, but in the cases where the charters are in favour of individuals it is impossible to discover whether the donation to the nunnery was made by the beneficiaries themselves or by a distant heir. Several of the charters are in favour of women, who may have been attached in some way to the community. A charter of 939, concerning a grant of five hides at Orchard in Dorset to a bishop (**10**), includes a passage in which the beneficiary transfers the land to a woman (probably a widow) named Beorhtwyn; the estate is not listed separately in Domesday Book, but could have been reckoned under one of the neighbouring Shaftesbury manors (it is a difficulty that the property in question still seems to have been in episcopal hands in 963; see pp. 42, 100). In 948 King Eadred gave eight hides in the Isle of Purbeck to a religious woman named Ælfthryth (**16**); by 1066 this had been combined with a neighbouring estate of seven hides granted to a thegn in 956 (**19**) to form Shaftesbury's sixteen-hide Domesday manor of Kingston (see pp. 68–9). Five years later Eadred transferred thirty hides at Felpham in Sussex to his mother, described in the charter as *famula Dei* (**17**); it is possible that Eadgifu, like her daughter-in-law Ælfgifu (see **28**) and Ælfgifu's mother, Wynflæd (see **13**, **26**), had some connection with Shaftesbury. A final female beneficiary was Brihtgifu, who received a grant of twenty-three *iugera* at an unidentified *Ealderescumbe* in 968 (**27**). It is far from certain that a grant made to a woman would necessarily have benefited Shaftesbury immediately or within a short time; caution is indicated by the example of Cheselbourne, which was granted to a nun in 942 but does not seem to have passed to Shaftesbury until after 1019 (see **13**, **30**).

ABBREVIATIONS

BL	British Library
Bodleian	Oxford, Bodleian Library
GDB	Great Domesday Book
s.	*saeculo*
TRE	*Tempore regis Edwardi*

BIBLIOGRAPHICAL ABBREVIATIONS

Abrams 1991	L. Abrams, 'A Single-Sheet Facsimile of a Diploma of King Ine for Glastonbury', *The Archaeology and History of Glastonbury*, ed. L. Abrams and J.P. Carley (Woodbridge, 1991), pp. 97–133
Æthelweard	*The Chronicle of Æthelweard*, ed. A. Campbell (London, 1962)
ASC	*Anglo-Saxon Chronicle*
Asser	*Asser's Life of King Alfred*, ed. W.H. Stevenson (Oxford, 1904)
BAFacs.	*Facsimiles of Anglo-Saxon Charters*, ed. S. Keynes, Anglo-Saxon Charters, Supplementary ser. i (London, 1991)
Barker 1949	E.E. Barker, 'Sussex Anglo-Saxon Charters: Part iii', *Sussex Archaeological Collections* lxxxviii (1949), pp. 51–113
BCS	For 'Birch' in citations of charters
Bede, *HE*	Bede, *Historia Ecclesiastica*
Birch	W. de G. Birch, *Cartularium Saxonicum*, 3 vols (London, 1885–93)
Bishop, *English Caroline Minuscule*	T.A.M. Bishop, *English Caroline Minuscule* (Oxford, 1971)
Bresslau, *Handbuch*	H. Bresslau, *Handbuch der Urkundenlehre für Deutschland und Italien*, 3 vols (Leipzig and Berlin, 1912–60)

Brooks, *Church of Canterbury*	N. Brooks, *The Early History of the Church of Canterbury: Christ Church from 597 to 1066* (Leicester, 1984)
BTSuppl.	*Supplement* to T.N. Toller, *An Anglo-Saxon Dictionary, based on the collections of J. Bosworth* (Oxford, 1928)
Chaplais 1965	P. Chaplais, 'The Origin and Authenticity of the Royal Anglo-Saxon Diploma', *Journal of the Society of Archivists* iii.2 (1965), pp. 48–61 (repr. in *Prisca Munimenta*, ed. F. Ranger (London, 1973), pp. 28–42)
Chaplais 1968	P. Chaplais, 'Some Early Anglo-Saxon Diplomas on Single Sheets: Originals or Copies?', *Journal of the Society of Archivists* iii.7 (1968), pp. 315–36 (repr. in *Prisca Munimenta*, ed. F. Ranger (London, 1973), pp. 63–87)
Chaplais 1969	P. Chaplais, 'Who Introduced Charters into England? The Case for Augustine', *Journal of the Society of Archivists* iii.10 (1969), pp. 526–42 (repr. in *Prisca Munimenta*, ed. F. Ranger (London, 1973), pp. 88–107)
Chaplais 1981	P. Chaplais, 'The Authenticity of the Royal Anglo-Saxon Diplomas of Exeter', in his *Essays in Medieval Diplomacy and Administration* (London, 1981), at pp. XV 1–34 and Addendum (originally publ. in *Bulletin of the Institute of Historical Research* xxxix (1966), pp. 1–34)
Chaplais 1985	P. Chaplais, 'The Royal Anglo-Saxon "Chancery" of the Tenth Century Revisited', *Studies in Medieval History presented to R.H.C. Davis*, ed. H. Mayr-Harting and R.I. Moore (London, 1985), pp. 41–51
Cooke 1982	K. Cooke, 'Shaftesbury Abbey in the Eleventh and Twelfth Centuries: the Nuns and their Estates', unpubl. M. Litt. thesis, Oxford University (1982)
Davis, *Cartularies*	G.R.C. Davis, *Medieval Cartularies of Great Britain: a Short Catalogue* (London, 1958)
De Ant. Glast.	J. Scott, *The Early History of Glastonbury: an Edition, Translation and Study of William of Malmesbury's 'De Antiquitate Glastonie Ecclesie'* (Woodbridge, 1981)
DEPN	E. Ekwall, *The Concise Oxford Dictionary of English Place-Names*, 4th edn (Oxford, 1960)
Drögereit 1935	R. Drögereit, 'Gab es eine angelsächsische Königskanzlei?', *Archiv für Urkundenforschung* xiii (1935), pp. 335–436

Dumville, *Wessex*	D.N. Dumville, *Wessex and England from Alfred to Edgar: Six Essays on Political, Cultural and Ecclesiastical Revival* (Woodbridge, 1992)
Earle	J. Earle, *A Handbook to the Land-Charters and other Saxonic Documents* (Oxford, 1888)
Edwards, *Charters*	H. Edwards, *The Charters of the Early West Saxon Kingdom*, British Archaeological Reports, British ser. cxcviii (Oxford, 1988)
Edwards 1986	H. Edwards, 'Two Documents from Aldhelm's Malmesbury', *Bulletin of the Institute of Historical Research* lix (1986), pp. 1–19
Ekwall, *River-Names*	E. Ekwall, *English River-Names* (Oxford, 1928)
EPNS	English Place-Name Society
Fell, *Edward*	C.E. Fell, *Edward King and Martyr*, Leeds Texts and Monographs. n.s. (Leeds, 1971)
Finberg, *Agrarian History*	H.P.R. Finberg, *The Agrarian History of England and Wales, I.ii: A.D. 43–1042* (Cambridge, 1972)
Finberg, *ECDC*	H.P.R. Finberg, *The Early Charters of Devon and Cornwall*, Department of English Local History, Occasional Papers ii, 2nd edn (Leicester, 1963)
Finberg, *ECW*	H.P.R. Finberg, *The Early Charters of Wessex* (Leicester, 1964)
Forsberg, *Contribution*	R. Forsberg, *A Contribution to a Dictionary of Old English Place-Names*, Nomina Germanica ix (Uppsala, 1950)
Forsberg 1942	R. Forsberg, 'Topographical Notes on some Anglo-Saxon Charters', *Namn och Bygd* xxx (1942), pp. 150–8
Forsberg 1970	R. Forsberg, 'On Old English *ad* in English Place-Names', *Namn och Bygd* lviii (1970), pp. 20–82
Gelling, *Place-Names*	M. Gelling, *Place-Names in the Landscape* (London, 1984)
Gelling, *Signposts*	M. Gelling, *Signposts to the Past: Place-Names and the History of England* (London, 1978)
GP	*Willelmi Malmesbiriensis Monachi De Gestis Pontificum Anglorum Libri Quinque*, ed. N.E.S.A. Hamilton, Rolls Series (London, 1870)
Grundy, *Somerset*	G.B. Grundy, *The Saxon Charters and Field-Names of Somerset* (Taunton, 1935) (also publ. as 8 parts in *Proceedings of the Somersetshire Archaeological and Natural History Society*, lxxiii-lxxx (1927–34), same pagination)
Grundy 1919, 1920	G.B. Grundy, 'The Saxon Land Charters of Wiltshire', *Archaeological Journal*, 2nd ser. xxvi (1919), pp. 143–301; xxvii (1920), pp. 8–126
Grundy, 1933, 1934, 1935, 1936, 1937, 1938	G.B. Grundy, 'Dorset Charters', *PDNHAS* lv (1933), pp. 239–68; lvi (1934), pp. 110–30; lvii

	(1935), pp. 114–39; lviii (1936), pp. 103–36; lix (1937), pp. 95–118; lx (1938), pp. 75–89
Harmer, *Writs*	F.E. Harmer, *Anglo-Saxon Writs* (Manchester, 1952)
Harrison, *Framework*	K. Harrison, *The Framework of Anglo-Saxon History to A.D. 900* (Cambridge, 1976)
Hart 1964	C.R. Hart, 'Some Dorset Charter Boundaries', *PDNHAS* lxxxvi (1964), pp. 158–63
Hart 1973	C.R. Hart, 'Athelstan "Half-King" and his Family', *Anglo-Saxon England* ii (1973), pp. 115–44
Haslam 1982	J. Haslam, 'The Towns of Wiltshire', *Anglo-Saxon Towns in Southern England*, ed. J. Haslam (Chichester, 1984), pp. 87–147
Hearne, *John of Glastonbury*	*Johannis ... Glastoniensis Chronica sive Historia de Rebus Glastoniensibus*, ed. T. Hearne, 2 vols (Oxford, 1726)
Hoare, *Wilts*	R.C. Hoare, *The History of Modern Wiltshire*, 6 vols (London, 1822–44)
Hutchins, *Dorset*	J. Hutchins, *The History and Antiquities of the County of Dorset*, 2 vols (London, 1774)
Hutchins, *Dorset* (3rd edn)	J. Hutchins, *The History and Antiquities of the County of Dorset*, ed. W. Shipp and J.W. Hodson, 4 vols (London, 1861–70)
Jackson 1984	R. Jackson, 'The Tisbury Landholding granted to Shaftesbury Monastery by the Saxon Kings', *WANHM* lxxix (1984), pp. 164–7
KCD	For 'Kemble' in citations of charters
Keen 1984	L. Keen, 'The Towns of Dorset', *Anglo-Saxon Towns in Southern England*, ed. J. Haslam (Chichester, 1984), pp. 203–47
Kelly, *St Augustine's*	*Charters of St Augustine's Abbey, Canterbury*, ed. S.E. Kelly, Anglo-Saxon Charters iv (London, 1995)
Kelly 1990	S.E. Kelly, 'Anglo-Saxon Lay Society and the Written Word', *The Uses of Literacy in Early Mediaeval Europe*, ed. R. McKitterick (Cambridge, 1990), pp. 36–62
Kemble	J.M. Kemble, *Codex Diplomaticus Aevi Saxonici*, 6 vols (London, 1839–48)
Keynes, *Diplomas*	S. Keynes, *The Diplomas of King Æthelred 'the Unready' 978–1016: a Study in their Use as Historical Evidence* (Cambridge, 1980)
Keynes 1985	S. Keynes, 'King Athelstan's Books', *Learning and Literature in Anglo-Saxon England: Studies presented to Peter Clemoes*, ed. M. Lapidge and H. Gneuss (Cambridge, 1985), pp. 143–201

Keynes 1989   S. Keynes, 'The Lost Cartulary of Abbotsbury',
                             Anglo-Saxon England xviii (1989), pp. 207–43
Keynes 1992   S. Keynes, 'The Fonthill Letter', *Words, Texts
                             and Manuscripts: Studies in Anglo-Saxon Culture
                             presented to Helmut Gneuss*, ed. M. Korhammer
                             (Cambridge, 1992), pp. 53–97
Keynes 1993   S. Keynes, 'A Charter of King Edward the Elder
                             for Islington', *Historical Research* lxvi (1993),
                             pp. 303–16
Keynes 1994a   S. Keynes, 'Cnut's Earls', *The Reign of Cnut,
                             King of England, Denmark and Norway*, ed. A.R.
                             Rumble (Leicester, 1994), pp. 43–87
Keynes 1994b   S. Keynes, 'The "Dunstan B" Charters', *Anglo-
                             Saxon England* xxiii (1994), pp. 165–93
Keynes 1994c   S. Keynes, 'The West Saxon Charters of King
                             Æthelwulf and his Sons', *English Historical Review*
                             cix (1994), pp. 109–49
Keynes (forthcoming)   S. Keynes, 'Addenda to Professor Sawyer's *An-
                             notated List*', *Anglo-Saxon England*, forthcoming
Keynes and Lapidge, *Alfred S. Keynes and M. Lapidge, *Alfred the Great:
the Great*   Asser's 'Life of King Alfred' and other Contem-
                             porary Sources* (Harmondsworth, 1983)
Lawson, *Cnut*   M.K. Lawson, *Cnut: the Danes in England in the
                             Early Eleventh Century* (London, 1993)
Levison, *England and the   W. Levison, *England and the Continent in the Eighth
Continent*   Century* (Oxford, 1946)
Liebermann, *Gesetze*   F. Liebermann, *Die Gesetze der Angelsachsen*, 3
                             vols (Halle, 1903–16)
Mon. Angl.   R. Dodsworth and W. Dugdale, *Monasticon
                             Anglicanum*, 3 vols (London, 1655–73)
Mon. Angl. (rev. edn)   W. Dugdale, *Monasticon Anglicanum*, ed. J. Caley,
                             H. Ellis and B. Bandinel, 6 vols in 8 (London,
                             1817–30)
Murphy 1992   E. Murphy, 'Anglo-Saxon Shaftesbury – Bectun's
                             Base or Alfred's Foundation?', *PDNHAS* cxiii
                             (1992), pp. 23–32
Nelson 1991   J.L. Nelson, 'Reconstructing a Royal Family: Re-
                             flections on Alfred, from Asser, chapter 2', *People
                             and Places in Northern Europe 500–1600: Essays
                             in Honour of Peter Hayes Sawyer*, ed. I. Wood
                             and N. Lund (Woodbridge, 1991), pp. 47–66
O'Donovan, *Sherborne*   *Charters of Sherborne*, ed. M.A. O'Donovan, An-
                             glo-Saxon Charters iii (London, 1988)
O'Donovan 1972   M.A. O'Donovan, 'An Interim Revision of Epis-
                             copal Dates for the Province of Canterbury, 850–
                             950: Part I', *Anglo-Saxon England* i (1972),
                             pp. 23–44

Pafford 1952   J.H.P. Pafford, 'Bradford-on-Avon, the Saxon Boundaries in Ethelred's Charter of 1001 A.D.', *WANHM* liv (1951–2), pp. 210–18

Pierquin, *Recueil*   H. Pierquin, *Recueil général des chartes anglo-saxonnes: les Saxons en Angleterre 604–1061* (Paris, 1912)

PDNHAS   *Proceedings of the Dorset Natural History and Archaeological Society*

PN Devon   J.E.B. Gover, A. Mawer and F.M. Stenton, *The Place-Names of Devon*, 2 vols, EPNS viii-ix (Cambridge, 1931–2)

PN Dorset   A.D. Mills, *The Place-Names of Dorset*, 3 vols, EPNS lii-iii, lix/lx (Cambridge, 1977–89)

PN Sussex   A. Mawer and F.M. Stenton, with J.E.B. Gover, *The Place-Names of Sussex*, EPNS vi-vii (Cambridge, 1929–30)

PN Wilts.   J.E.B. Gover, A. Mawer and F.M. Stenton, *The Place-Names of Wiltshire*, EPNS xvi (Cambridge, 1939)

Rackham, *Countryside*   O. Rackham, *The History of the Countryside* (London, 1986)

RCHM Dorset iv   *An Inventory of Historical Monuments in the County of Dorset: iv, North Dorset*, Royal Commission on Historical Monuments (England) (London, 1972)

Ridyard, *Royal Saints*   S. Ridyard, *The Royal Saints of Anglo-Saxon England: a Study of West Saxon and East Anglian Cults* (Cambridge, 1989)

Robertson, *Charters*   *Anglo-Saxon Charters*, ed. A.J. Robertson, 2nd edn (Cambridge, 1956)

Robinson, *Dunstan*   J.A. Robinson, *The Times of St Dunstan* (Oxford, 1923)

Rutter 1989   J. Rutter, 'The Search for a Small Anglo-Saxon Bound at Shaftesbury', *PDNHAS* cxi (1989), pp. 125–7

S   For 'Sawyer' in citations of charters

S (Add.)   For 'Addenda to Professor Sawyer's *Annotated List*' (Keynes, forthcoming) in citations of charters

Sawyer   P.H. Sawyer, *Anglo-Saxon Charters: an Annotated List and Bibliography*, Royal Historical Society Guides and Handbooks viii (London, 1968)

Sims-Williams 1975   P. Sims-Williams, 'Continental Influence at Bath Monastery in the Seventh Century', *Anglo-Saxon England* iv (1975), pp. 1–10

Sims-Williams 1988   P. Sims-Williams, 'St Wilfrid and Two Charters dated 676 and 680', *Journal of Ecclesiastical History* xxxix (1988), pp. 163–83

Smith, *EPNE*	A.H. Smith, *English Place-Name Elements*, 2 vols, EPNS xxv-xxvi (Cambridge, 1956)
Taylor, *Dorset*	C. Taylor, *Dorset* (London, 1970)
Taylor and Taylor, *Anglo-Saxon Architecture*	H.M. Taylor and J. Taylor, *Anglo-Saxon Architecture*, 3 vols (Cambridge, 1965–78)
Tengvik, *Bynames*	G. Tengvik, *Old English Bynames*, Nomina Germanica iv (Uppsala, 1938)
Thomson 1958–60	T.R. Thomson, 'The Early Bounds of Wanborough and Little Hinton', *WANHM* lvii (1958–60), pp. 203–11
VCH Dorset II	*Victoria History of the County of Dorset* II, ed. W. Page (London, 1908)
VCH Dorset III	*A History of Dorset* III, ed. R.B. Pugh, Victoria History of the Counties of England (Oxford, 1968)
VCH Wilts. VIII	*A History of Wiltshire* VIII, ed. E. Crittall, Victoria History of the Counties of England (London, 1965)
VCH Wilts. XIII	*A History of Wiltshire* XIII, ed. D. Crowley, Victoria History of the Counties of England (Oxford, 1987)
VSB	*Vitae S. Bonifatii Archiepiscopi Moguntini*, ed. W. Levison, Monumenta Germaniae Historica, Scriptores Rerum Germanicarum (Hanover, 1905)
WANHM	*Wiltshire Archaeological and Natural History Magazine*
Whitelock, *EHD*	*English Historical Documents* c. *500–1042*, ed. D. Whitelock, English Historical Documents i, 2nd edn (London, 1979)
Whitelock, *Wills*	*Anglo-Saxon Wills*, ed. D. Whitelock (Cambridge, 1930)
Wormald 1985	P. Wormald, *Bede and the Conversion of England: the Charter Evidence*, Jarrow Lecture 1984 ([1985])

LIST OF CHARTERS

CHARTERS OF SHAFTESBURY ABBEY

1. a. Cenred grants thirty hides by Fontmell Brook, Dorset, to Bectun, abbot. [A.D. 670 × 676]

b. Cyneheard, bishop [of Winchester] describes the settlement of a dispute over the land in favour of Abbot Ecgwald and his *familia* at Tisbury minster, Wiltshire. A.D. 759

2. Ecgberht, king of the West Saxons, confirms the possession by three sisters, Beornwyn, Ælfflæd and *Walenburch*, of ten hides at Woolland, Dorset. A.D. 833

3. Æthelbald, king of West Saxons, grants fourteen hides at Teffont, Wiltshire, to Osmund, *minister*. A.D. 860

4. Æthelberht, king of the West [Saxons], grants three hides at Dinton, Wiltshire, to Osmund, *minister*. A.D. 860

5. Æthelred, king of the Saxons, grants two hides at Cheselbourne, Dorset, to Ælfstan, *princeps*. A.D. 859 [for 867/8 × 871, ? 869 or 870]

6. Æthelred, king of the West Saxons, grants give hides at Cheselbourne, Dorset, to Ealdorman Ælfstan. [A.D. 867/8 × 871, ? 869 or 870]

7. Alfred, king, grants forty hides at Donhead, Wiltshire, and Compton Abbas, Dorset; twenty at Sixpenny Handley and Gussage St Andrew, Dorset; ten at Tarrant Hinton, Dorset; fifteen at Iwerne Minster, Dorset; and fifteen at Fontmell, Dorset, with various privileges, to Shaftesbury Abbey. [A.D. 871 × 877]

8. King Æthelstan grants eleven and a half hides at Fontmell Magna, Dorset, to the *familia* at Shaftesbury. A.D. 932

9. King Æthelstan grants twelve hides at Tarrant Hinton, Dorset, to the nuns of Shaftesbury. A.D. 935

10. a. King Æthelstan grants five hides at West Orchard, Dorset, to Ælfric (? Ælfred), bishop. A.D. 939

b. Ælfred, bishop [? of Sherborne], grants the land to Beorhtwyn, daughter of Wulfhelm.

11. King Eadmund grants ten hides at Liddington, Wiltshire, to *Adulf* (Eadwulf), his man. A.D. 940

12. King Eadmund grants two hides at Beechingstoke, Wiltshire, to Eadric, his *uassallus*. A.D. 941

13. King Eadmund restores and confirms seven hides at Cheselbourne, Dorset, to Wynflæd, a nun, and grants her a further eight hides in the same place. A.D. 942 With a vernacular note concerning land at Winterborne Tomson, Dorset.

14. King Eadmund grants eleven hides at Mapperton on Almer, Dorset, to Eadric, *comes*. A.D. 943

15. King Eadmund grants five hides at Hinton St Mary, Dorset, to Wulfgar, *minister*. A.D. 944

16. King Eadred grants eight hides in the Isle of Purbeck, Dorset, to Ælfthryth, a religious woman. A.D. 948

17. King Eadred grants thirty hides at Felpham, Sussex, to Eadgifu, his mother. A.D. 953

18. King Eadred grants five hides at Henstridge, Somerset, to Brihtric, *minister*. A.D. 956 [? for 953 × 955]

19. King Eadwig grants seven hides at Corfe and Blashenwell, Dorset, to Wihtsige, *minister*. A.D. 956

20. King Eadred grants sixteen hides at Corfe and Blashenwell, Dorset, to Wihtsige, *minister*. A.D. 956

21. King Eadwig grants eighty or ninety hides to the minster at Shaftesbury. A.D. 956. With the bounds of Donhead and Easton Basset in Wiltshire, and Compton Abbas, Sixpenny Handley and Iwerne Minster in Dorset.

22. King Eadwig grants land at Shaftesbury, Dorset, to Wulfgar Leofa. A.D. 958

23. King Eadric (*for* Eadwig) grants three hides at Thornton in Marnhull and at Iwerne Courtney, Dorset, to Wulfgar, *minister*. A.D. 958

24. King Edgar grants five hides at East Orchard, Dorset, to Ælfsige, *minister*. A.D. 963

25. King Edgar grants five hides at Teffont, Wiltshire, to Sigestan, *minister*. A.D. 964

26. King Edgar confirms ten hides at *Uppidelen* (Piddletrenthide), Dorset, to the church at Shaftesbury, A.D. 966

27. King Edgar grants three *iugera* of farmland and twenty *iugera* of woodland at *Ealderes cumbe* to Brihtgifu. A.D. 968

28. King Æthelred confirms Shaftesbury's possession of twenty hides at Tisbury, Wiltshire. A.D. 984

29. King Æthelred grants the *cenobium* of Bradford-on-Avon, Wiltshire, and its appurtenant lands, to the nuns of Shaftesbury. A.D. 1001

30. King Cnut grants sixteen hides at Cheselbourne, Dorset, to *Agemund* (Aghmundr), *minister*. A.D. 1019

CONCORDANCE OF THIS EDITION WITH SAWYER'S LIST AND THE EDITIONS OF BIRCH, KEMBLE AND ROBERTSON

	Sawyer	Birch	Kemble	Robertson
1	1164	107	104	
	1256	186		
2	277	410	232	
3	326	500	284	
4	329	499	283	
5	334	525	300	
6	342	526	302	12
7	357	531	310	13
		532		
8	419	691	361	
9	429	708	366	
10	445	744	376	
11	459	754	386	
12	478	769	390	
13	485	775	392	
14	490	781	394	
15	502	793	397	
16	534	868	418	
17	562	898	432	
18	570	923	455	
19	632			
20	573	910	435	
21	630	970	447	
22	655	1026	470	
23	656	1033	474	
24	710	1115	501	
25	730	1138	513	
26	744	1186	522	
27	762	1218	547	
28	850		641	
29	899		706	
30	955		730	

NOTE ON THE METHOD OF EDITING

The pre-Conquest charters of Shaftesbury have been preserved in a single fifteenth-century cartulary, BL Harley 61. This has been given the siglum C (in this series the sigla A and B are reserved for originals and later copies on single sheets). Dodsworth's transcription of the first eight texts in the cartulary (Bodleian, Dodsworth 38, 1–8v) has been given the siglum D. Among the papers of Henry Spelman appears a transcript of **29**, clearly taken from BL Harley 61 (Lawrence, Kansas, University of Kansas, Kenneth Spenser Research Library, Dept of Special Collections, MS E. 107, pp. 13–14); this has been given the siglum E.

The texts of the pre-Conquest charters in BL Harley 61 appear to be several removes from the original charters, and are often in a rather poor condition. My aim has been to make the individual documents comprehensible, and so I have adopted modern punctuation, and have supplied deficiencies and corrected corruption wherever this could be done with some confidence; elsewhere I have suggested emendations in the apparatus. Personal names and place-names have been capitalized.

In places the manuscript is no longer legible, perhaps through the action of damp. The rubrics, written in red ink, have been particularly affected, but these are of little significance. More serious is the loss of text in two charters. In **8** some words of the Latin proem are missing, but can happily be supplied through comparison with contemporary diplomas. The loss of part of the boundary clause in **21** is not so easily remedied. Kemble (followed by Birch) does give readings for the defective sections, and these have been noted in the text, since it is possible that the manuscript was in better condition in his day (although it has to be said that his suggestions do not look very credible).

THE CHARTERS

1

a. *Coenred grants thirty hides* (manentes) *by Fontmell Brook, Dorset, to Bectun, abbot.* [A.D. 670 × 676]

b. *Cyneheard, bishop* [*of Winchester*]*, describes the settlement of a dispute over the land in favour of Abbot Ecgwald and his* familia *at Tisbury Minster, Wiltshire.* A.D. 759

C. BL Harley 61, 19v–20r: copy, s. xv
  Rubric: + Donum regis Coin[. . . . .] ª
Ed.: a. Kemble 104
    b. Birch 107, 186
    c. Pierquin, *Recueil*, pt I, no. 47
Translated: Whitelock, *EHD*, no. 55
Listed: Sawyer 1164, 1256; Finberg, *ECW*, nos 551, 557

(*a*)

In nomine Domini nostri Iesu Christi saluatoris. Ea que secundum ecclesiasticam disciplinam ac sinodalia decreta salubriter definiuntur, quamuis solus sermo sufficeret, tamen pro euitanda futura temporis ambiguitate[b] fidelissimis scripturis[c] documentis sunt commendanda. Quapropter ego Coinredus, pro remedio anime mee et relaxacione piaculorum meorum, aliquam terre particulam donare decreuerim uenerabili uiro Bectune abbati, id est .xxx. manentes.[d] De aquilone riuus nomine Funtamel,[e] ex meredie habet terram beate memorie Leotheri episcopi.[f] Nam earundem supradictarum[g] cespites pro ampliori firmitate euuangelium superposui, ita ut ab hac die tenendi, habendi, pussidendi[h] in omnibus liberam et firmam habeat potestatem. Si quis uero episcoporum seu regum contra hanc definicionis cartulam propria temeritate uel potius sacrilega debacacione[i] uenire temptauerit, inprimis iram Dei incurrat,[j] a liminibus sancte ecclesie et seperatur, et hoc quod repetit, uendicare non ualeat.

Ego Coinredus qui hanc cartulam donacionis mee per omnia in manu propria signaui et ad roborandum fidelibus testibus tradidi. +
Ego Leotherius quamuis indignus episcopus hanc cartulam donacionis subscripsi. +
Ego Cunibertus abbas subscripsi. +
Ego Hadde abbas subscripsi. +
Ego Wimbertus presbiter qui hanc cartulam rogante[k] supraeffato abbate scripsi et subscripsi et ceteri. +

3

(b)

Hoc signum ego Cyniheardus indignus episcopus impressi ad confirmandam roborandamque hanc cartulam quam huiusmodi conscriptum*[l]* esse fateor. Successor abbatis prenominati Bectuni, Catuuali nomine, dedit terram supra designatam .xxx. manencium Wintran abbati pro pecunia sua et scripsit libellum alium donacionis huius atque possessionis suprascripte. Subtraxit tamen et donacionis prime litteras et subscripciones regum, episcoporum, abbatum atque principum quia inter cetera terrarum suarum testimonia hec eadem terre particula conscripta non facile potuit eripi neque adhuc potest. Et propterea, decedentibus primis testibus, longa deceptacio*[m]* inter familias duorum monasteriorum orta est et perseuerat usque nunc. Habeant autem hanc terram semper ex quo a prefato abbate primo data est Wintran*[n]* successores eius, et alterius familie et successores primum libellum que manibus predictorum testium roboratur. Iccirco ego nunc atque rex noster*[c]* ceteri quorum testificacio et subscripcio infra*[o]* notatur reconciliauimus eos in pace, partim data pecunia, partim iuramento adhibito, in tantum ut deinceps successores Wintran*[p]* abbatis, id est Eguuald*[q]* et familia eius que est in monasterio quod dicitur Tissebiri, cum licencia alterius familie cui preest Tidbald abbas, habeant possideantque perpetualiter terram de qua diu*[r]* altercacio erat, et presens libellum ego discripsi*[s]* atque excerpsi ab illo primitus dato Bectuno*[t]* abbati, concedente scilicet Tidbaldo abbate et familia eius, et dedi Eguualdo abbati, testibus infra notatis consencientibus atque confirmantibus hanc scripturam, reprobantibus*[u]* autem alia scriptura*[v]* que sunt edita de hac terra. Et hec acta sunt ⟨anno⟩*[w]* ab incarnacione Domini nostri Iesu Christi .dcclviiii., indiccione .xii.

Kinewlf regis + Herewald episcopi + Scilling prefecti*[x]* + Cerdic prefecti*[x]* et ceteri. +

[a] *Rubric partly illegible*   *[b]* ambiguitatem C
[c] *A word such as* et *or* ac *may have fallen out here*   *[d]* manientes C   *[e]* ffuntamel C
[f] *See commentary for the punctuation and interpretation of the boundary details (this section was probably revised by Bishop Cyneheard)*
[g] *A word such as* terrarum *may have fallen out here*   *[h]* *A spelling for* possidendi
[i] *A spelling for* debacchatione   *[j]* demicurrat C   *[k]* rogantes C
[l] *For* conscriptam   *[m]* *A spelling for* disceptatio   *[n]* Wirtrun C   *[o]* infra; C
[p] Wintrun C   *[q]* Eguuabo C   *[r]* quamdiu C   *[s]* *A spelling for* descripsi
[t] Betuno C   *[u]* reprobrantibus C   *[v]* *For* alias scripturas
[w] *The word* anno *has fallen out here*
[x] pr' C *(Kemble and Birch wrongly expand this to* presbiter)

This document was put together in its present form by Cyneheard, bishop of Winchester, in 759. It consists of a revised version of a charter of Coenred, issued in the 670s, followed by a statement in which the bishop explains the circumstances which made it necessary to adapt the charter in this way. Coenred's charter was in favour of an Abbot Bectun, and it apparently conveyed extensive property, including thirty hides by Fontmell Brook. It emerges from Cyneheard's statement that Bectun's successor, Catwali, sold the thirty hides to Wintra, the abbot of Tisbury minster, and drew up a charter recording this transaction. In normal circumstances the original title-deed (that is, Coenred's charter) would have been transferred with the land to the new owner, but in this case Catwali retained the title-deed because it also covered other estates belonging to his minster. Some time later, when all the witnesses to the original grant were dead, the successors of Bectun and Catwali laid claim to the Fontmell property on the basis of Coenred's original charter. In 759 King Cynewulf and Bishop Cyneheard negotiated a settlement, which left Abbot Ecgwald and his community at Tisbury in continued possession of the land, but seems also to have involved the payment of compensation to their opponents in return for a formal waiving of their claim. Bishop Cyneheard drew up the present document for Tisbury minster as proof of its rightful title, incorporating a revised copy of Coenred's charter which he had edited to remove the references to the other estates granted to Bectun, so that it now applied only to the thirty hides in the Fontmell area.

Cyneheard's account of the genesis and resolution of the dispute is of great interest for the insight it provides into the development of the use of legal documentation in Anglo-Saxon England. The churchmen who were producing and promoting written charters as valid title to land were still working out the legal procedures for their application. In this case, the consequences of a certain transaction (the alienation of part of a minster's endowment) had not been considered in terms of the legal documentation involved. Abbot Catwali could not hand over Coenred's charter with the estate because it was also the title-deed for other properties (compare, for example, S 235 and S 1171, which record grants to early minsters of land in several places). So he seems to have improvised, drawing up a private charter recording the sale, but keeping back the formal diploma which served as title-deed to his minster's endowment. This solution was flawed, as became apparent in a later generation when the witnesses to the original transactions were dead. In order to resolve the subsequent dispute, Bishop Cyneheard himself was forced to improvise, and the result was the present double document. It is perhaps misleading to treat this text as an 'insertion' (as Chaplais 1965, p. 56 [pp. 36–7]), since that is a technical term for an 'authentic copy', produced according to strict legal procedures (and really a later medieval phenomenon): for discussion, see Bresslau, *Handbuch*, i. 89–93, ii. 301–8. 1 can hardly be considered an 'authentic copy' of Coenred's charter, since the bishop, on his own initiative, has radically tampered with the text of the earlier document and significantly altered its nature, a bizarre proceeding in formal diplomatic terms and evidently not based upon legal precedent. We are not told in the present document whether the dispute-settlement also involved emendation of Coenred's original charter, still in the possession of Bectun's community, but it seems likely that any reference to the thirty hides at Fontmell Brook was expunged. Something similar seems to have happened in the case of a contemporary Barking charter, originally covering seventy-five hides in several places, where the hidage has been reduced to forty in both text and endorsement (S 1171; see Chaplais 1968,

p. 330 [p. 80]); compare also Archbishop Wulfred's insistence in the early ninth century that Abbess Cwoenthryth delete from her hereditary charters all references to the estates which she had ceded to him in compensation (S 1436). The experiences of the Tisbury community may have directly influenced the treatment in Canterbury three years later of another case in which one charter dealt with several estates. The archive of St Augustine's Abbey preserves a document dated 762 in which a layman, about to travel to Rome, announces his intention of bequeathing to the abbey one of a number of properties which had been granted to him by King Æthelberht II of Kent (S 1182; Kelly, *St Augustine's*, no. 12); the wording is rather ambiguous, but it seems that a note of the bequest was added to the original charter and S 1182 itself drawn up separately and handed over to the abbey in order to guarantee its position. Canterbury familiarity with the West Saxon case may account for certain minor similarities in the formulation of S 1182 and 1 (noted by Chaplais 1965, p. 56 [pp. 36–7]).

1 is without doubt an authentic document of 759. The first section, comprising Coenred's charter, is technically not authentic as it stands, since by Cyneheard's own admission he has reworked the dispositive section in order to delete references to the property which remained in the possession of Abbot Bectun's successors. It can be assumed that it was the section between *id est .xxx. manentes* and *Nam earundem* which bore the brunt of Cyneheard's revision. The hidage was presumably changed and the rudimentary bounds either added in their entirety or altered in some way, which might explain their confusing structure (see further discussion below). The eighth-century revision would also adequately account for the apparently ana-chronistic reference to Bishop Leuthere as *beate memorie*, a designation very rarely applied to living persons (Levison, *England and the Continent*, pp. 226–7; Chaplais 1965, p. 55 [p. 36]); this last detail probably represents Cyneheard's automatic homage to a venerable predecessor.

In all other respects, Coenred's charter seems acceptable as one of the very earliest surviving Anglo-Saxon diplomas. It has no formal dating clause, but is datable to the pontificate of Bishop Leuthere of Wessex, one of the witnesses (A.D. 670 × 676; for a slightly different calculation of the pontificate, to A.D. 669 × 675, see Edwards, *Charters*, pp. 232–3). The donor is probably the father of King Ine, who is mentioned in the latter's lawcode as an adviser (Liebermann, *Gesetze*, i. 88). In an Abingdon charter that seems to be based on some genuine early records (S 241) he appears as joint-donor with Ine of land in Berkshire; in S 45 from Selsey (A.D. 692) he is styled *rex Westsaxonum*, while Ine attests without a style (this may owe something to revision by a later Chichester cartularist). Coenred's status is unclear to the modern historian, but he was evidently a significant figure after his son's accession in 688 (Stenton, *ASE*, p. 72; Edwards, *Charters*, p. 233). His charter in favour of Abbot Bectun, which makes no reference to royal consent or approval, indicates that he already enjoyed a degree of power in the 670s; the fact that he is not styled *rex* in the text agrees with the other evidence that he was not generally regarded as a king. Bectun does not occur elsewhere. His name has probably been corrupted in transmission; it may originally have been Beorhthun (Bercthun), the name of a contemporary ealdorman of Sussex and of an abbot of Beverley (Bede, *HE*, iv. 15; v. 2). His minster cannot now be identified. Suggestions that it was a predecessor of Alfred's foundation at Shaftesbury (for example, Keen 1984, pp. 213–14) are based largely on the circumstance that the charter was preserved in the Shaftesbury archive; but it is far more likely that **1** was acquired by the nunnery as part of the earlier documentation of the estate at Fontmell Magna which it was granted in 932, than that it was inherited from a defunct early minster at Shaftesbury (see further below, and also discussion in Murphy 1992, pp. 28–9). It may be a valid observation that Catwali, Bectun's successor, is more likely to have disposed of land which was situated some distance from his minster than of land in its close vicinity (Edwards, *Charters*, p. 233). The witnesses to Coenred's charter certainly seem compatible with the implied date. Apart from Bishop Leuthere, these comprise Cyneberht, probably the abbot of a minster at Redbridge (near Southampton) who insisted upon baptising two Wight princes fleeing from Cædwalla of Wessex (Bede, *HE*, iv. 16); Hædde, who was to be Leuthere's successor at Winchester; and a priest named Wynberht, who attests several other West Saxon charters from the later seventh century (S 239, 243, 1170 and 1245 [a Malmesbury forgery incorporating a genuine witness-list]), and who later became abbot of the minster at Nursling (*VSB*, p. 9).

Wynberht attests Coenred's charter with what appears to be a notarial subscription; his subscription to S 239 (not entirely genuine as it stands, but based on an authentic charter) is in a similar form ('Ego Winberctus hanc cartam scripsi et subscripsi'), and in S 243 also he appears to be claiming some responsibility for the production of the charter (' . . . hanc donationem dictans subscripsi'). Although it is a standard feature of Roman and later Continental diplomatic, the notarial subscription is virtually absent from surviving Anglo-Saxon deeds; the only real exceptions are in a handful of early West Saxon charters (see Edwards, *Charters*, pp. 12–13) and in some late diplomas associated with foreign scribes (S 1028, 1390; see also Keynes, *Diplomas*, pp. 26–8, for discussion of tenth-century formulas of attestation which imply personal responsibility for producing the charter). Apart from including a notarial subscription, Coenred's charter inclines towards the Continental tradition in the formulation of the sanction. This is most noticeable in the concluding phrase, 'et hoc quod repetit uendicare non ualeat', which is meaningless in the context of a religious sanction. This is a common formula in Merovingian charters, where it usually follows details of the fine to be paid by an invader, and is intended to emphasize that payment of the fine did not entail any claim to future possession of the estate; the only other instance in a diploma from Anglo-Saxon England is in an Exeter charter of 1044 (S 1003; see Chaplais 1965, p. 55 [p. 36], and *idem* 1966, p. 26). The use of this Merovingian formula, together with other elements of the wording of the sanction, suggests that the draftsman may have been familiar with contemporary Frankish charters (Levison, *England and the Continent*, pp. 227–8). Another Continental and perhaps Frankish symptom which appears in West Saxon charters in this period is the occasional inclusion of the word *feliciter* in dating clauses (see S 234, 236, 245; Edwards, *Charters*, p. 12). In the second half of the seventh century Wessex had two bishops of Frankish origin, Leuthere himself and his uncle Agilbert (Bede, *HE*, iii. 7), and the resulting contact between the two churches could provide a context for the diffusion of some knowledge of Frankish diplomatic practice into Wessex. But this Continental influence was superficial and transient. In Coenred's charter, as in the other comparable West Saxon texts, the structure and formulation conform to the usual Anglo-Saxon pattern. The straightforward verbal invocation is of the commonest type (see S 1171, 10, 45, 235 etc.); the proem, with minor variations in expression but the same theme, was in frequent use in this period (see S 241, 248, 1169, 1248, 1787; and discussion in Wormald 1985, pp. 10–11); the formulation of the dispositive section has been compared to that of S 51 (Harrison, *Framework*, p. 69); the statement of powers, while owing something to Continental antecedents, has close parallels in contemporary English charters (see especially S 235, 1799, 1800; and Edwards, *Charters*, p. 232), and there are also parallels to the wording of part of the sanction (Sims-Williams 1975, pp. 5–6). Despite the Continental elements, Coenred's charter is unmistakably an Anglo-Saxon text, and the same is true of the other West Saxon charters with formulas that may have a Frankish origin. This implies that the Anglo-Saxon diplomatic tradition was already firmly established by the 670s, a conclusion in line with the arguments that charter-production was taking place in England in the earlier seventh century (see Chaplais 1969; Wormald 1985; Kelly 1990). These 'alien' formulas seen in West Saxon charters of the seventh century had no permanent influence and had disappeared by the second quarter of the eighth century; their brief appearance was presumably due to experimentation by a few charter-scribes who had been exposed to Continental documents. In the instance of Coenred's charter it seems possible that the Continental features may be due to the involvement of Bishop Leuthere in drawing up the charter; his subscription contains the 'humility' formula which may signal participation in the drafting process (also found in his subscriptions to S 51 and S 1245: see Sims-Williams 1988, p. 166). The mixture of Anglo-Saxon and Frankish formulas could perhaps be explained if the bishop added some modifications to a sample draft drawn up by an Anglo-Saxon (Wynberht).

Coenred's charter is one of a small number of early Anglo-Saxon diplomas which include a reference to a formal ceremony intended to mark the conveyance in the eyes of the witnesses and to give it a religious guarantee (for the background, see Chaplais 1965, pp. 52–3 [p. 33]). In this case sods from the land conveyed were placed on a gospel-book. A similar procedure is mentioned in S 239 from Abingdon and in three early documents from the minster at *Medeshamstede* (S 1804–6); in S 1804 we are told that the event took place before witnesses in King Æthelred's chamber in the Mercian royal vill at Tamworth, and that the king joined hands with his queen and Bishop Seaxwulf to perform the ceremony. A variant of this, which involved placing the sods on an altar, is mentioned in two early Kentish charters from Minster-in-Thanet (S 14, 15); a later Canterbury document recording the settlement of a dispute about land at Cookham notes that the original donor, King Æthelbald of Mercia, had sent a sod of the estate with the charter to be placed on the altar of Christ Church (S 1258). The Bath foundation charter (S 51) refers to the *cespitis conditione*. See also S 30, 1258.

Apart from the donor, all the witnesses to Coenred's charter are clerics. It is possible that Bishop Cyneheard abbreviated the witness-list and omitted any secular subscriptions when he revised the text, but there does seem some scope for suggesting that West Saxon land-charters might be witnessed entirely by clerics (by contrast, in Kentish charters of this period most witnesses are laymen: see S 8, 19 etc.). S 248, a charter of Ine from Glastonbury, survives as a single-sheet copy which may be a facsimile of the lost original (Abrams 1991); all the witnesses here are bishops. Similarly, in the witness-list of S 1245 (A.D. 675) all but one of the witnesses has an ecclesiasticial style (the last is unstyled). But the case cannot be pressed too far, since early West Saxon texts generally survive only as cartulary copies with very short and possibly abbreviated witness-lists; it should be noted that S 235, the only trustworthy seventh-century charter preserved in the cartulary of Old Minster, Winchester, which usually gives texts in full, has twenty-one witnesses, ten of them of ecclesiastics. In Coenred's charter the formulation of the subscriptions seems to be contemporary.

The second part of **1**, the account of the subsequent dispute and its resolution, also appears entirely acceptable. The beginning of Cyneheard's statement has a close resemblance to his subscription in a Malmesbury charter of 758 (S 260): 'Hoc signum ego Kyneheardus episcopus iussus a rege supranominato inscripsi et subscripsi'. A slightly later charter of uncertain provenance (S 264, A.D. 778) also begins with the words *Hoc signum* (this was issued after Cyneheard's death). The formulation of the dating clause in **1** is also very close to that in S 260. There is no reason to question the substance of the narrative. Wintra, abbot of Tisbury, is also mentioned in the Life of St Boniface (*VSB*, p. 14); he attests S 245 (A.D. 704), Ine's grant of privileges to the West Saxon churches (for which see Edwards 1986), and is mentioned in the text of S 241 (A.D. 699), which is a concoction based on more than one seventh-century record. Bishop Cyneheard's statement concludes with a (presumably) abbreviated witness-list, consisting of four subscriptions; the witnesses are King Cynewulf, Bishop Herewald of Sherborne and two *prefecti* (for whom see also S 96, 261–4).

1 covers an area of thirty hides in the vicinity of Fontmell Brook. The details of the rudimentary bounds are rather ambiguous, no doubt due to Bishop Cyneheard's reworking of the dispositive section (see above); it is possible that they represent a new insertion into the text, intended to distinguish the thirty hides more particularly from neighbouring property still retained by Bectun's minster. Whitelock (*EHD*, p. 481), respecting the punctuation of the manuscript, translated the relevant section: ' ... 30 hides north of the stream Fontmell by name; it has on the south the land of Bishop Leuthere ...' This interpretation is not really satisfactory; *riuus* should not be a genitive form, and it is odd that both references should be to the southern boundary. It seems preferable to supply punctuation between *manentes* and *de aquilone*, and to translate: 'In the north [is] the stream called Fontmell; on the south it [the estate] has the land of Bishop Leuthere' (the construction favoured by Finberg, *ECW*, p. 155). The two statements do not balance properly, due to the lack of a verb in the first, but the discrepancy can probably be explained as the result of Bishop Cyneheard's adaptation of an existing text. On this construction, the thirty hides would lie south of Fontmell Brook and would therefore incorporate the land later known as Fontmell Magna, where Shaftesbury was granted eleven and a half hides in 932 (**8**), and where it held a manor assessed at fifteen hides in 1066 (GDB 78v). Attempts have been made to locate the thirty hides more precisely (see Murphy 1992), but the evidence is extremely tenuous, and no firm conclusions are possible. **1** probably represents part of the earlier documentation of the Fontmell Magna estate, which passed into the nuns' hands when they acquired the land; if this was the case, then the larger land-unit in existence in the seventh and eighth centuries would appear to have been broken up by the tenth century. An alternative possibility is that Shaftesbury acquired **1** as part of the archive of the disbanded Tisbury minster; by the reign of King Eadmund (A.D. 939 × 945) the community had come into possession of an estate centred on Tisbury, presumably representing at least part of the endowment of the ancient minster (see **28**).

2

Ecgberht, king of the West Saxons, confirms the possession by three sisters, Beornwyn, Ælfflæd and Walenburch, *of ten hides* (manentes) *at Woolland, Dorset.* A.D. 833 (26 December)

C. BL Harley 61, 17v–18r: copy, s. xv
   Rubric: Hec est scripcio Ageberti regis Saxonum de decem mansis terre dividende inter tres sorores loco ubi dicitur Þennland ecclesie sancti Edwardi Shafton'.
Ed.: a. Kemble 232 (with the bounds in vol. iii, p. 390)
    b. Birch 410
    c. Pierquin, *Recueil*, pt 1, no. 136
Listed: Sawyer 277; Finberg, *ECDC*, no. 9; Finberg, *ECW*, no. 565

In nomine Domini nostri Iesu Christi. Ego Agebertus gratia Dei occidentalium Saxonum rex, cum consensu et communi consilio episcoporum et principum meorum ac tocius plebis mee seniorum, hanc testimonii cartulam conscribere[a] iussi, id est decem manencium terre illius ubi dicitur Þennland ut firmiter iuxta[b] antiquam conscriptionem ipsis postsessoribus[c] quorum propria hereditas, id sunt tres sorores Beornpyn, Alfled, Walenburch,[d] assignata permaneat, cum eiusdem territoriis et omnibus rebus ad se pertinentibus, absque ulla contradiccione firma stabilitate perseueret.[e] Et iccirco fecimus quia nescimus pro qua causa contingit quod anteriora scripsiuncula perdita fuissent. Et si unquam eueniat ut ab alicui[f] hominum inuenta reperiantur, nisi in substanciam et sustentacionem hiisdem heredibus perueniant, sint semper diiudicata atque proscripta[g] ab omnibus catholicis erectam fidem colentibus. Illam utraque terram easdem[h] prenominate sorores inter se diuidentes, unusquisque[i] illa re accepit .iii. cassatos et quarte terciam partem sibi in proprium ius. Contigit autem post annorum curriculam[j] ut, easdem[h] prenominate sorores plus de paterna hereditate suscipientes, Bearnwine recessit in Domnoniam et ibi partem suum[k] sumpsit in loco qui uocatur Derentune homm, et aliis duobus has .x. manentes prout illis placuit diuidendas dimisit. At illi[l] uero inter se diuidentes, Alfled accepit sibi in occidentali parte in dominium peculiare duos cassatos.

Territoria uero huius agelli ista sunt. Primitus of alor riðe uppe on anne þoure,[m] þanen on anne walle dich, þannen þurh reoþe on delesburg middenwearde, þanen to cylberge, þanen on pyrtruman,[n] þanen on burg, þanne on anne dich, one þane ealdene hage, þanen anlang ðies hagen oð anne þorn on hacggen hamme, þanen on anne hege ðat on irichte on anne oc, ðonne*º* est ouer melenbroc on anne þ,*ᵖ* on anne stapel, eft to anne aler riðe.*�q* Scripta est uero huius priuilegii scedula anno dominice incarnacionis .dcccxxxiii., indiccione .xii., die qua sancti Stephani prothomartiris solempnitas celebretur in uilla regali qui*ʳ* uocatur Dornwerecestre, coram ydoneis adstipulatoribus quorum nomina subter notata patescunt. Siquis autem tyrannica potestate inflatus et diabolica fraude deceptus hoc infringere aut minuere ausus sit, sciat se excommunicatum et a societate sanctorum seperatum*ˢ* et ante tribunal Christi racionem redditurum.

+ Ego Agebertus rex hanc nostram communem coroboracionem propria manu signo sancte crucis sic confirmo.
Ego Alstanus episcopus consensi et subscripsi.

ᵃ For conscriberi   *ᵇ* iuxta ut firmiter iuxta C   *ᶜ Perhaps a spelling for* possessoribus
ᵈ This name seems to be corrupt (perhaps Ealhburh)
ᵉ The syntax of the passage from ut firmiter *to* perseueret *appears confused (see commentary)*
ᶠ For aliquo   *ᵍ* prescripta C   *ʰ For* eaedem   *ⁱ For* unaquaeque
ʲ For curriculum   *ᵏ For* suam   *ˡ For* ille
ᵐ Or þonre *or* poure *(since the scribe does not distinguish between* þ *and* p); *probably an error for* þorne *(see commentary)*
ⁿ pyrtrum' C   *º* donne C   *ᵖ Probably for* þorne   *�q* ride C   *ʳ For* que   *ˢ For* separatum

---

2 is unlikely to be authentic in its present form, although there can be little doubt that it is based to a large degree upon authentic early documentation (in two places the scribe has reproduced the Insular abbreviation for *autem*, which had fallen out of use by the post-Conquest period). The boundary clause appears to be an addition, and there is to be some reason to believe that the preceding section covering the two divisions of the property (from *Illam utraque terram* to *duos cassatos*) has also been interpolated into a charter of Ecgberht that was originally concerned only with the confirmation of ten hides at Woolland. It will be argued below that the charter has been altered, probably in the tenth or eleventh century, to create a title-deed for the five-hide Shaftesbury manor at Stoke Wake.

The basis of the extant text appears to have been a charter in the name of Ecgberht which was drawn up to confirm the ownership of ten hides in Dorset for which the earlier documentation was missing. Several such substitute diplomas were produced during the reign of Edward the Elder, probably to replace charters lost during the Viking incursions of the previous decades (S 361, 367–9, 371; see also S 222, 225, and Keynes 1993), and there are a number of similar documents from later in the tenth century (for example, **26**; see further Keynes, *Diplomas*, p. 32 n. 53), but **2** is a unique survival of such a confirmation from the pre-Viking period. The charter is said to have been issued on St Stephen's Day (26 December) 833 in the royal vill at Dorchester. A number of other ninth-century West Saxon charters were issued or ratified on St Stephen's day: S 290 (O'Donovan, *Sherborne*, no. 3) at an unknown

Æscantun in 840, S 298 at an unspecified location in 846, S 333 (O'Donovan, *Sherborne*, no. 6) at Dorchester in 864, and a charter underlying S 272–6 (all apparently spurious in their present form) at Southampton in 825 (see also S 120–1, 172 from Mercia). There may be a slight inconsistency between the incarnation year and the indiction, easily explicable in terms of a mistake by the original scribe or the omission of a minim by a later copyist. At this period the incarnation year and indiction in the dating clauses of Anglo-Saxon charters seem both generally to have been reckoned from Christmas Day (Harrison, *Framework*, p. 116 n. 17; O'Donovan, *Sherborne*, p. 24); thus 26 December 833 would be cited as the twelfth indiction, which it is, but given the incarnation year 834. However, the possibilities for minor error in this situation are obvious, and there is no reason to believe that the Anglo-Saxons recognised rigid rules in this area. The formulation of the dating clause and sanction and of the two surviving subscriptions seems acceptable (compare, for instance, S 290 and 300). The syntax of the central part of the dispositive section is distinctly confused. This can perhaps be explained by the incapacity of the draftsman, who was here forced by the nature of the transaction to depart from any existing model available to him. Few charter-scribes in mid-ninth-century England seem to have had sufficient grasp of Latin grammar to compose independently, and some could not even cope successfully with the deployment of standard formulas (see, for instance, **3, 4, 5**); at least standards in Wessex were superior to those in the Canterbury scriptorium, where standards dropped to an appalling level by *c.* 870 (see Brooks, *Church of Canterbury*, pp. 170–4). But the confusion in the dispositive section of Ecgberht's confirmation could also be due to later interference. If, as is suggested below, the later section detailing the two divisions of the estate between the three sisters was interpolated into an existing document, it is possible that the dispositive section of Ecgberht's charter was modified at the same time in order to stress their joint ownership of the property. Indeed, the confirmation may originally have been in favour of the person from whom they inherited it, or even of a much earlier owner; it is possible that the word *postsessores* used in the disposition is not simply a version of *possessores* but rather a neologism with the force of 'later owner'. It should be noted that there is no other example before the tenth century of a royal diploma in favour of a woman who was not an abbess or connected in some way to a religious house. In the truncated witness-list the only subscriptions are those of Ecgberht and of Ealhstan, bishop of Sherborne, who took office between 816 and 825 and died in 867.

It is difficult to be certain whether or not the narrative section preceding the bounds is an addition. This states that the three sisters divided the land among themselves, each taking three hides and 'the third part of a fourth' (presumably meaning three and a third hides). After some years they received more of their *paterna hereditas*, which led to a new division of their property. Beornwyn went to Devon and took her share at a place called *Derentune homm* (the *hamm* associated with Dartington; for the significance of this, see *PN Devon*, i. 265, 297), leaving her land at Woolland to be reallocated between Ælfflæd and *Walenburh*. We are told that Ælfflæd took two hides in the western part, presumably adding them to her existing share of three and a third hides. If this section of the charter did form an integral part of Ecgberht's confirmation of 833, then it might be suggested that this new division between Ælfflæd and *Walenburh* was the incentive that prompted the sisters to apply for a charter to replace the one which had been mislaid. But if this were indeed the case then it is difficult to understand why the main dispositive section should stress that all three sisters were the 'possessors' of Woolland, although Beornwyn had now resigned her share. It is not possible to assert with confidence that a ninth-century scribe would *not* in those circumstances produce a document such as **2**, but there does seem to be some scope to suspect that the details about the two divisions of the property may represent a later addition to the text, intended to bring the estate history up to date. A close parallel can be found in a document from Christ Church, Canterbury, which was originally a charter of King Æthelwulf, probably issued in the 840s, granting land at Horton to Eadred (S 319). In the following decades the land changed hands several times and parts of it were hived off, as a result of which a certain Eadwulf came into possession of half a hide. He also apparently acquired the original landbook of Eadred or a copy of it, for this diploma was adapted at Christ Church, apparently in 874, to create a title-deed for Eadwulf's half-hide; details of the subsequent transaction were inserted into the original dispositive section and a new boundary clause inserted. The resulting document is a diplomatic travesty, but it presumably fulfilled Eadwulf's requirement for a valid landbook for his half hide at Horton. (As a further complication, S 319 is now extant as an eleventh-century single-sheet copy; it is possible that further interference with the text took place at this stage.) In a similar way, the extant text of **2** seems to have been drawn up or adapted to provide a title-deed for Ælfflæd's share of the land at Woolland (it is noticeable that the charter gives details of Ælfflæd's final allocation, but not that of *Walenburh*).

The second division left Ælfflæd with slightly more than half of the original ten-hide estate at Woolland. The two hides which she acquired from Beornwyn were located *in occidentali parte*, and it seems likely that her whole share lay in the western part of the estate. At this stage it is possible to see a connection with the later tenurial history of the area. In 1066 the manor at Woolland, assessed at five hides, was held by Milton Abbey (GDB 78r); immediately to the west was Shaftesbury's five-hide manor of Stoke Wake, which may have originated as a dependency of Woolland (GDB 78v). The combined territory of these two manors almost certainly represents the ten hides confirmed in Ecgberht's charter of 833, and the five hides belonging to Shaftesbury at Stoke Wake were probably those which fell to Ælfflæd's share after the division with *Walenburh*. This explains why the charter was preserved at Shaftesbury, and it also supports the suggestion that in its present form **2** represents an adaptation of Ecgberht's charter which was intended to provide a title-deed to Ælfflæd's share of the divided estate.

The crucial confirmation of this interpretation should lie in the boundary clause, which ought to refer only to Stoke Wake and not to the whole ten-hide Woolland property, and should presumably date from the ninth century. But interpretation of this survey is far from straightforward, and it is difficult to date. There is no problem in accepting that a West Saxon charter of 833 might include a detailed vernacular boundary clause, even though the other charters of Ecgberht which have such a clause seem to be spurious; in the second half of the eighth century it is not uncommon to find lengthy Latin bounds in charters dealing with land in Wessex (see S 262, 264, 267–8), and by the 840s West Saxon charter-scribes were certainly providing vernacular bounds (S 298, an original, and see S 290, 292). But the boundary clause in **2** has been judged to be much later than the ninth century, perhaps as late as the eleventh century (Peter Kitson and Margaret Gelling, pers. comms; Edwards, *Charters*, p. 234). It seems probable that the existing bounds were added to the text at some stage, perhaps as a substitute for an existing Latin or vernacular clause. This substitution may have been independent of the suspected interpolation detailing the two divisions of the property between the sisters, but is more likely to have taken place at the same time. It is also difficult to establish whether the bounds do indeed cover Stoke Wake. It has been argued by Hart (1964, pp. 158–9) that they outline the modern parish of Woolland, which would exclude Stoke Wake, but it should be noted that none of the boundary marks can be positively identified and it will be demonstrated below that the survey can also be made to fit the bounds of Stoke Wake parish. The meaning of the individual boundary marks is discussed in *PN Dorset*, iii. 232–8; Mills here follows Hart's interpretation.

The name Woolland (*Wennland*) derives from OE *wynn-land*, 'meadow-land' (*PN Dorset*, iii. 232–3). This was a hilly area, which would be used more for pasture than for arable cultivation. The survey begins and ends with an 'alder stream' (*alor, rið*), which appears to be one of the many feeders of the river Divelish. Hart identifies the boundary mark with a stretch of one stream running from ST 777087 to 785075, in the north-eastern part of Woolland parish. *PN Dorset* (iii. 233), accepts this identification, but links it with the place-name Aldermore which is found in several forms in an area to the south of Woolland (Broad Aldermore, Long Aldermore, Little Aldermore etc.; see also *PN Dorset*, iii. 229). Little Aldermore and Aldermore Copse lie in Stoke Wake, and an alternative identification for this boundary mark would be with the stream that runs parallel to the north-eastern section of the Stoke Wake parish boundary from ST 760081 to 770062, which in its upper stretches is associated with the woodland known as Little Aldermore. The next boundary mark appears to be corrupt; Hart's suggestion that it should be *þorne*, 'thorn-tree', may be preferable to the alternative *torr*, 'rocky crag', of *PN Dorset* (iii. 238), given the frequency with which thorn-trees occur as boundary marks in Dorset surveys. The boundary then touches on a 'ditch with an embankment' (*weall-dic*) and a 'row' (*ræw*), perhaps a row of trees or a hedge-row, before passing through the middle of *delesburg*. Hart associates this with the feature later known as Delcombe Head and interprets it as 'hill at the top of the dell' (*dell, beorg*); *PN Dorset* (iii. 221–2), relying on later forms, suggests that the present reading is corrupt, and that the feature may originally have been *deorlea(ge)sbeorg*, 'hill of the wood or clearing frequented by animals (perhaps more specifically deer)' (*deor, leah, beorg*). The identification of *delesburg* with Delcombe Head is far from certain, given the very different later forms associated with the modern place-name. If the survey is actually following the Stoke Wake boundary here, then an alternative identification would be with the tumulus known as Bul Barrow (ST 776057), which lies on the Stoke Wake/Woolland boundary to the south-east of Little Aldermore, or with Bulbarrow Hill itself. The next boundary mark is *cylberge*, which Hart identifies with a tumulus at ST 778055, close to the Stoke Wake/Woolland boundary and just to the south-east of Bul Barrow; this would fit both interpretations of the survey, but makes better sense in the context of the Stoke Wake parish boundary, where the tumulus marks the furthest point of an easterly spur. Hart takes the first element of *cylberge* to be a personal name *Cyla*, so 'Cyla's barrow or hill' (*beorg*); *PN Dorset* (iii. 237) suggests an alternative etymology of *ci(e)gel-beorg*, 'barrow marked by a pole'. A third alternative may be *cyll*, 'flagon, vessel, leather bottle', perhaps a reference to the shape of a particular barrow. *Wyrt-(t)ruma* (*wyrtrume*) and the related *wyrtwala* occur quite frequently in boundary-clauses, apparently indicating to a linear feature generally associated with wood-land. The meaning is disputed, but a plausible explanation is that these words referred to the banks whch demarcated the boundaries of a wood (Rackham, *Countryside*, p. 82). If the survey is here following the Stoke Wake boundary, it would at this point be running west along the southern edge of the protruding spur. Hart identifies the next boundary mark (*burg*) with Bul Barrow, assuming confusion of *beorg* with *burh* (see also *PN Dorset*, iii. 233). An alternative identification on the Stoke Wake parish boundary would be with the Iron Age hillfort known as Rawlsbury Camp (ST 767058), where *burh* would indeed be appropriate (*PN Dorset*, iii. 210–11). After this the survey touches on a ditch, and then runs along the old *hage* (perhaps *haga*, 'hedge, enclosure', but note that in this late manuscript it is difficult to distinguish *hege* and *hage* and similar words) to a thorn-tree. *Hacggen hamme* may be 'Hæcga's meadow or enclosure' (pers. n. Hæcga, *hamm*) or 'meadow or enclosure where haws grow' (*hagga, hamm*): see *PN Dorset*, iii. 237. According to Hart's interpretation this is a reference to the water-meadows now known as Woolland Dairy Farm (ST 764073); this would be about a mile to the north of Bul Barrow, the last boundary mark which he identifies. Alternatively, if the survey is here following the Stoke Wake boundary then it would run west to meet a stream (a feeder of the river Lydden) just to the north of Hatherly Farm (ST 755054). This would be an appropriate terrain for river-meadow, and there is also a possibility of some connection between the second interpretation of *hacggen hamme* and the etymology of Hatherly, thought to derive from *hagu*, 'hawthorn', and *leah*, 'clearing' (*PN Dorset*, iii. 210). From here the boundary goes past a hedge (*hege*) and an oak tree (*oc, ac*) and then crosses 'mill brook' (*myln, broc*). The next boundary mark is probably another thorn-tree. Finally the survey passes a (boundary-) post (*stapel*) and returns to 'alder stream'. Hart interprets these details in connection with the north-western section of the Woolland parish bounds (see *PN Dorset*, iii. 236, for a comment on 'mill brook'), but they could also be appropriate for the Stoke Wake parish boundary, which forms a bulge to the west of the stream on which Hatherly Farm is located (perhaps touching on the hedge and the oak-tree) before joining a second stream (perhaps the 'mill brook') and following it to approximately ST 743070, where it turns to the north-east. The word *ofer* is difficult to accommodate in this context, since the boundary follows the stream for some distance (unless it refers to the fact that the survey joins the stream from the west and leaves it on the east bank). From this point the Stoke Wake boundary runs directly north-east to join the proposed 'alder stream' at ST 760081. The boundary-post could have been located at the extreme northerly point of the parish, where there is a sharp angle in the parish boundary.

The survey can thus be made to fit the later parish boundaries of both Stoke Wake and Woolland, and there is no internal detail which conclusively favours one interpretation over the other. However, in view of the later tenurial history of the area, it seems more likely that the boundary clause covers Stoke Wake. In its present form **2** appears to be the title-deed for the five hides of the original ten-hide Woolland estate which came into the possession of Ælfflæd; her share seems to have been located in the western part of the estate. **2** was preserved at Shaftesbury, which held a five-hide Domesday manor at Stoke Wake, while the corresponding Woolland manor belonged to Milton Abbey. The probability is that **2** is the land-book for the western half of the Woolland estate, which later became known as Stoke Wake.

3

Æthelbald, king of the West Saxons, grants fourteen hides (cassati) *at Teffont, Wiltshire, to Osmund,* minister. A.D. 860

C. BL Harley 61, 18rv: copy, s. xv
  Rubric: + Hec est concessio regis Athelbaldi de .xiiii. cassatis terre iuxta Tefuntam qua ut in subsequente notatur pagina omni tempore dicta re concessit.
Ed.: a. Kemble 284 (with the bounds in vol. iii, p. 395)
    b. Birch 500
Listed: Sawyer 326; Finberg, *ECW,* no. 209

Regnante imperpetuum Deo et Domino Iesu Christo, cum cuius imperio hic labentis seculi prosperitas in aduersis successoribus sedulo*ᵃ* permixta et conturbata cernuntur*ᵇ* et omnia uisibilia atque desiderabilia ornamenta huius mundi ab ipsis amatoribus cotidie transeunt. Ideo beati quique ac*ᶜ* sapientes cum hiis fugitiuis seculi diuitiis eterna et iugiter permansura gaudia celestis patrie magno opere adipisci properant. Quapropter ego Adelbaldus gratia Dei occidentalium Saxonum rex dono atque concedo dilecto ac uenerabili ministro meo pro eius humili ob[ ]*ᵈ* Osmunde*ᵉ* terram .xiiii. cassatorum in loco qui appellatur be Tefunte, hoc est ut habeat et possideat prefatam terram in perpetuam hereditatem cum omnibus utilitatibus ad eam pertinentibus, campis, siluis, pratis, pascuis, atque omnia in omnibus quamdiu in ista transitoria uita demoratus fuerit, et post finem uite illius heredi cuicumque uoluerit liberam habeat donandi uel concedendi potestatem. Sit hec terra prefata secura et inmunis omnium rerum legalium*ᶠ* et principalium tributum et ui*ᵍ* exactorum operum, furisque comprehencione,*ʰ* simulque et omni populari grauidine,*ⁱ* nisi expedicione et pontis factione et arcium municione. Hec sunt termini terre.

Arest on þane reanden*ʲ* peg, ðat on ðone forde to Teofunte, þanen on brochenenberge, ðat on hoddes clif, þanen on abbenbeorg, ðat on scortencumb, on ðes linkes hauede suthward and northward, þanen on leon berg, þat on ða ealden dich, þanne onne þat furch ðe is aðe riuen*ᵏ* to Nodre, þannen on funtnesford,*ˡ* þannen on herepaþ, on þe reden wege, on*ᵐ* þa two meades oþer be Nodre oþer be Þilig ðe ðar to herað.

Siquis hanc meam ⟨donationem⟩*ⁿ* augere et amplificare uoluerit, augeat omnipotens Deus dies eius prosperos. Si uero quis infringere uel mutare presumpserit, noscat se ante tribunal eterni iudicis in die iudicii coram Christo et omnibus sanctis racionem redditurum esse, nisi prius satisfaccione emendauerit. Scripta est hec cartula anno dominice incarnacionis .d.ccc.lx., indiccione .iiii., istis testibus consencientibus quorum nomina infra scripta uidentur esse.

Adelbald rex. + Aedelbert rex. + Iudith regis filius.*[o]* + Suidhun episcopus. + Alhstan episcopus. + Osric dux, et ceteri. +

[a] scedulo C   *[b] For* cernitur   *[c]* ac et C   *[d]* ob *followed by blank space* C (*for* obsequio *or* obedientia)
[e] For Osmundo   *[f] For* regalium   *[g]* in C   *[h] A spelling for* comprehensione
[i] The grammatical construction of the immunity clause is confused, but was probably copied from a model (compare S 298)   *[j] Probably for* readen (*see final boundary mark*)
[k] For adrifen   *[l] Probably for* funtesford   *[m] For* and
[n] The word donationem *has fallen out here*
[o] The scribe seems to have omitted Judith's style and the names of one or more of Æthelbald's younger brothers, to whom the style regis filius *would properly apply*

Osmund is also the beneficiary of **4**, which covers three hides at Dinton, a short distance to the east of Teffont Magna. Both charters belong to 860, and were apparently issued respectively before and after the death of King Æthelbald. In most respects these seem to be authentic documents, but it is a difficulty that both are dated to the fourth indiction, although 860 would normally have been reckoned as the eighth indiction (in the dating clauses of ninth-century charters the incarnation year and the indiction are generally treated as if both began on 25 December, although technically the indiction should begin in September: see Harrison, *Framework*, pp. 115–16). The most likely explanation would be that the original dating clauses did not include an indiction (this is the case in the majority of West Saxon diplomas issued between 858 and end of the ninth century: see S 1274, 335–6, 340–1, 539); the present faulty indictions may both have been added by a later copyist.

The West Saxon charters of Kings Æthelbald, Æthelberht and Æthelred are intimately related in terms of structure and formulation, and may be the work of a royal scribe attached to the West Saxon court (see Keynes 1994c, pp. 1131–4). This group comprises three Shaftesbury diplomas (**3**, **4**, **5**; and see also **6**), three from Old Minster, Winchester (S 1274, 336, 340), two from Abingdon (S 335, 539) and one each from Glastonbury (S 341) and Sherborne (S 333, a vernacular translation); see also S 202, a forgery based on a West Saxon charter of this date. The formulation of the dispositive section and sanction of **3** has close links with that of the corresponding sections of the other texts in this group (see especially **4** and S 335–6). Most West Saxon charters of this period begin with an extended verbal invocation; that in **3** appears also in two charters of Æthelwulf dated 850 (S 300, 301). The closest parallel for the immunity clause is also to be found in a charter of Æthelwulf (S 298). The witness-list consists of a simple list of names with crosses (compare **4** and S 1274). The subscription of the donor's brother King Æthelberht is noteworthy.

In 858 Æthelwulf's territory had been divided between his two eldest sons; elsewhere they are seen to act independently in their separate realms (see S 328, 1274), but **3** indicates that they did meet on occasion (see further discussion in Keynes 1994c, pp. 1128–31). **3** may also have been witnessed by one or both of the younger brothers of the two kings, Æthelred and Alfred; the style *filius regis* which is mistakenly applied to Queen Judith would properly belong to them, and it can probably be assumed that the scribe has inadvertently omitted some part of the witness-list. The episcopal witnesses are Swithhun of Winchester and Ealhstan of Sherborne, and Osric was evidently ealdorman of Hampshire (*ASC s.a.* 860). The brief lacuna in the text suggests that the scribe may have found her exemplar difficult to read; she appears to have had similar problems with the boundary clause of **16**.

Osmund may have been a relative of Ealdorman Osric or of King Æthelwulf's first wife, Osburh, daughter of Oslac (Stevenson, *Asser*, p. 4; for speculation on the significance for West Saxon dynastic history of names beginning in Os-, see Nelson 1991). The name Osmund is common in witness-lists of the period; the beneficiary of this charter can probably be identified with the thegn who attests prominently in S 298, 1274, 333 and 335.

There are two neighbouring settlements called Teffont, lying on a stream flowing south to the river Nadder about ten miles north-east of Shaftesbury. The northern village is Teffont Magna, located near the source of the stream, on the lower slopes of the downs; immediately to the south is Teffont Evias. Teffont Magna was certainly a Shaftesbury possession in the later medieval period; in the Domesday survey it seems to have been reckoned under the community's twenty-hide manor at Dinton (GDB 67v). The dependency of Teffont on Dinton is highlighted by the fact that Teffont Magna remained a chapelry of Dinton parish until the nineteenth century (see *VCH Wilts.* VIII, p. 74). Teffont Evias was in different hands in 1086; it is listed among the lands of Alfred of Marlborough, with an assessment of six and a half hides TRE (GDB 70r). The two manors were probably regarded as distinct from a fairly earlier date, since they were situated in different hundreds (Teffont Evias in Dunworth, Teffont Magna in Warrington). A later charter in the archive (**25**) records a grant in 964 to a thegn named Sigestan of five hides in the common land at Teffont; it is likely that the five hides lay in Teffont Magna, with its later Shaftesbury connection, but in the absence of a boundary clause we cannot be certain of this.

Grundy (1919, pp. 181–3) has suggested that the fourteen-hide estate granted in **3** probably covered an area equivalent to the later parishes of both Teffont Magna and Teffont Evias. He bases his case in large part on the fact that the estate included two separate areas of appurtenant river-meadow, on the Nadder and the Wylye, apparently deducing that this indicated that two settlements were involved in the grant. This is hardly a convincing argument, since there is no reason why a single estate should not have rights in the river-meadow of two areas. The bounds of **3** are difficult to interpret on the ground and, while they clearly cover at least part of the later Teffont Magna parish, it is impossible to be certain whether they include or exclude Teffont Evias. On balance, it seems most likely that the fourteen-hide estate of 860 does represent the whole of the district known as 'Teffont' (that is, both Teffont Magna and Teffont Evias); this early land-unit would then have been divided up at some stage, with the northern part descending to Shaftesbury and being combined with Dinton, and the southern part passing into other hands.

The place-name Teffont appears to be formed from OE *teo, corresponding to OFris tia, 'boundary, boundary-line', and OE funta, 'spring, stream' (PN Wilts., pp. 193-4); Fovant, located directly across the Nadder, also includes the funta element (ibid., p. 214). To the north-west lie Fonthill Gifford and Fonthill Bishop; here the first element is thought to be a British river-name Font (DEPN, p. 183). This cluster seems significant (see Gelling, Signposts, p. 84), and may point to the existence of a local district-name Font or Funt. The element also occurs in funtesford in the bounds of 3, and in funtes hricg in the Tisbury survey (28). The fourteen-hide estate covered in 3 probably stretched from the Nadder valley in the south to the crest of the downs overlooking the Wylye valley. The northern boundary appears to have been partly defined by the ancient earthwork known as Grim's Ditch (ða ealden dich), as was the northern boundary of Teffont Magna parish; a charter of 940 covering ten hides on the Wylye (S 469) mentions Teofuntinga gemære in association with Grim's Ditch. The earthwork is also mentioned in the surveys of several other estates in this area (Forsberg 1942, p. 143): see 4 (Dinton), S 469 (Baverstock), S 766 (Sherrington), S 612 and 1811 (Little Langford). 'The old ditch' is the only boundary mark in 3 that can be identified with some confidence. The survey begins and ends at 'the red way' (read, weg), which apparently led to the ford 'to' Teffont. These points are likely to be on the southern boundary, somewhere in the Nadder valley; the ford may have been over the Nadder, at the south-western angle of Teffont Evias parish (ST 986300). After this there is a string of boundary marks appropriate for the downland terrain to the north: 'broken hill or barrow' (brocen, beorg), 'Hodd's escarpment' (pers. n. Hod(d), clif), 'Æbba's hill or barrow' (pers. n. Æbba, beorg) and 'the short combe' (sc(e)ort, cumb). The next feature is associated with a hlinc, in this case probably one of the ancient cultivation terraces known as known as strip-lynchets (Gelling, Place-Names, pp. 163-5); the 'headland' of the hlinc would presumably have been a projecting portion of the terrace (for heafod, see Gelling, ibid., pp. 159-60). Leon berg is another barrow or hill (beorg); the first element should probably be leou, for hleow, 'sheltered, sunny' (Smith, EPNE, i. 251). Then comes 'the old ditch' or Grim's Ditch, after which the next boundary mark is a furrow or trench (furh) which has been 'driven' to the Nadder. Grim's Ditch in the Teffont area is more than three miles from the Nadder, which seems a considerable distance to 'drive' anything that might be described as a furh. It is possible that, as Grundy supposed, some boundary marks have fallen out; or this passage may have become slightly corrupt. The eastern boundary of Teffont Magna parish did not reach the Nadder, but cut across from the downland to the Teffont stream; this was probably the location of funtes ford (for the first element, funt, see above). The boundary then ran along a highway (herepæð) back to 'the red way'.

4

Æthelberht, king of the West [Saxons], grants three hides (cassati) *at Dinton, Wiltshire, to Osmund,* minister. A.D. 860

C. BL Harley 61, 17v: copy, s. xv
    Rubric: Hec est donacio Athelberti regis de tribus cassatis in loco qui dicitur Duninghelande Deo et ecclesie sancti Edwardi Shafton' imperpetuum.
Ed.: a. Kemble 283 (with the bounds in vol. iii, p. 395)
      b. Birch 499
Listed: Sawyer 329; Finberg, *ECW*, no. 210

Regnante imperpetuum Domino nostro Iesu Christo summo et ineffabili rerum creatori ac moderatori omnium, in*ᵃ* sua multimoda disponens potencia temporibus ut uoluerit finem imponet. Iccirco cunctis agendum est ut hic bonis actibus future beatitudinis felicitatem adipisci mereantur. Quapropter ego Athelbert gracia Dei occidentalium ⟨Saxonum⟩*ᵇ* rex dono atque concedo dilecto ac uenerabili ministro Osmundo ⟨terram⟩*ᶜ* .iii. cassatorum*ᵈ* in loco qui dicitur Duningland sibi suisque heredibus in propriam atque perpetuam hereditatem, hoc est ut habeat ac possideat prefatam terram cum omnibus ad se pertinentibus, campis, siluis, pratis, atque omnia in omnibus ad eandem terram pertinentibus, quamdiu in hac uita uixerit; post uero suum ab luce decessum, liberam habeat donandi uel concedendi potestatem cuicumque donare uel concedere uoluerit. Sit hec prefata terra libera ab omni regali seruicio et omnium regularium*ᵉ* seruitute preter expedicionem. Si quis hanc nostro*ᶠ* satisfaccionis donacionem augere uel amplificare uoluerit, augeat omnipotens Deus dies eius prosperos. Si uero quis*ᵍ* infringere uel mutare ⟨presumpserit⟩,*ʰ* noscat se ante tribunal Christi redditurum racionem, nisi huius*ⁱ* satisfaccione emendauerit. Hiis terminis circumdatis.

Arest a norward þan londe on ða ealden dic, þanen ut þurch Suinleah,*ʲ* suð þið ðere*ᵏ* heren wike, þanen þið slahgraues, þanen on erðerburg, þanen on ceadenford, þanen þar suth ouer on þare oþer ea, þanen up on Nodre on þat rede clif, þanen north on dic, þanen on hrycg leah estward.

Scriptum quidem hec est cartula*ˡ* anno incarnacionis dominice .dccclx., indiccione .iiii., in loco qui dicitur Sumertun, testibus hiis consencientibus quorum nomina infra scripta uidentur esse.

Aþelberd rex. Adelstan*ᵐ* episcopus. Suiðhun episcopus. Aþeldred filius regis et ceteri.

    ᵃ Other examples of this invocation have the words tempora qui *instead of* in
    ᵇ The word Saxonum *has fallen out here*   *ᶜ The word* terram *has probably fallen out here*

^d carattorum C   ^e *For* secularium   ^f *For* nostre   ^g eius C
^h *The word* presumpserit *has fallen out here*   ⁱ *Probably for* prius
^j *Earlier editions read* sinnleah (*the* i *is not distinguished*)   ^k pid dere C
^l *Perhaps read* Scripta quidem est hec cartula   ^m *For* Alhstan (Ealhstan)

4 is in favour of the same individual as **3** and would appear to have been issued later in the same year. Both documents belong to an inter-related group of charters in the names of Æthelbald, Æthelberht and Æthelred (see **3**, and Keynes 1994c, pp. 1123–34). **4** shares with **3** an incorrect indiction; it is likely that in both cases this was inserted by a later copyist and that, as in the majority of West Saxon charters issued between 858 and the end of the ninth century, the dating clause of **4** did not originally include an indiction. **4** seems otherwise to be entirely acceptable. It begins with an extended invocation, which shades into a proem; this particular formula is also found in S 1274 (A.D. 858) and S 341 (A.D. 869), as well as in the 'Decimation' charters of 854 (S 303–5, 307–8; for the fundamental authenticity of these documents see S.E. Kelly, 'King Æthelwulf's Decimations', forthcoming). The formulation of the dispositive section seems contemporary (compare **3** and S 335–6, 340–1, 539); the anathema was also used in **3** (and see S 1274 and 335). The reservation clause is unusual in that it mentions only one of the three customary burdens; the same feature is found in S 330 (Kelly, *St Augustine's*, no. 22), which was drawn up at a royal vill in Surrey in 861 (but which has largely Kentish formulation). **4** was issued at Somerton in Somerset. The episcopal witnesses are Ealhstan of Sherborne (here corrupted to *Adelstan*) and Swithhun of Winchester. That Æthelberht's brothers did attest his charters as *filius regis* is indicated by S 327 (an original charter in which date and beneficiary have been altered).

Forsberg (1942, pp. 153–4) has convincingly located the three hides at *Duningland* in the eastern part of the later parish of Dinton. In 1066 Shaftesbury held a twenty-hide manor centred on Dinton (GDB 67v). This appears to have included land at Teffont Magna, perhaps representing part of the estate granted to Osmund in **3** (see also **25**, the record of a grant of five hides in the common land at Teffont). The Dinton manor was evidently a composite estate, built up by Shaftesbury or an earlier land-owner (presumably some time after **25** was issued in 964); it is not known at what date Shaftesbury came into possession of these lands. The early forms of Dinton point to an original *Duningtun*, 'Dun's farm or enclosure' (*PN Wilts.*, p. 160); *Duningland* may have been a secondary settlement to the east, or an alternative form of *Duningtun* (for the occasional overlap between *land* and *tun*, see Gelling, *Place-Names*, pp. 245–6). The survey begins to the north of the estate at 'the old ditch', which was the ancient earthworth known as Grim's Ditch, also mentioned in the bounds of Teffont (**3**), Baverstock (S 469), Sherrington (S 766) and Little Langford (S 612, 1811). From here the boundary seems to have descended south to the Nadder valley, west along the river and then north again into the downland. *Suinleah* is 'swine wood or clearing' (*swin, leah*), surviving as Swindley Copse (SU 105337; *PN Wilts.*, p. 161). The next boundary mark appears to be 'the hoary wych-elm' (*har*, gen. *haran, wice*); it is also mentioned in the Baverstock boundary clause in S 766 (*on haran wic westeweardne*). From here the boundary goes towards a 'sloe-tree grove' (*sla, graf*), before reaching an earthwork (*eorðburh*) and 'Ceada's ford' (pers. n. Cead(d)a, *ford*), after which it runs south to 'the other river' (the Nadder has two branches in this area). The boundary then follows the Nadder (probably westwards) to 'the red bank or slope' (*read*, *clif*), then goes north along a ditch and eastwards in a 'wood or clearing on a ridge' (*hrcyg*, *leah*); this last boundary mark may be the *Rygley* (also *Riggle* and *Ryggley*) mentioned in the 1570 survey of the lands of the Earl of Pembroke (Forsberg 1942, p. 154).

5

Æthelred, king of the Saxons, grants two hides (cassati) *at Cheselbourne, Dorset, to Ælfstan*, princeps. A.D. 859 [for 867/8 × 871, ? 869 or 870]

C. BL Harley 61, 18v–19v: copy, s. xv
    Rubric: Aeþeldredus rex ista subscripcione litterarum .ii. cassatos iuxta Cheselburnam ut presens notatur inscripcio in hereditatem concedit perhennem.
Ed.: a. Kemble 300 (with the bounds in vol. iii, p. 397)
      b. Birch 525
      c. Pierquin, *Recueil*, pt 2, no. 36
Listed: Sawyer 334; Finberg, *ECW*, no. 574

Regnante imperpetuum Domino nostro Iesu Christo. Omnia que uidentur temporalia sunt et que non uidentur eterna sunt; iccirco terrenis et caducis eterna et iugiter mansura mercanda sunt. Quapropter ego Atheldred Deo donante Saxonum rex, cum consensu et licencia omnibus optimatibus*ᵃ* gentis nostre, amantissimo atque fidelissimo meo principi Alfstano aliquam terre partem, id est duos cassatos in loco qui dicitur be Chiselburne, ut liberam habeat et uiuente et post obitum eius cuicumque uoluerit dare in eternam hereditatem, libenter impendo et deuota mente liberam, id est ut omnium regalium debitum et principalium rerum ceterarumque causarum furisque comprehencione*ᵇ* et ab omnium secularium seruitutum molestia secura et inmunis equaliter, sine expedicione et arcis municione, permaneat,*ᶜ* ut michi clemens et misericors rerum conditor ad uicissitudinem huius munificencie emulamentum largitur, ercata*ᵈ* piaculorum preterita indulgeat, presencia emendet, contra futura clipeum potentatus apponat. Si quis uero hanc donacionem atque libertatem augere uoluerit, sit mercis*ᵉ* eius cum sanctis angelis Dei; alioquin si quis diabolica fraude deceptus infringeret uel mutare desiderat, sciat se separatum*ᶠ* a consorcio sanctorum, nisi satisfactione emendauerit.

Ðis is þes landes imare þus uten ymsald.*ᵍ* Arest on land scorhlinc to Chiselburne, þannen anlang streames, þannen up of streame on anne hlincheshˌeaued, þanen be suþe scaftesbury*ʰ* on þane hlinc, of þat ihlinche on anne castel at swindune upward, of ðycastele to burnstowe, þanen on anne linkes heaued, þanen to anne castel, of ðicastele on anne herepaþ, westward

ouer herepaþ on hlinc reawe, þanen on anne crundel to burnstowe,[i] on anne
cnap, on anne ierð londe northward, þanen wið anne crundeles, of þane
crundele on þes heges hirne, þanen eft to herepaðe, of herepaðe on heandene
beorg, on Deuelisc, of dune anlang streames, up of streame on anne furch,
on anne stan castel, of ða icastele on bleomannes[j] berge, of þa iberge on
land scarlinc, an[k] sex made eres[l] be Frome be[m] Deuelisc made þe ierþ on
þise lande.

Scripta est hec signigrafa[n] in publico loco qui dicitur at Wdegeate, anno ab
incarnacione Domini nostri Iesu Christi .d.ccc.lix., indiccione .iii., coram
ydoneis testibus quorum nomina infra clare patescit.[o]

Ego Aþeldred rex hanc donacionis cartulam propria manu cum signo sancte
crucis confirmaui. +

Signum manus[p] Alfherð[q] episcopi. +

Signum Heahmundi episcopi, et ceteri. +

[a] *For* omnium optimatum   [b] *A spelling for* comprehensione
[c] *The various elements of the immunity clause are grammatically incompatible*
[d] *? For* errata   [e] *A spelling for* merces   [f] reparatum C
[g] *See the commentary for the meaning of this phase*   [h] *Error for* ceatpanberge (*see* **6**)
[i] burstowe C   [j] *Probably for* blæcmannes (*compare* **6** *and* **30**)   [k] *For* and
[l] *For* æceras   [m] wið *in* **6**   [n] *A spelling for* syngrapha   [o] *For* patescunt   [p] manu C
[q] *For* Alhferð (Ealhferð)

For commentary on this charter see that on **6**, pp. 24–8.

6

*Æthelred, king of the West Saxons, grants five hides at Cheselbourne,
Dorset, to Ealdorman Ælfstan.* [A.D. 867/8 × 871, ? 869 or 870]

C. BL Harley 61, 20rv: copy s. xv
  Rubric: + Atheldredus rex huius carminis inscripcione dimisit et uendidit v. hidas ad
  Cheselburniam cum omnibus rite pertinentibus ut in subsequente scripto subnotatur.
Ed.: a. Kemble 302 (with the bounds in vol. iii, p. 398)
     b. Birch 526
     c. Robertson, *Charters*, no. 12 (pp. 22–5), with translation
Listed: Sawyer 342; Finberg, *ECW*, no. 575

Regnante imperpetuum Domino nostro Iesu Christo. Rixiende ure dritte
halende Crist. Ich Atheldred mid Godes giue Westsaxne king mid leue and
eþeafunghe mine ðare seleste þiotene, ich forgiue and selle for me selfne
minre saule to alesnesse minne ðam leueste and itreweste alderman Elfstane

alchene idal landes in þare istowe þe is inemned be Chiselburne fif hide, him to habbene and to brukende on elche halue, þat is þanne þat it bie i.sien[a] fre of al ikenelricre and alderdomelere þinghe an i.witradenne, an of elchene þinghe buten fierde and angieldes. And het it acheliche fre þurgwine habbe suelcman suo al se ich it habbe gief donne huelman[b] be segen[a] þat he þis giue, and sale ieche oð manifelde wille, i.ache him almigti God alle goode here for wolde and his igaste furch, agiue þa ache reste in ðam towarde liue. If þat ilimpe þat oniman þurch deules lore and for þeses middelerdes idle þinghe on onni idale ilitel oþer michel þis ibreke oþer iwanie, wite he hine fram alle leaffulle inne þese iworlde asceaden, and he des sel in domes deghe beforen Criste rich agieldende bute he it are her on worlde mid richte ibete.

Ðis land is þisen imare, þus ute þinsald.[c] Arest on landscar hlinc to Cheselburne, þannen anlang streames, þanen up of streame on anne linkes haued, þanen be suðe ceatpanberge on þanne hlinc, of þanne i.hlinche on anne castel at swindone uuepearde, of þe castele to burnstowe, þanen up anlang burnstowe, þanen on anne linkes heued, þanen to anne castele, of þo icastel on þere herepaþ westward, ep[d] ðe herepað on þat hlinc reawe, þanen on anne crundel to burnstowe, on anne cinep, on ðan gerðe lande nordewarde, þanen wið anne crundeles, of þi crundele on ðes[e] heges hirnen, þanen eft to herepað, of þe ereðe[f] on Hendune beorch, on Deflisch, of dune anlang streames, up on streame on anne furch, on anne stancastel, of þi castele on blieq;mannes[g] beorg, of þa iberge on land scare hlinc, and sex made eres[h] be Frume wið Deuliscmad ierð to þise land.

Ðises landes freols was iwriten in þare stowe þat is inemned at Þudegate[i] beforen þese wetene þe here namen her beneþen amerkede standen.

Aþeldred Rex. + Ealferð episcopus. + Heahmund episcopus, et ceteri. +

---

[a] ? past participle of OE seon, 'to see' (Robertson, Charters, p. 282)
[b] oniman written above line C   [c] Probably for ymsald as in 5 (see commentary)
[d] Probably for of   [e] des C   [f] Probably for herepaðe (compare 5)
[g] bleomannes in 5; blacmannes in 30   [h] For æceras   [i] Pudegate C

---

5 and 6 are both charters of King Æthelred in favour of Ealdorman Ælfstan, apparently issued at at the same place (Woodyates in Dorset, about ten miles west of Shaftesbury) and covering land at Cheselbourne. They have the same boundary clause but different assessments; 5 allegedly covers two hides and 6 five. This discrepancy could be the result of scribal confusion at one stage between *ii* and *v*, but may also have some connection with the complex history of the Cheselbourne estate, which is discussed below. 6 is undated, while 5 is attributed to 859, which is incompatible with the donor (Æthelred was king between 865 and 871) and with

the attestation of Bishop Heahmund of Sherborne, who was appointed in 867 or 868 and died in 871; an easy emendation would be to 869. **5** is also dated to the third indiction, which would be more appropriate for 870 (the indiction technically ran from September to September, but in ninth-century charters was usually calculated from Christmas Day: see Harrison, *Framework*, pp. 115–16). However, West Saxon charters from this period did not usually include an indiction and there is some reason to believe that the examples in **3** and **4** were added by a later Shaftesbury copyist; it is possible that the indiction in **5** is also an addition, in which case the broader dating limits of 867/8 × 871 would apply. **5** is diplomatically acceptable as a charter of that date, although its boundary clause is probably a later substitution. Its formulation is very similar to that of other West Saxon charters issued by Æthelred and his older brothers, among them **3** and **4** (see pp. 17, 21; and Keynes 1994c, pp. 1123–34). The proem is a standard formula which recurs, with minor variations in its wording, in charters from the seventh to the eleventh century; a very similar proem appears in S 539, which is probably from 868 (see also S 340). West Saxon kings in this period were usually styled *rex occidentalium Saxonum*, but *rex Saxonum* was often used in the eighth century and was revived in Alfred's reign, so there is no real difficulty with its appearance in **5** (it is also possible that the adjective was omitted by a copyist, just as *Saxonum* disappeared from the same formula in **4**). The wording of the dispositive section and sanction seems contemporary, although it is difficult to parallel precisely; the immunity clause is comparable with that in **3** (and see also S 288, 290). The syntax of the immunity clause is faulty, probably because the scribe was here combining elements from two different models. It is followed by a unique passage in which the king expresses his hopes that the grant will bring him future divine indulgence and protection; the draftsman may have had in mind the threat posed by the Viking forces in Mercia, which was to materialise in the invasion of Wessex in 871. For the wording of the dating clause, see also S 335 and 336 (neither of which includes an indiction). In the truncated witness-list the episcopal witnesses are Ealhferth of Winchester and Heahmund of Sherborne. Little is known about the beneficiary, Ealdorman Ælfstan. Several charters issued between 862 and *c.* 875 were witnessed by an Ælfstan *dux*; the witness-list in S 340 suggests that two individuals of that name and status may have been attesting over the same period.

6 almost certainly represents a translation of **5**. Robertson (*Charters*, pp. 281–3) came to the opposite conclusion, arguing that the differences between the two texts are significant and that they indicate that the Middle English document had an Old English predecessor which was drawn up independently of **5**. The principal divergence between **5** and **6** occurs in the immunity clause. **5** includes among the exemptions the item *furis comprehensio* (equivalent to *infangenetheof*, the right to try a thief captured on the property and to take the profits), which is quite often mentioned in West Saxon charters in the mid ninth century (compare **3**, and S 288, 290, 292 etc.). **6** has instead *witerӕden*, which refers to the payment of fines (all fines paid were to go to the owner of the estate instead of the king). It seems that the vernacular privilege is here using a blanket term for profits of justice and perhaps therefore claiming a wider exemption; this is not incompatible with the suggestion that **6** is basically a translation of **5**. Similarly, in the reservation clause the Latin text specifies military service and fortress construction, while **6** refers to *fyrd*, military service, and to *angild*, which is a common term in lawcodes and an obligation sometimes mentioned in earlier ninth-century charters under the term *singulare pretium* (see S 171, 185, 186 etc.); it means that in criminal cases only simple compensation was to be paid to the plaintiff outside the estate, with no punitive fines (these were to be paid to the owner of the estate instead, so *angild* in the reservation clause balances *witeræden* in the immunity clause). Robertson concluded that these variations show that the two texts were essentially independent and that the vernacular version was not taken directly from the Latin; she suggested that two land-grants were involved, and that the common boundary clause belonged to only one of them, but was later wrongly associated with the other as well. An alternative explanation, which seems preferable, is that **6** represents a free translation of the Latin text, in which the scribe expressed the immunities enjoyed by the estate in different terms, paying more attention to the jurisdictional aspect than the original draftsman. It is difficult to believe that Ealdorman Ælfstan was the beneficiary of two separate grants of land at Cheselbourne, apparently made on the same occasion. **6** is far more likely to be the result of translation, probably of an initial translation into Old English which was modernized in the later medieval period.

To seek a better understanding of the relationship between these two documents, it is necessary to look more closely at the history of the Cheselbourne estate. In 1019 Cnut granted sixteen hides at Cheselbourne to one of his Danish followers, an area roughly corresponding with the later parish (**30**); Shaftesbury's Domesday manor had the same assessment and probably covered the same territory (GDB 78v). The estate which we see in 1019 seems effectively to have been created in 942, when King Eadmund restored to a nun named Wynflæd seven hides at Cheselbourne and also granted her another eight hides there from his own patrimony (**13**). In Eadmund's charter the boundary clause is incomplete; it describes only the northern and eastern boundaries of the Cheselbourne estate, and omits to define the southern boundary. It seems likely that the draftsman was concerned only to cover the eight hides that were being added to Wynflæd's existing holding, and that he saw no reason to give details of the common boundary of the two areas (we can deduce from this that Wynflæd already owned land in the southern and western part of Cheselbourne). The implication is that Wynflæd already had a charter or charters with a boundary clause providing title to the seven hides of her original Cheselbourne property. **13** also provides some extra information about these seven hides. The passage is difficult to interpret, but it seems to state that Wynflæd had been given five hides by a certain Ælfsige, and that two hides had later been added by Eadmund himself; these two hides were not at Cheselbourne itself, but in a dependency some miles away on the river Winterborne. These details are of some help in understanding **5** and **6**. The different assessments in the two documents now gain significance; it seems likely that at some stage **5** and **6** were regarded as complementary, respectively giving title to the two-hide and five-hide territories which made up Wynflæd's original seven-hide holding.

Their common boundary clause adds a further dimension of complication. It appears to describe almost the whole of the later Cheselbourne parish, effectively the same area as the sixteen-hide estate granted by Cnut in **30** (the only difference is that the survey in **5** and **6** omits the section of the estate lying east of Devil's Brook, but this may be due to scribal error – see below). If **5** and **6** are supposed to represent the earlier documentation of Wynflæd's seven-hide holding, then their boundary clause seems out of place. It is possible that the texts were worked over by more than one revisor, with different intentions, or perhaps they were created by a single forger who was not consistent in his approach. What is clear is that **5** and **6** cannot be confidently accepted as a genuine Latin diploma and a free translation. Although **5** is clearly based on a ninth-century charter, its present form appears to reflect the preoccupations of a fabricator; the boundary clause at least would appear to be a substitution or insertion, and it is impossible to be certain that the model did actually record a grant of land at Cheselbourne.

The context for the creation of these texts may have been an eleventh-century dispute over Cheselbourne. The sixteen hides granted to Aghmundr in 1019 (**30**) had passed to Shaftesbury by the Confessor's reign. The Domesday entry for Shaftesbury's manor (GDB 78v) notes that Earl Harold had seized Cheselbourne along with other Shaftesbury estates, and that King Edward had issued a writ ordering its restitution; this was apparently not implemented, but after the Conquest the writ was discovered in the abbey church and King William restored the estate (see p. xxiii). These events would explain why the Shaftesbury community might be very anxious about the validity and adequacy of the documentation supporting to its claim to Cheselbourne, and would provide a context for the production of a translation and for some tampering with earlier diplomas.

The boundary clause common to the two charters has been well discussed by Grundy, in the context of all the Cheselbourne surveys (Grundy 1934, pp. 115–30); better interpretations of some of the boundary-marks are to be found in *PN Dorset* (iii. 205–8). Generally the survey seems to correspond with the later parish boundary of Cheselbourne, beginning on the southern boundary at a point between Cheselbourne stream and Devil's Brook, and then proceeding in a clockwise direction. It omits the section of the parish around Lyscombe Bottom in the north-west, which is a relatively recent addition, and it also leaves out that part which lies to the east of Devil's Brook; in this case there is some possibility that a copyist has made a mistake and conflated two references to the *Deuelisc*, omitting the intervening section of the survey. In both **5** and **6** the survey is introduced by a unique vernacular phrase; it should probably read (preferring the version in **5**): 'Ðis is þæs landes gemære þus utan ymbsæled' ('This is the boundary of the land thus bound on the outside'). The first boundary mark was a strip-linchet or ancient ploughing terrace (*hlinc*) lying on a boundary (*landscearu*); it was apparently located to the east of Cheselbourne stream, just above Chebbard Farm (SY 762982). The boundary follows the stream for a very short distance, and then turns westwards, where it encounters the 'headland' or projecting portion (*heafod*) of another linchet before passing to the south of 'Ceatwa's barrow' (pers. n. Ceatwa, *beorg*), which scribal inattention has transformed to *scaftesbury* in **5**; the name Ceatwa is also found in nearby Chebbard Farm (see *PN Dorset*, i. 303–4). The next boundary marks are another linchet and a 'heap of stones' (*ceastel*) on 'swine down' (*swin*, *dun*); Grundy associates the latter with the hill to the south of Hog Leaze now occupied by Dole's Hill plantation. *Burnstow* in this instance probably means 'the channel or bed or an intermittent stream'; it appears to refer to the stream flowing south from Lyscombe Farm which is called *lisc broc* in **13** and **30** (see *PN Dorset*, iii. 205). The boundary, now running north, follows this feature for a distance, then turns to take in an area to the west of the stream, defined by another 'headland of the linchet', another 'heap of stones', a highway (*herepæð*), a 'linchet row' (*hlinc-ræw*) and a gully or quarry (*crundel*); it then re-encounters the *burnstow* at a point further north. The hill-top or hillock (*cnæp*) may mark the north-western corner of the estate. From here the boundary (now probably running east) goes north of a piece of ploughland (*ierðland*), past another gully, and then reaches a 'bend in the hedge' (*hege, hyrne*) and another highway. The next boundary mark is a barrow (*beorg*) on 'high down' (*heah*, wk. obl., *hean, dun*), which is probably Henning Hill to the north of Cheselbourne (*PN Dorset*, iii. 218); the barrow may be the feature known as Giant's Grave (ST 757017). The boundary passes west to Devil's Brook and appears to follow the stream for some distance. It is here that the survey in **5** and **6** diverges from those in **13** and **30**, which briefly follow Devil's Brook but then turn to take in an area to the east of the brook before bending back to meet it once more further south. It is possible that an early scribe confused the two references to the Devil's Brook and inadvertently omitted the intervening boundary marks. From the stream the survey in **5** and **6** (now running west again) rises to a furrow or ditch (*furh*) and another heap of stones (apparently equivalent to the *stancyste* of **30**). The feature called *bleomannes berge* in **5** and *blieq;mannes beorg* in **6** is *blacmanne berge* in **30**; this would appear to be a personal name Blæcmann, with *beorg*, probably here 'barrow'. The survey now returns to its starting point. The property included six acres of meadow on the river Frome and (?) by Devil's Brook.

7

Alfred, king, grants forty hides at Donhead, Wiltshire, and Compton Abbas, Dorset; twenty at Sixpenny Handley and Gussage, Dorset; ten at Tarrant Hinton, Dorset; fifteen at Iwerne Minster, Dorset; and fifteen at Fontmell Magna, Dorset, with various privileges of jurisdiction, to Shaftesbury Abbey. [A.D. 871 × 877]

C. London, BL Harley 61, 21v–22r: copy, s. xv
  Rubric (*before both versions*): Hoc est testamentum regis Aluredi quod propria uoluntate
  ecclesie de Sheftesbury facere adquieuit.
Ed.: a. Hutchins, *Dorset*, ii. 21
      b. Kemble 310
      c. *Mon. Angl.* (rev. edn), ii. 477 (no. 2)
      d. Birch 531 (English), 532 (Latin)
      e. Pierquin, *Recueil*, pt 2, no. 42
      f. Robertson, *Charters*, no. 13 (p. 24), English only, with translation, p. 25
Listed: Sawyer 357; Finberg, *ECW*, no. 212

Ðis is þe quide þat Alured king ian in to Sceaftesburi, Gode to loue and seint Marie and alre Godes halegen, mine saule to þearue on halre tungan, þ is an hund hide mid mete and mid manne al so it stant, and mine dochte Agelyue forð mid þare erie in to þan menstre for þanne hie was onbroken

ihadod, and mine socne in to þan menstre þat ic selue achte, þat is forsteal
and hamsocne and mundebreche. And þis sent þare landiname þe ic þider
iunnen habbe, þat is at Dunheued and at Cumtune .xl. hide, and at Hanlee
and Gissic .xx. hide, and at Terente .x. hide 7 at Ywern .xv. hide and
Funtemel*a* .xv. hiden. And þis is to witnesse Adward mine sune and Aþered
arceb' and Alcheferd bissop and Adelheach b' and Wlfhere alderman and
Adwlf alderman and Cuðred alderman and Tumbert abb' and Midred mine
þegen and Aþelþulf et Osric and Berthful and Cyma. And loke hþa þeses
awande, habbe he Godes curs et sainte Marien and alle Godes haleges ac
on ecnesse. Amen.

Ego Rex Aluredus in honore Dei et sancte Marie uirginis et omnium
sanctorum dono et concedo, uiuens et in prosperitate adhuc uigens, Sceptoniensis*b* ecclesie centum hidas terre cum hominibus et aliis pertinenciis
quemadmodum modo se habent*c* et Ayleuam filiam meam cum eisdem, que
cogente infirmitate in eadem ecclesia facta est sanctimonialis, preter hec iura
que ad corona mea*d* pertinent, scilicet forsteal et hamsokne et munbrech. Et
hec sunt nomina terrarum qua*e* supradicte ecclesie dedi et concessi: Dunehefda et Kuntune quadraginta hidas, in Henlee et Gersicg uiginti hidas, in
Tarente decem hidas, in Hywerna quindecim hidas, in Funtemel quindecim
hidas. Huius rei testes sunt Edwardus filius meus, Athelredus archiepiscopus,
Alfredus episcopus, et Adelheacus episcopus et Wlfere, Raduulfus, Kudredus
ealdreman, Turebertus abbas, Mildredus et Atelwlfus et Osricus et Berthwlfus
et Cuna mei.*f* Quicumque hec auerterit sit a Deo et sancta Maria uirgine et
omnibus sanctis maledictus in eternum. Amen.

a ffuntemel C   *b* *For* Sceptoniensi   *c* he'bent C   *d* *For* coronam meam
e *For* quas   *f* *The word* ministri *has probably fallen out here*

7 is clearly spurious, although certain of its details (such as the information that
Æthelgifu had poor health) may be based on the community's records and valid
traditions about its early history. It was probably composed in Old English; the
present vernacular text has been considerably modernized by later copyists, and the
Latin version is evidently a late translation. It is difficult to suggest a date for the
fabrication, but the likelihood is that it took place in the late eleventh or twelfth
century; the privileges of jurisdiction to which the document refers are often mentioned
in royal writs from the eleventh century onwards (for the meaning of the terms, see
Harmer, *Writs*, pp. 79–81). The forgery may not have had much currency; it is
probably significant that it comes at the end of the pre-Conquest charters in the
Shaftesbury cartulary, although its importance as a foundation document should
have merited a more prominent position. The forger has drawn upon a genuine
document of Alfred's reign for the witness-list. The episcopal witnesses are Archbishop

Æthelred, Ealhferth of Winchester and Æthelheah of Sherborne. Ealhferth died between 871 and 877, and this provides the dating limits for the forger's source; these are difficult to reconcile with the subscription of the ætheling Edward, who can hardly have been old enough to act as a witness by 877 (he does not attest other charters until the 890s: see S 348, 350, 354–6), so perhaps the forger was using more than one source. The subscriptions of the three ealdormen are compatible with a date in the 870s: Wulfhere was the beneficiary of S 341 (A.D. 869) and attests several charters in the 850s and 860s; Ealdorman Eadwulf subscribes after Wulfhere in S 340 and 1201 (both A.D. 868); Cuthred is the beneficiary of a Winchester lease of 871 × 877 (S 1275), which is subscribed by Abbot Tumberht.

As a guide to the initial endowment of Shaftesbury 7 is clearly untrustworthy. Two of the places mentioned (Tarrant Hinton and Fontmell Magna) were not granted to the community until the reign of Æthelstan (see 9, 8). There is also some reason to believe that Iwerne Minster was still in royal possession in 963 (see 21 and 24). Nothing is known about the acquisition of the other estates said to have been given by Alfred; they are located within a fifteen-mile radius of Shaftesbury and could conceivably have formed part of the core endowment, but there is no other evidence to confirm the claim (see further discussion, pp. xxiii–xxvi). 7 must be considered in relation to 21, a charter in the name of Eadwig which purports to record the grant of eighty (or ninety) hides to the abbey; although the location of this land is not specified, 21 includes bounds for all the estates mentioned in 7, with the significant exception of Tarrant Hinton and Fontmell Magna. (The Gussage mentioned in 7 but not in 21 is Gussage St Andrew, a secondary settlement in the manor of Sixpenny Handley.) The authenticity of 21 is highly debatable, but it seems most likely to be spurious as it stands. Since it attributes the grant of these estates to Eadwig rather than Alfred, the supposed founder of Shaftesbury and thus a more charismatic donor as far as the community was concerned, it can probably be assumed that it represents an earlier tradition about the acquisition of this property than does 7. The forger of 7 probably knew 21, and was perhaps intending to improve upon it as a title-deed to part of the abbey's central endowment (with references to Tarrant Hinton and Fontmell Magna thrown in for good measure). For more detail on the history of these estates, see 21 (and for Tarrant Hinton and Fontmell Magna see 9 and 8).

8

King Æthelstan grants eleven and a half hides (carattae *for* cassati) *at Fontmell, Dorset, to the* familia *at Shaftesbury.* A.D. 932 (24 December)

C. BL Harley 61, 11r–12r: copy, s. xv
  Rubric: Hoc est donum Aþelstani regis de .xi. carr' terre ut uocant solicoli iuxta Funtemel.
Ed.: a. Kemble 361 (with the bounds in vol. iii, pp. 409–10)
      b. Birch 691
Listed: Sawyer 419; Finberg, *ECW*, no. 577

Flebilia fortiter detestanda totillantis seculi piacùla, diris obscene horendeque
mortalitatis circumsepta latratibus, non nos patria indepte pacis securos sed
quasi fetide coruptele in uoraginem[a] cassuros prouocando ammonent, ut ea
toto mentis conamine cum curribus[b] suis non solum dispiciendo[c] sed eciam
uelut fastidiosam melancolie iniuriam[d] abhominando fugiamus, tententes[e]
ad illud euuangelicum, 'Date et dabitur uobis'.[1] Qua de re infima quasi
[peripsema quisquiliarum abiciens, superna ad instar preciosorum monilium][f]
eligens, adipiscendam[g] melliflue dulcedinis [misericordiam][h] perfruendamque
infinite leticie iocunditatem, ego Aþelstanus rex Anglorum, per omnipotentis[i]
dexteram tocius Britannie regni solio sublimatus, quandam telluris particulam fidelissime familie monialium que sub regulari deuote exercitacionis
uita in monasterio ciuitatis que Schaftesbiry uocatur Deo militat, id est .xi.
et dimidia adtecta carattarum[j] in loco quem solicole et Funtemel uocitant,
ea interiacente condicione, ut omni die usque magne discrecionis[k] iudicii
anno[l] illa successoresque eius cotidie post primam quinquaginta decantent
psalmos, anime pro excessibus mee, horaque mediante tercia missam per-
celebrent, ut diuinam consequi plenissime ualeam misericordiam, tribuo.
Quatinus illa eam sine iugo detestande seruitutis cum pratis, pascuis, siluis,
riuulis omnibusque ad illam utilitatibus rite pertinentibus liberaliter ac
eternaliter quamdiu uiuat habeat, et post generalem qui omnibus certus
incertusque constat transitum subsequentibus sibi fidelibus imperpetuum
derelinquat. Predicta siquidem tellus hiis terminis circumcincta clarescit.
Arest on Wde brigthe and þanen up on beteswirþe sled, þanen to snelles
hamme weghe, þanen on þurch þo aelres to holencumbe, of þanne cumbe to
holenwelle, of þan welle on hamelendune north ecge, þanen to Langencumbes
hauede, þanen on dollen berch, an[m] þanne to wde, on ðon hagen, oð þas
soces seað, ðanen on holewei, of holleweie on sledwich,[n] of sledweie on
hrigcspeg,[o] þannen anlang hricg þeges, of rig wei ut to þe wines weie, þanen
to burch linken, ðannen[p] on þa gereþrenc withinne ða[q] chealc seðas, þanen
to holebroke, þanen on ðies littlen Seaxpennes suð eke,[r] þane on sandhellesled, þanen on ða riþe to Styrd,[s] þanen anlang streames eft to Wde
bricge, þanen on halgan weies[t] lake, þanen to þanen welle siluen, þanen on
þa hege reawe to þane shamelen, an[u] to þan herepaþe, þonne west be
wintrintune[v] ut þurch sulan graf, þanne one þe hegen, be weste hegen paðe
and þar of dune to þare stigele, þanne west anlang hegen to heldmannes
wrthe suthward, þanen north to ludmannes putte, þanen be wntrune[w] on
blinches broc, of þanne broke to wigheardes stapele, fram wigheardes stapele
to cludesleghe,[x] of þare lege to þanen ealden herepaþe þ schet to blinchesfelde,
þanen forð be þyrttrune to scearpenhame, þanen one þat lake to Stirchel,
anlang streames eft to Wdebrige, and at Suttune ligð .xxiiii. akeres meade

þat hirð in to Funtmel, on*^m* ðes horderes land oþer half hewisse of Suttune erþe in to þis land.

Si autem quod absit aliquis diabolico inflatus spiritu et hanc mee composicionis*^y* ac confirmacionis breuiculam demere uel infringere temptauerit, sciat se nouissima ac magna examinacionis die, tuba perstrepente archangeli, bustis sponte dehiscentibus, somata diu fessa relinquentibus, elimentis omnibus pauefactis, cum Iuda proditore qui a satoris*^z* pio sato filius perdicionis dicitur eterna confusione edacibus ineffabilium tormentorum flammis periturum. Huius namque a Deo Dominoque Iesu Christo inspirante atque inuente uoluntatis scedula anno dominice incarnacionis .d.cccc.xxxii., regni mei gratis mihi commisi octauo, indiccione .v., concurrente septimo, epacta .xi., kalendis Ianuarii nonis, luna rotigere uagacionis terciodecimo, in uilla omnibus notissima que Ambresburch nuncupatur, episcopis, abbatibus, ducibus, patrie procuratoribus regia dapsilitate ouantibus, perscripta est, cuius eciam inconcusse firmitatis auctoritas hiis testibus roborata constat quorum nomina subtus carretteribus*^a2* depicta annotantur.

Ego Athelstanus singularis priuilegii monarchia preditus*^b2* rex et huius indiculi fulcimentum cum signo sancte crucis corroboraui et subscripsi. +
Ego Wlfhelmus Doroborasensis*^c2* ecclesie archiepiscopus consensi et subscripsi. +
Ego Wlfstanus ecclesie Eboracensis archiepiscopus consensi et subscripsi et ceteri. +

^a uoragine C   *^b* *Probably for* casibus   *^c* *A spelling for* despiciendo
^d *Probably an error for* nauseam   *^e* *A spelling for* tendentes
^f *In this section the MS is mostly illegible, and some parts have been supplied from*
S 416   *^g* *Other examples of this formula read* ad adipiscendam
^h *Word illegible in MS, supplied from* S 416
^i *Other examples of this formula read* omnipatrantis   *^j* *For* cassatorum
^k *Probably for* districtionis (*compare* S 418)
^l S 418 *also reads* anno (*perhaps error for* die)   *^m* *For* and   *^n* *Probably for* sledweie
^o hriycspeg C   *^p* dannen C   *^q* da C   *^r* *Probably for* ecge
^s *Probably error for* Styrchel (Stirchel)   *^t* *Error for* welles   *^u* *Probably for* on *or* and
^v winteintune *in earlier editions* (*probably for* wirtrume)   *^w* *For* wirtrume
^x tudesleghe *in* 23   *^y* compocionis C   *^z* sadoris C   *^a2* *For* caracteribus
^b2 monachia predutus C   *^c2* *For* Dorobernensis

[1] Luc. 6: 38

The great majority of the royal diplomas issued between 928 and 934 conform to a very distinctive model, characterized by a high level of standardization, by lush and vivid language and imagery, and in particular by a dating clause incorporating a variety of unusual details (probably read off from an Easter table) and a very long witness-list, which might include more than a hundred subscriptions (see further, *BAFacs.*, p. 9). The two surviving originals from this period were written by a single scribe, designated 'Æthelstan A' by Drögereit (1935, pp. 345–8) and 'Scribe 1' by Chaplais (1965, p. 60 [p. 41]), and it is generally assumed that this scribe was also responsible for drafting the texts. Chaplais (*ibid.*) believes that he was attached to the Winchester scriptorium, to which charter-production had been temporarily delegated (see also Chaplais 1985, pp. 47–9); Keynes (*Diplomas*, pp. 42–4) argues that he was a royal scribe, working directly on the king's orders. **8** conforms closely to the pattern of 'Æthelstan A' diplomas, lacking only the extended witness-list (understandably curtailed by the cartularist or in her exemplar). Its proem was the one which 'Æthelstan A' used exclusively between 931 and 933 (in 934 he switched to a different formula, beginning *Fortuna fallentis saeculi*). **8** is one of a small sub-group of 'Æthelstan A' diplomas issued between 24 December 932 and 26 January 933 which impose certain religious conditions in return for the grant; lay beneficiaries are required to feed a specified number of paupers (S 418, 379 [a forgery modelled on a charter of Æthelstan]) and religious houses are required to offer up prayers for the king, either on an daily or an annual basis (**8**, S 422, 423 [O'Donovan, *Sherborne*, nos 7, 8]). The condition imposed here upon the Shaftesbury nuns, the obligation to sing fifty psalms and a mass every day for the king's soul, recalls the provision in Æthelstan's Exeter code (V Athelstan 3; Liebermann, *Gesetze*, i. 168) that required every minster community to sing fifty psalms for the king every Friday. The Sherborne community, in return for the estates covered in S 422 and 423, was obliged to sing the whole psalter on All Saints' Day, a considerably less onerous condition than that imposed on Shaftesbury. **8** was issued on the same day and at the same place (the royal vill at Amesbury in Wiltshire) as S 418, a grant of land in Hampshire to a layman conditional on the daily feeding of 120 paupers; the truncated witness-list of **8** may have been identical to that of S 418. The two texts have in common some minor variants in the standard formulation, notably in the anathema. The simultaneous drafting of the two documents probably explains an unexpected feature of **8**, the inclusion of a clause permitting posthumous alienation of the property, which seems inappropriate in a grant to a religious house; the wording is the same as in S 418. The regnal year is calculated from 1 January 925 (for the significance of this, see Keynes 1985, p. 187).

Fontmell Magna lies about three miles south of Shaftesbury, on the edge of the Vale of Blackmoor and at the foot of Cranborne Chase. Fontmell is a British name, probably meaning 'stream or spring by the bare hill'; it originally applied to Fontmell Brook (*DEPN*, p. 184; *PN Dorset*, iii. 103; Ekwall, *River-Names*, pp. 161–2). Shaftesbury's Domesday manor there was assessed at fifteen hides (GDB 78v). The composite charter edited as **1**, which covers an area of thirty hides in the vicinity of Fontmell Brook, probably represents part of the earlier documentation of the estate transferred in **8**; it would appear that the earlier thirty-hide land-unit had been broken up by the tenth century. The boundary clause seems to describe the whole of the later parish of Fontmell Magna (see Grundy 1936, pp. 103–10, and *PN Dorset*, iii. 103–13 for better interpretations of some of the boundary-marks). The estate, like the later parish, was divided into two parts, linked by a narrow neck in the vicinity of Woodbridge; one section extended to the east, between the parishes of Compton Abbas and Sutton Waldron, while the other lay to the north-west of

Woodbridge. It is possible that the present estate resulted from the amalgamation of two smaller units. The appurtenances included twenty-four acres of meadow at Sutton Waldron, and there is a note that one and a half hides of the 'treasurer's' land at Sutton Waldron belonged to the property.

The survey first describes the eastern section, moving in a clockwise direction. From Woodbridge (ST 847180) the boundary follows 'the valley of Biedi's enclosure' (pers. n.*Biedi or Bæde, *wyrth*, *slæd*), which may be the stream valley running from Woodbridge towards Twyford; the first element is also found in nearby Bedchester (*PN Dorset*, iii. 104). The next mark is 'the way by or to Snell's enclosure' (pers. n. Snell, *hamm*, *weg*), after which the boundary passes through a group of alder-trees (*alor*) to 'hollow combe' (*hol*, *cumb*); the latter is remembered in Hawkcombe Lane in Compton Abbas, originally named from a group of fields near the parish boundary (*PN Dorset*, iii. 99–100). This boundary mark is mentioned in the Compton Abbas bounds (**21**) as is the next, 'hollow spring or spring in a hollow' (*hol*, *wella*). The Fontmell survey then follows the north edge of 'scarred or flat-topped hill' (*hamol*, *hamel*, *dun*), an old name for Fontmell Down (see *PN Dorset*, iii. 106), to 'the upper end (*heafod*) of Longcombe (Bottom)' (ST 885177; see *PN Dorset*, iii. 104). 'Dolla's barrow or hill' (pers. n. Dol(l)a, *beorg*), which is also mentioned in the Compton bounds (**21**), is probably the nearby tumulus at ST 889182. After this the boundary (now running south) comes to a wood (*wudu*), which is probably Fontmell Wood, and then touches on a hedge or enclosure (*haga*) and 'the pit in the marsh' (*soc*, *seath*); this last appears to be the feature called Washers Pit in Ashmore (ST 898167). From here the survey follows a sequence of 'ways': first 'hollow way' (*hol*), which appears to be the path running south from Washers Pit through Balfour's Wood, then (turning westwards) 'valley way' (*slæd*), 'ridge way' (*hrycg*) and 'the friend or retainer's way' (*wine*). The next boundary mark, (*to*) *burch linken*, refers to the group of strip linchets at ST 875167; the first element could be *birce*, 'birch-tree', with *-en* representing dative plural *-um* (as *PN Dorset*, iii. 110), but it could also be uninflected *burh*, 'fortified place', given the frequent spelling *-ch* for final *-h* in this manuscript. After this the boundary meets the *gereprenc* 'within the chalk pits' (*cealc seað*); *gereprenc* is obscure and probably corrupt (see discussion in *PN Dorset*, iii. 110). 'Hollow brook' (*hol*, *broc*) survives as a field-name Holbrook to the south-west of Fontmell Magna (*PN Dorset*, iii. 108–9); it may refer to part of Fontmell Brook, which the boundary crosses in this area. The boundary then runs along the southern edge of a hill called Little *Seaxpenn*, which is Pen Hill in Sutton Waldron (ST 850165); the second element is PrWelsh *penn*, 'hill', and the first is probably *Seaxe*, 'Saxons' (see *PN Dorset*, iii 104–5). The name survives in Sixpenny Farm (ST 844169); the hill also gave its name to the hundred (*PN Dorset*, iii. 89). From Pen Hill the survey follows 'the valley by the sandy hill' (*sand*, *hyll*, *slæd*) and a small stream (*rið*). The stream runs into another waterway called *Styrd*, which seems to be a mistake for *Stirchel*, the name of the stream which flows north-south through Woodbridge, where the first part of the bounds now ends (see Ekwall, *River-Names*, p. 382, under Sturkel).

The second part of the boundary clause defines the area of the estate which lay to the north-west of Woodbridge, again running clockwise. The survey begins at Woodbridge in the south-east, and then corresponds for some distance with the northern boundary of East Orchard (**24**); the East Orchard bounds are much simpler, referring to *higna (ge)mære*, 'the boundary of the religious community' (i.e. to Shaftesbury's estate at Fontmell), and omitting some of the detailed boundary marks. In **8** the survey follows 'the stream flowing from the holy spring' (*halig, welle, lacu*) to the spring itself, and then runs along a hedge-row (*hege-rǽwe*) to the *shamelen*; this seems to derive from OE *sceamol* and to refer to a shelf of land or a ledge (*PN Dorset*, iii. 136). The boundary then joins a highway before turning west by a woodbank (*wyrtrume*, taking *wintrintune* as a corruption) and emerging through *sulan graf*, which may be 'Sula's grove' (pers. n. *Sula, *graf*) or 'grove of the bog or miry place' (*syle, sylu*; see *PN Dorset*, iii. 112). The next boundary mark is 'the *hegen*', after which the survey goes west 'by the *hegen* path'. *PN Dorset* (iii. 110) speculates that this is an actual occurrence of the postulated OE *hægen, 'enclosure' (thus, 'to the enclosure and west of the enclosure path'), but it is perhaps unwise to rely too heavily on the orthography of this late manuscript, where the vernacular sections are heavily modernized and often corrupt; the possibility of confusion with *haga, hege* and similar words should be borne in mind. After this the boundary descends to a stile (*stigel*), and proceeds west along a *hegen* (perhaps *hægen again) to the southern part of 'Ealdmann's enclosure', which is also mentioned in the bounds of East Orchard (**24**), West Orchard (**10**) and Thornton (**23**); this must have been located at approximately ST 822182. From this point the Fontmell survey (now moving north) parts company with the East Orchard estate and a little later picks up the Thornton bounds. The next boundary marks are 'Ludmann's pit' (pers. n. Ludmann, *pyt*), and another wood-bank (*wyrtrume*). The first element of *blinches broc* may be an Old English river-name, *Blinc*, meaning 'glittering'; it recurs later in the Fontmell survey in *blinchesfeld* ('the tract of open land by the *Blinc* or into which the *Blinc* flows'), which is *blinnesfeld* in the Thornton bounds and survives in the name of Blynfield Farm, located further up the brook (see discussion in *PN Dorset*, iii. 91–3). The Fontmell boundary is then defined by 'Wigheard's (boundary-)post' (*stapel*), 'the wood or clearing of the rocky outcrop' (*clud, leah*), 'the old highway which goes (shoots) to *blinchesfeld*', another woodbank and 'the rough(-surfaced) enclosure' (*scearp, hamm*). The survey finally reaches a stream (*lacu*) which joins the *Stirchel*, and then follows the latter south back to Woodbridge.

9

King Æthelstan grants twelve hides (manentes) *at Tarrant Hinton, Dorset, to the nuns of Shaftesbury.* A.D. 935

C. London, BL Harley 61, 15rv: copy, s. xv
    Rubric: Aþelstanus rex hec in scripto bis sex manentes ad Tarentam Deo et ecclesie sancti
    Edwardi roboratum.
Ed.: a. Kemble 366 (with the bounds in vol. iii, pp. 410–11)
    b. Birch 708
Listed: Sawyer 429; Finberg, *ECW*, no. 581

Regem*ᵃ* regum Dominoque dominorum regnorum regnum sublimiter regente cunctorumque*ᵇ* creaturarum, quas ipse ante secula et in seculis seculorum ineffabiliter preordinatos[c] moderando condicionis statum regulauit, usuique terregeno ineffabiliter[d] creata prolataque ad antropon salutem concessit duo inesse,[e] quibus tunc humanorum constat effectus actuum, uoluntas scilicet atque potestas. Iccirco ille diuicie cum mentis intencione diligende sunt que numquam decipiunt, habentem nec in ipsa morte admittuntur, sed plus habundant dum cernitur quod amatur. Quapropter ego Aþelstanus, nodante[f] Dei gracia basileos Anglorum et eque tocius Britannie orbis Deicolarumque fylos atque curanculus[g] eorum, non innocenter[h] diuinam amonicionem obaudiens, partem ruris proprii iuris mei dicione subactam, in feruore amoris illius qui dixit, 'Date et dabitur uobis',[1] libens perpetuali libertate tribuendo condono Christicolis uirginibus etare matris Iesum seruientibus in loco celebri at Schaftesbiri, bis sex manencium in loco qui uulgari dictione et appellatiua relacione nuncupatur ad Terentam seu[i] supradiximus, eatinus ut sanctis conaminibus mellita assistentina[j] oramina cateruatim importuniis precibus perpetrata crimina altithronum archontem ueniam impetrent ⟨ … ⟩[k] omnimodo interdicamus, ita ut hec nostra donacio in sempiterno graphio cum signaculo sancte crucis confirmata sit. Eciam si quilibet altas[l] litterarum discrepciones[m] conferat uel antiquam cartulam, nichil aduersum hanc pretitulant constitucionem, sed [n]nostri iudicii et signo sancte crucis erectione[n] contempta fiant et ad nichillum ualeant. Sit autem predictum rus cum omnibus ad se rite pertinentibus, campis, pratis, liber excepto hiis tribus, pontis et arcis constructione expedicionisque adiuuamine in cunctis successoribus. Hoc ius donacionis augendo conseruantibus feliciter perueniant inter celibes celestium turmarum et sine fine in eterna doxa letentur. Siquis autem quod non optamus infringere temptauerit hoc nostrum donum, sciat se in examine tremendi iudicii redditurum temeritatis audacium perpessum esse, nisi pura emendacione et singulta lamentacione emendauerit. Istis terminibus circumgirata esse uidetur.

Arest of Pimpern welle, and þanen to þare rede hane, and þanen to þare hþitendich, and þanen andlang dich to dungete, ut þurch þane wde, 7 þanen to þan stanegan crundel, 7 þanen to fildene lane uppende, 7 þanen to Terrente, 7 þanen anlang streames oð þanne ford, 7 þanen eft[o] anlang herepaþes oð littlen wde, 7 þanne anlang þere fures one ðat[p] dich, 7 þanen to tatanbeorge, and of þane berge anlang pic herepaþes to Chircelford, 7 of þanne forde to bacging berghe, 7 þanen on þane oþerne beoit,[q] 7 þannen to horsedich, 7 þannen on porres berg, of þane beorge est[r] on þone med ham suðewardne, 7 þanen on þat beorhlem be westen cockes þorne, 7 þanen þiyres ouer chelesberghe, 7 þanen wið norþen þanen graetem beorge, 7 þanne of dune to Pimpern on þa burnestowe middewardde, 7 þanen eft to Pimpernwelle.

Incipiente anno .xi. predicti regis prefatum donum consignatum est, anno
ab incarnacione Domini nostri Iesu Christi .d.cccc.xxxv., indiccione .vii.

Ego Athelstanus gracia Dei rex Anglorum prefatum donum cum sigillo
sancte crucis confirmaui atque roboraui. +
Ego Wlfhelm Durubernensis*s* ecclesie archiepiscopus titulaui triumphale
signum superni rectoris. +
Ego Alfech Þintaniensis*t* ecclesie hierarchus tripudium sancte crucis impressi
et ceteri. +

a For Rege (*S 469 has* Regi)   *b For* cunctarumque (*same error in S 469*)
c For preordinatas   *d* inuiolabiliter *in S 469*   *e* inee C
f Probably for donante (*see commentary, and also* 11)   *g Probably error for* curagulus
h non inhianter *in S 469*   *i For* ceu   *j Probably for* assistentia
*k Some text (incorporating the beginning of the prohibition) appears to have been lost
between* impetrent *and* omnimodo   *l Probably for* alias   *m A spelling for* descriptiones
n ... n This section appears to be corrupt   *o Perhaps for* est   *p* dat C
q Perhaps error for beorg(e)   *r Perhaps error for* pest   *s For* Dorobernensis
t Þitaniensis C

¹ Luc. 6: 38

9 is a characteristic example of the type of diploma which was being issued in the
last years of Æthelstan's reign, after the cumbrous 'Æthelstan A' model (see **8**) was
phased out in the course of 935 in favour of a simpler and more flexible construction,
which itself evolved into a standard type that dominated charter-production in the
940s and beyond. This new type of diploma initially had a standard layout, which
emphasized the significant words and formulas in the text: the names of the donor,
beneficiary and estate were generally isolated by the use of capitals, spacing and
punctuation; the bounds were written in smaller script, sometimes with a thinner
pen; the dating clause was given on a separate line, with the elements separated by
spaces; the witness-list (much shorter than in the 'Æthelstan A' diplomas) was
arranged in neat columns. There are two surviving originals from 939, which were
written by different scribes but conform to the new layout (S 447, 449); they are
probably a good guide to the original appearance of **9**.

   The formulation of **9** is contemporary, and there is no reason to question its
authenticity. The first part of the extended invocation appears almost verbatim a
charter of 940 (S 469 from Wilton), which has other links with **9**; the second part
(from *ad antropon*) occurs in a charter of 937 (S 438, also from Wilton), and the
final sentence (*Idcirco ... amatur*) is also to be found in another charter of that year
(S 437, Thorney). The long royal style is not precisely paralleled elsewhere, but the
first part (to *orbis*) occurs in several charters of these years (S 430–1, 438, 446, 448
etc); the curious participle *nodante*, which is regularly found in the formula *nodante
Dei gratia*, is probably a perverse inversion of *donante*. *Fylos* is a grecism, as is *etare*
in the dispositive section; *curanculus* may be a corruption of *curagulus*, a word often
found in contemporary royal styles (see S 430, 438, 446 etc.). The dispositive section

begins in a leisurely fashion, with claims of pious motivation; this is partly reproduced in **10** and in other charters of the period (compare 469, 493 etc.). The dispositive phrase, from *libens* to *condono*, also occurs in **10** and S 469 (compare the corresponding phrases in S 430, 438, 446). The reference to the beneficiaries (the nuns of Shaftesbury) is partly paralleled in S 438 from 937, in favour of the Wilton community: 'uenerabili collegio Christicolarum in illo celebri loco qui dicitur Wiltun ad ecclesiam sancte Marie matris Domini'. The apologetic disclaimer for the Anglo-Saxon place-name is typical of the period, and paralleled precisely in S 431, 469 etc. (see also S 438, 446). There is no statement of powers, perhaps because the draftsman was distracted by the requirement to insert a prayer-condition in the position where this formula would usually appear (although it is also possible that the lack of a statement of powers is to be connected with the apparent loss of some text after the prayer condition). The beneficiaries are requested to intercede through prayer for the faults of the donor, a provision which recalls the more specific prayer requirement in **8**; a similar condition appears (after a statement of powers) in S 438: 'eatenus ut uestra ueneranda monastice classis caterua medullata orationum holocaustamata con-corditer nostri memoriam summotonanti commendare non pigeat'. There follows a proscription of all other charters relating to the property, which implies that the earlier landbook(s) for Tarrant Hinton had been lost or mislaid. The simple immunity clause is contemporary; the expression of the reservation clause is the same as in in S 431, which also has an identical blessing and anathema (both are standard formulas). The wording of the dating clause is unusual. The regnal year is calculated from the king's coronation in September 925 (on the significance of this, see Keynes 1985, p. 187).

Several Dorset settlements took their name from the river Tarrant (a variant of Trent; see Ekwall, *River-Names*, p. 416). The second part of Tarrant Hinton commemorates Shaftesbury's ownership; it derives from *higna-tun*, (*hiwan*, gen. *higna*, 'members of a religious house', and *tun*: see *PN Dorset*, ii. 120). Shaftesbury's Domesday manor at Tarrant Hinton was still reckoned at twelve hides in 1066 (GDB 78v). The boundary clause defines the whole of the later parish (part of which was transferred to Pimperne parish in 1933): see discussion by Grundy (1938, pp. 82–6), and explanation of the individual boundary-marks in *PN Dorset*, ii. 119–22. The survey begins in the south-western part of the circuit, near Pimperne village, and proceeds in a clockwise direction. The first and last boundary mark is the spring (*wella*) which gives rise to the stream known as Pimperne, flowing from Pimperne Down past the village to join the river Stour at Blandford (Ekwall, *River-Names*, p. 326; *PN Dorset*, ii. 110–12). The survey then passes 'the red stone' (*read, han*) and 'the white ditch' (*hwit, dic*); Grundy identifies the latter with an ancient dyke by Pimperne Long Barrow (ST 918106). Next come 'down gate or gap' (*dun, gæt*; wrongly associated with Tarrant Hinton Down in *PN Dorset*, ii. 121), a wood (probably in the area of Hinton Bushes and Pimperne Bushes; see *ibid.*) and 'the stony quarry' (*stanig, crundel*). The next boundary mark is difficult; it appears to mean 'the upper end of the dwellers in open country' (see *PN Dorset*, ii. 122) unless *fildena* is from an adjective *filden*, 'fielden' (see Kitson, *Folia Linguistica Historica* xiv/1–2 (1994), pp. 61–9). After this the boundary reaches the Tarrant, which it follows for a short distance south to a ford crossed by a highway (at ST 931119); it then passes along the highway to a little wood (see Little Wood in Eastbury Park) and goes along a furrow or trench (*furh*) to a ditch or dyke, which is probably the place marked as 'British Settlement' on older Ordnance Survey maps (ST 944126). 'Tata's barrow' (pers. n. Tata, *beorg*) appears to be the long barrow at ST 964131, while the '*wic* highway' was a stretch of the Salisbury-Blandford Forum road known as Week Street (*PN Dorset*, ii. pp. 144–5); the *wic* may have been a simple dairy farm, but it is speculated that the word could refer to a nearby Romano-British village (Latin *vicus*). *Chirchelford* lay on the stream which runs through Long Crichel and Moor Crichel (see *PN Dorset*, ii. 274); the ford itself was probably at ST 960127. 'Bacga's barrow' (pers. n. Bacga, *ing*, *beorg*) is likely to be the tumulus at ST 957123, and 'the other barrow' that at ST 955119. Grundy identifies *horsedich* (*hors*, gen. pl. *horsa*, *dic*) with an ancient earthwork to the east of Tarrant Hinton village (ST 947110). 'Worr's barrow' (pers. n. Worr, *beorg*) appears to be the tumulus at ST 948108. After this the boundary skirts the south side of 'the meadow enclosure' (*mæd*, *ham*); this must have been river-meadow on the Tarrant, which the boundary crosses just south of Tarrant Hinton village. The survey is moving west here, so the directional indicator *est* is likely to be an error for *west*. It has been suggested that *beorhlem* is a compound of *beorg*, 'barrow', and *leam*, dative plural of *leah*, 'wood, clearing' (*PN Dorset*, ii. 122); there are a large number of tumuli and barrows in the area to the south-west of Tarrant Hinton. From here the boundary passes to the west of 'Cocc's thorn-tree' (pers. n. Cocc, *thorn*), across 'Ceol's barrow' (pers. n. Ceol, *beorg*) and to the north of 'the great barrow' (perhaps the long barrow at ST 923093). It then descends once more to the Pimperne and proceeds along the middle of the *burnstow* back to Pimperne spring; *burnstow* here probably means 'the channel or bed of an intermittent stream', as in the case of *lisc broc* in Cheselbourne (see *PN Dorset*, ii. 205).

10

a. *King Æthelstan grants five hides* (mansae) *at West Orchard, Dorset, to Ælfric* (? *Ælfred*), *bishop.* A.D. 939

b. *Ælfred, bishop, grants the land to Beorhtwyn, daughter of Wulfhelm.*

C. BL Harley 61, 15v–16v: copy s.xv
   Rubric: Hec carta inscripta est de .v. mansis terre ad Archet et adiacentibus.
Ed.: a. Kemble 376 (with the bounds in vol. iii, p. 413)
     b. Birch 744
     c. Pierquin, *Recueil*, pt 2, no. 68
Listed: Sawyer 445; Finberg, *ECW*, no. 583

Regnante Theo in eona eonum.*^a* Neminem quippe in mortali solo, quamuis uniuersam cousmi*^b* seriem quisque sollerti mentis acumine perlustret, expertem reperiet debite mortis extitisse illamque iuste seueritatis sentenciam protoplasti preuaricacionis noxam delatam euasisse, ut dicitur, 'Et*^c* in terra ibis, puluis es et in puluerem reuerteris'.[1] Quapropter ego Aþelstanus rex, diuina fauente gracia tocius Britannie primatum[d] regalis regiminis obtinens, partem ruris proprii iuris mei dicione subactam in feruore amoris illius qui dixit, 'Date et dabitur uobis',[2] et pro deuoto famulatu et fideli seruicio libens perpetuali libertate tribuendo condono Alfrico fideli meo in Christo ministro et episcopo .v. mansas in loco qui uulgari dictione et appellatiua relacione nuncupatur at Archet. [e]Et ego Alfridus episcopus dabo illas .v. mansas Beorhtwne filia Wlfhelmi que fuit uxor fratris illius Beorhtere,[e] cum omnibus ad se rite pertinentibus, campis, siluis siluorumque[f] nemoribus, ut hec prospere possideat ac eternaliter teneat dum huius eui fragilis cursum uti audebit, post se autem ueluti affirmauimus cuicumque uoluerit heredi derelinquat ceu supradiximus in eternam hereditatem. Fiat uero prefata terra ab omni seruili iugo libera cum omnibus sibi recte pertinentibus, exceptis hiis tribus, expedicione, pontis arcisue coedificacione. Hanc uero prelatiuam donacionem sublimiter a patre luminum instigatam quisquis beniuola ac fideli mente augendo amplificare satagerit, augeat amplificetque[g] cunctiparens genitor in hoc presenti seculo uitam illius et cum suis omnibus prospera feliciter longiturne uite gaudia et in futuro audiat illam dominicam uocem dicentem sibi, 'Uenite benedicti patris mei, percipite regnum quod uobis paratum est ab origine mundi'.[3] Minuentibus uero atque frangentibus hanc donacionem, quod opto absit a fidelium mentibus, terrat[h] pars eorum cum illis de quibus econtra fatur, 'Discedite a me maledicti in ignem eternum qui paratus est Sathane et satellitibus[i] eius',[4] nisi prius digna Deo penitencia ueniam legali satisfaccione emendent. Istis terminibus predicta terra circumgirata esse uidetur. Acta est prefata donacio anno ab incarnacione Domini nostri Iesu Christi .d.cccc.xxxix., indictione .xii.

þis sent þa land imare to Archet þare westere[j] fif hide. Arest suthþard of ealdmannes pyrðe[k] at lang[l] hecgan to sugging made, þane on irichte to Stirthel[m] on þane alr beneþen scealden forde,[n] 7 þanen anlang higþeges, þ of higeweges ande[o] [p]Funtemel þry akeres wið[q] eastem þane broc,[p] þonne anlang Funtmeales oþ eadelmes melne, of Funtemel to þane twam þornen, þat forð on irichte to stigel hege, ouer Stirtel,[m] 7 þonun on irichte to ginum hocum, to þrem land sharen, þat on Archet hamm, and þanen Cagbroc,[r] up anlang Cagbroges to land share hegen, þonne anlang heges to ealdmannes wyrþe.

Ego Athelstanus rex tocius Britannie prefatam donacionem cum sigillo sancte crucis confirmaui. +

Ego Wlfhelm Dorobernensis ecclesie archiepiscopus eiusdem regis donacionem cum tropheo agie crucis consignaui. +

Ego Alfech Wintoniensis ecclesie episcopus triumphalem tropheum agie crucis impressi et ceteri. +

 a eom C   *b* *A spelling for* cosmi
c *The words* Terra es *have dropped out before* Et (*compare* S 430, 438)   *d* priuatum C
e···e *Perhaps an interpolation* (*see commentary*)   *f* *For* siluarumque
g amplificet qui C   *h* *Error for* fiat   *i* satellibus C   *j* *Probably for* westerne
k pyrde C   *l* *Probably for* andlang   *m* *For* Stirchel   *n* forð C   *o* *For* ende
p···p *The meaning of this section is unclear, perhaps because some text has been lost or because it is an interpolation*   *q* wid C
r *A word such as* on *has dropped out before* Cagbroc

1 cf. Gen. 3: 19
2 Luc. 6: 38
3 cf. Matt. 25: 34
4 cf. Matt. 25: 41

This document records two transactions: an initial grant of land to *Alfricus*, described as thegn and bishop; and a transfer of the land by *Alfridus*, bishop, to a woman named Beorhtwyn. There can be no doubt that a genuine royal diploma of 939 underlies this text, but in its current form it presents some difficulty. An initial problem is deciding whether or not the passage recording the second transaction should be regarded as an interpolation. This certainly seems to be the most likely explanation; the motive would be to bring the history of the estate up to date by inserting the details of a subsequent transaction. But it is also possible that the passage in question was an original part of an unconventional diploma; on this interpretation, it would have been agreed before the diploma was drawn up that the beneficiary of Æthelstan's initial donation should give the land to Beorhtwyn as soon as he received it (there is a possible parallel in S 362, although the relevant passage in that document could also be a later addition). Crucial to the second interpretation is the supposition that the beneficiary of the original grant and the bishop reassigning the land to Beorhtwyn were the same individual, and that one of the names has been corrupted in the course of transmission. The best candidate for an identification would be Ælfred, the contemporary bishop of Sherborne, in whose diocese the estate was located. There was also a Bishop Ælfric at Hereford at around this time, but his dates are uncertain and it seems unlikely that he would be the beneficiary of a grant of a Dorset estate. So it seems reasonable to conclude that it was the bishop of Sherborne who was the original beneficiary and also the donor of the land to Beorhtwyn. This identification would be compatible with the view that the original diploma contained details of both transactions, but it certainly does not rule out the possibility that the passage in Ælfred's name is a later addition. Ælfred of Sherborne was dead by 943, so his transfer of the land to Beorhtwyn could not have taken place long after the original grant. It is worth noting that the relevant passage gives two details about Beorhtwyn; she was the daughter of Wulfhelm and also the wife of 'his' brother (presumably the bishop's brother rather than her own uncle). Detail of this kind is more often to be found in a will than in a diploma, and this raises the possibility that the information about the regrant of the estate may have been taken from a separate document, such as Bishop Ælfred's testament, and inserted into the diploma when it passed into Beorhtwyn's possession. A final complication is the implication in the bounds of East Orchard (**24**) that West Orchard belonged to a bishop in 963 (the relevant boundary is called *bissopes imare*). If this is correct, then it would indicate that Ælfred's grant to Beorhtwyn had not taken effect and that the land had remained among the possessions of the bishops of Sherborne, or perhaps that Beorhtwyn had been given only a life-interest in the property (an alternative possibility is that the bounds copied into **24** were out of date).

In the last resort, the question of interpolation must remain open, but it does seem probable that **10** is either in its entirety a genuine and unorthodox charter of 939 or an interpolated text that reached its present form shortly after that date. The basic formulation of the diploma is clearly contemporary. The verbal invocation and proem are found together in three other charters of the later 930s (S 430, 438, 446); the proem is identical in S 430, has a long extension in S 438 and diverges after *euasisse* in S 446. The royal style has no exact parallels, but is acceptable as a contemporary coinage. The wording of the dispositive section is very close to that in **9**. The reference to the beneficiary as 'fideli meo in Christo ministro et episcopo' seems awkward, but can be paralleled in S 506 (A.D. 945), a charter in favour of another Bishop Ælfred, this time of Selsey ('cuidam mihi fidelissmo in Christo ministro et episcopo nomine Ælfredo'). The passage in the name of Bishop Ælfred appears awkwardly between the place-name and the list of appurtenances, which certainly gives the impression that it is an interpolation; but it is not impossible that the original draftsman, in diverging from his model, was himself responsible for this infelicity. The statement of powers and immunity clause are standard formulas which were used together in S 441 and 442, both from 938, and in S 351, a forgery based on a charter of 939 (and see also S 1013); the immunity clause alone was used regularly between 938 and 946 and occasionally revived. The wording of the blessing and anathema seems contemporary; the phrase *cunctiparens genitor* recurs in S 446 from 939. The form of the dating clause is acceptable, although its position between the introduction to the bounds and the boundary clause itself is unusual; the formulation of the surviving subscriptions is contemporary (compare S 447, an original of 939).

10 is concerned with an estate of five hides at West Orchard, lying about five miles south-west of Shaftesbury. The introduction to the bounds in **10** refers to the estate as the *westere fif hide*, thus distinguishing it from the five hides at East Orchard which were granted to a layman in 963 (**24**); this detail may have been added at a later date, when both properties came in Shaftesbury's possession. As mentioned above, the bounds in **24** suggest that West Orchard belonged to a bishop in 963. Neither East nor West Orchard has a separate Domesday entry, and it seems likely that they were reckoned under a neighbouring manor or manors in 1086. Shaftesbury certainly owned both estates in the later medieval period, and it also held much of the surrounding land in 1066. To the east lay Fontmell Magna, where the community was granted eleven and a half hides in 932 (**8**); Shaftesbury's Domesday manor there was assessed at fifteen hides TRE (GDB 78v), and the discrepancy could perhaps be accounted for by supposing that the eleventh-century manor included a dependency at West Orchard. It may be significant that at a later date West Orchard was treated as a chapelry of Fontmell Magna parish, while East Orchard was a chapelry of Iwerne Minster (Hutchins, *Dorset* (3rd edn), iii. 557, 550)

Archet is a British name meaning '(place) beside the wood', from PrWelsh **ced*, 'wood', with **ar*, 'beside, in front of, facing'; it is identical with the Welsh place-name Argoed (see *PN Dorset*, iii. 133). The bounds are discussed by Grundy (1937, pp. 105–7), and the separate boundary marks are examined in *PN Dorset*, iii. 137–9. The survey appears to describe the whole of the later parish of West Orchard, starting at the most northerly point and proceeding in a clockwise direction. It begins at 'Ealdmann's enclosure' (pers. n. Ealdmann, *wyrth*), which is also mentioned in the bounds of Fontmell (**8**), Thornton in Marnhull (**23**) and East Orchard (**24**), and which must have been situated at approximately ST 822182. From here the boundary runs south along a hedge (*hecg*) to *sugging mead*, which occurs in the East Orchard bounds as *sucgimade* and survives as a field-name 'Sow Mead'. *PN Dorset* (iii. 138) suggests a derivation from *sug(g)a*, 'swamp', with *ing*, to form an adjective, 'swampy': thus, 'swampy meadow' or 'the meadow at the swampy place' (*mæd*). From here the survey proceeds directly to the *Stirchel*, which was the stream running north-south through Woodbridge (Ekwall, *River-Names*, p. 382, under Sturkel). The boundary meets the *Stirchel* by an alder-tree (*alor*) below 'shallow ford' (*sceald, ford*); the ford was probably situated where the later parish boundary crosses the stream (ST 833165). From here the boundary follows a 'hay way' (*hig, weg*) to its end (*ende*); this was evidently on the line of the minor road running from Winchells Farm, which the parish boundary follows south to the point where it turns sharply west. The meaning of the next part of the boundary clause is not clear. Fontmell is the name of the *broc* subsequently mentioned (which gave its name to Fontmell Magna); the *pry akeres* apparently lay to the east of the brook. It is possible that the survey is here alluding to an appurtenance of the estate, presumably river-meadow associated with the brook. Perhaps this represents an interpolation into the boundary clause; alternatively, it may be the case that some text has dropped out here which would clarify the relationship of these features. It is likely that the survey here followed the line of the later parish boundary, which joined Fontmell Brook at ST 835155. It then continues along the brook (westwards) as far as 'Eadhelm's mill' (*myln*), probably located at ST 829152. This was the extreme southerly point of the estate; from here the boundary turns to the north-west, where it passes two thorn-trees and goes directly to a hedge with a stile (*stigel, hege*). It then crosses the *Stirchel*, here known as Manston Brook, at approximately ST 823159. The next boundary mark is *ginum* (or *ginun*) *hocum*, where the second word is presumably the dative plural of *hoc*, a fairly common element in place-names, where it has the sense 'bend', 'projecting corner' or 'spur of hill' (*DEPN*, p. 243). The first element of the boundary mark is obscure; if the original spelling was *ginnum*, it could be *ginne*, 'wide, spacious' (see *PN Dorset*, iii. 138). From here the survey proceeds to 'the place where three boundaries meet' (*ðrie, landscearu*), the three in question being West Orchard, Thornton (**23**) and Manston (for which no pre-Conquest charter survives); the junction was at ST 817172. *Archet hamm*, 'the river-meadow of Orchard', is the place where the Thornton bounds begin and end; it would have been located on the stream known as Key Brook. From here the boundary follows Key Brook and 'boundary hedge' (*landscearu, hege*) back to 'Ealdmann's enclosure'.

11

King Eadmund grants ten hides (mansae) *at Liddington, Wiltshire, to* Adulf (*Eadwulf*)*, his man.* A.D. 940

C. BL Harley 61, 9v–10r: copy, s. xv
　　Rubric: Hec est impendicio Admundi regis quam ut scriptum est imperpetuum servaturum impendit scilicet Lidentune.
Ed.: a. Kemble 386 (with the bounds in vol. iii, p. 415)
　　b. Birch 754
　　c. Pierquin, *Recueil*, pt 2, no. 73
Listed: Sawyer 459; Finberg, *ECW*, no. 252

Regnante Deo imperpetuum architectorio qui sua ineffabili rite potencia omnia disponit atque gubernat uicesque temporum hominumque mirabiliter discernens terminumque incertum prout uult equanimiter imponens. Quapropter ego Admundus nutu Dei gracia*ᵃ* basileos Anglorum cuidam meo homine Adulfo .x. mansas perhenniter impenderem ubi ruricoli antico usu nomen imposuerunt at Lidentune, ut ille bene perfruatur ac possideat quamdiu uiuat et post obitum sui*ᵇ* heredes et posteri illius, quamdiu unus ex illa geneologia superfuerit, habeat et possideat cui libenter tradita fuerit ab illo. Sit autem predicta terra cum omnibus ad se rite pertinentibus libera, campis, pascuis, pratis, excepto istis tribus, expedicione, pontis arcisue construccione. Si quis uero quod non optamus contra nostrum hoc decretum machinari uel infringere aliquid uoluerit, sciat se racionem grauiter redditurum in die iudicii ante tribunal Domini nisi prius hic digna emendauerit penitencia ante mortem. Istis terminibus predicta terra circumgirata esse uidetur.

þis sand þe land imare to Lidentune. Arest of Dorcyn on ða*ᶜ* to brokene strate, anlang strate on Lyden, up anlang Liden on þe estre Lyde cumb, þanen of*ᵈ* feden þorn, of feden þorne on wlleuestan,*ᵉ* þanen on badherdes slede estward, of dun slede anlang ðere*ᶠ* dich on bechilde treu, þanan anlang bergedune on þane red stan, of þane stane west onlang weies on þere tweie iberges,*ᵍ* of þo iberghen on þe foer stanes, þanen on teppen cnolle, of þane cnolle on olencumb, þanen on grinescumb, þanen on þere herepaðe,*ʰ* on þane pet, of þane pitte on bicendich, þanen ut ðurth ðone*ⁱ* ordceard, of þane ordcearde on þare oðere*ʲ* herepað, on ðone pet, þanen on gosanwelle, of gosanwelle on Medeburne, up one þat strate,*ᵏ* of þare strate on ðet*ˡ* rede sloh, of þane slo on snodeshelle, of snodeshelle eft on Dorcyn.

Acta est hec prefata donacio anno ab incarnacione Domini nostri Iesu Christi .dcccxl., indiccione .xiii.

Ego Admundus rex Anglorum prefato^m donacionem sigillo sancte crucis confirma'ui. +

Ego Adred eiusdem regis frater consignaui. +

Ego Alfech Wintoniensis ecclesie episcopus triumphalem tropheum agie crucis impressi et ceteri. +

^{a} *Probably for* nodante Dei gratia (*see* **9**)　　^{b} *For* suum
^{c} *A word seems to have dropped out here*　　^{d} *For* on *or* oþ　　^{e} Wullafes stan *in S 1588*
^{f} dere C　　^{g} therges C　　^{h} herepade C　　^{i} durth done C　　^{j} odere C　　^{k} state C
^{l} det C　　^{m} *For* prefatam

11 seems to be authentic. Its closest parallels are with a charter of Æthelstan in favour of a nun, dated 939 and preserved at Abingdon (S 448). The invocation is more commonly found in the form *Regnante theo* . . . . (see S 395, 448, 513, 639, 707, 1379 and cf. S 727, 1214); in four instances it is followed by a longer version of the extension beginning *qui sua ineffabili* (S 448, 707, 1214, 1379). The royal style is a variant on a current formula beginning *nodante Dei gratia* (see **9**). The routine disclaimer introducing the vernacular place-name and the standard immunity clause and anathema are all found in S 448 and elsewhere, and the formulation of the dating clause and surviving subscriptions is also contemporary (compare the subscriptions with those in S 464 and 470, originals from 940). It is not unusual for a beneficiary to be referred to as the king's 'man', rather than his thegn (see, for instance, S 518, 522, 552); it does not necessarily denote a different legal status.

The only section of **11** which is at all remarkable is the statement of powers. Here the draftsman has departed from the wording of his models and has expressed the beneficiary's right of posthumous alienation in unparalleled terms (and in doing so has run into syntactical difficulties; the verbs *habeat* and *possideat* should be in the plural, to agree with *heredes et posteri illius*). The beneficiary is to enjoy and possess the land during his lifetime, and after his death his heirs and descendants are to hold it, as long as *unus ex illa geneologia* survives (*genealogia* here may refer to offspring, or more generally to the beneficiary's kindred). In most surviving Anglo-Saxon diplomas the statement of powers refers simply to the beneficiary's right to leave the estate after his death to whomsoever he wishes. Only occasionally does a draftsman elaborate upon this general provision. An original charter in the name of Offa (S 114, A.D. 779) stipulates that the land is to pass to a man of the beneficiary's kindred (*suae propinquitatis homini*), and seems to indicate (the single sheet is unfortunately damaged in this area) that it was to remain in his family. In S 214 (A.D. 869), another apparently original Mercian charter, the beneficiary is told that the land should be bequeathed to his brother, if still alive, and after that should remain in the paternal line ('et sic semper in sanguinitate paterne generationis sexuque uirili perpetualiter consistat adscripta'). A closer parallel to the condition in **11** occurs in a charter of Eadwig from 956, where the beneficiary can leave the estate to any heir *in genere suo* (S 606). A similar restriction to the beneficiary's kindred may be implied in **12**. In some instances these departures from the norm may represent idiosyncratic drafting, but it is clear from S 114 and 214 that on occasion they relate to specific conditions of the grant. Charters covering bookland of which the inheritance was restricted to the kindred can have passed only rarely into ecclesiastical archives, and were unlikely to survive if they did not do so; so it may have been the case that landbooks with such overt restrictions were more common than the small number of surviving examples suggests. A context for such charters is provided by a provision in Alfred's lawcode (§ 41; Liebermann, *Gesetze*, i. 74), which states that a man who inherited bookland from his kinsmen could not dispose of it outside his kindred if there was a document or witness to the effect that the men who had first acquired the land or who gave it to him had specified that he could not do so (see comment in Keynes and Lapidge, *Alfred the Great*, p. 309). Alfred's own will makes provision for the retention of bookland within his kindred (S 1507), and there is a similar preoccupation in the will of the contemporary Ealdorman Ælfred (S 1508). Diplomas such as **11** would seem to represent instances where the original beneficiary of the landgrant asked for his intentions about inheritance to be mentioned in the landbook, although in some case it was perhaps the wish of the royal donor for the descent to be restricted to male heirs (see further discussion in the commentary to **12**).

Liddington is located in north Wiltshire, near Swindon, almost fifty miles north of Shaftesbury. It was the community's most northerly Domesday manor and was a considerable distance from the rest of the abbey's pre-Conquest estates. The Domesday assessment was thirty-eight hides (GDB 67v), which may indicate that the land covered in **11** formed only part of the later manor. The bounds are discussed by Grundy (1920, pp. 12–16), and there are also helpful comments on the eastern boundary in T.R. Thomson's analysis of the bounds of S 312 and S 1588, which cover neighbouring estates (Thomson 1958–60). Liddington is named from a stream called *Hlyde*, 'the noisy one' (*PN Wilts.*, pp. 282–3; Ekwall, *River-Names*, pp. 272–3), later known as the 'Liden Brook', which forms part of the eastern boundary. The survey appears to outline the whole of the area of the later parish, beginning in the north-west and proceeding clockwise. The northern boundary is formed by a tributary of the river Cole which used to be known as Dorcan (from *dorce*, 'the bright one'); the stream also formed part of the boundaries of Badbury (S 568) and Chiseldon (S 366). The Liddington boundary follows the Dorcan from SU 183847 to approximately SU 193849, and then joins the Roman road to Mildenhall, the 'broken street' of the survey (*brocen*, pp. of *brecan*, *stræt*); an intervening boundary mark seems to have dropped out. The survey proceeds south along the road until it reaches the *Hlyde* (at SU 193833), and then follows the stream south-east to just beyond Liddington village where the combe to the east is evidently 'the eastern *Hlyde* combe' (*cumb*). The first element of *feden thorn* is obscure; according to Thomson, this thorn-tree was probably located at the place where the boundary crossed the Ridge Way (SU 218806). The next boundary mark was 'Wulflaf's stone' (pers. n. Wulflaf, *stan*), also mentioned in S 1588, which Thomson identifies with a sarsen at SU 222799. From here the Liddington boundary goes to the east of 'Bædheard's valley' (pers. n. Bædheard, *slæd*) and then from 'down valley' (*dun*, *slæd*) along a ditch or dyke to 'Beaghild's tree' (fem. pers. n. Beaghild, *treow*); the Wanborough bounds mention 'Beaghild's mire' (*sloh*). The boundary continues along 'barrow down' (*beorg*, *dun*) to 'the red stone' (*read*, *stan*), which would appear to have been at the extreme south-eastern point of the boundary (SU 236788). From here the survey turns west, following a 'way' which is evidently the ancient track known as the Sugar

Way. 'The two barrows' (*twa, beorg*) were probably the tumuli at SU 229785. In the next section of the survey the boundary marks are far more difficult to identify and may be very close together; the boundary here appears to follow the southern and western flanks of Liddington Hill past the hillfort known as Liddington Castle. The survey touches on 'the four stones' (*feower, stan*) and then a feature called *teppen cnolle*; the first element may be a personal name Tæppa or perhaps *tæppe*, 'tape, ribbon' (there are wandering linear earthworks in this area), and the second is *cnoll*, 'hilltop, summit of hill'. The next boundary marks are 'hollow combe' (*holu, cumb*), and 'combe of the trap or snare' (*grin*). After this the boundary follows a highway (*herepæð*), probably the branch of the north-south ridge way running towards Badbury, to a pit (*pytt*) and to *bicendich* (where the first element is either *bice, bicce*, 'bitch', or a personal name Bica), which may be the *olde dich* of the Badbury bounds (S 568). It then passes through 'the orchard' and follows another highway to a second pit. The first element in *gosanwelle* is probably a personal name *Gosa* (see *DEPN*, p. 201, Gossington): thus, 'Gosa's spring' (*wella*). This spring may have been the source of the stream call *mæd-burna* ('meadow stream'), which gave its name to the nearby settlement of Medbourne and which is also mentioned in the Badbury bounds. After this the boundary rejoins the Roman road to Mildenhall, the 'broken street' of the earlier part of the survey, and then passes further north-west to 'the reed marsh' (*hreod, sloh*). *Snodeshelle* is 'Snod's hill' (pers. n. Snod, *hyll*); older maps notice a house called Upper Snodshill at the northern end of Chiseldon parish (SU 182837). The survey now returns to the Dorcan brook.

12

King Eadmund grants two hides (mansae) *at Beechingstoke, Wiltshire, to Eadric, his* uassallus. A.D. 941

C. BL Harley 61, 4v–6r: copy, s. xv
    Rubric: Admundus rex apud Stokes .ii. terre mansas adiacentes imperpetua graphii custodia dono commisit.
D. Bodleian, Dodsworth 38, 4r–5v: copy of C, s. xvii
Ed.: a. *Mon. Angl.*, i. 213–14
    b. Kemble 390 (with the bounds in vol. iii, p. 416)
    c. *Mon. Angl.* (rev. edn), ii. 477–8 (no. 4)
    d. Birch 769
Listed: Sawyer 478; Finberg, *ECW*, no. 255
Edited from C

In nomine trine et une deitatis. Omnipotens supernare*ᵃ* temporaliumque uerus arbiter rerum, ante omnia tempora et ante omnia sidera duas originales de nichillo creaturas fieri disposuit, angelicam uidelicet lucem et informem materiam. Ex qua siquidem informi materia omnia que uidetur et que temporalia sunt secundum temporis discreccionem producens, insuper forma- uit hominem, qui spiritu uite inflatus et ad ymaginem et similitudinem Dei factus diuina dispensacione potestatem super alia cuncta elimenta dominandi habuit, quique paradisi cum omnibus sede perhenniter si uellet locatus diuinis imperiis humiliter obedire nollens, sed prona uoluntate et serpentina suasione inobedienter contra Deum superbire mallens, de superiori statu in inferiorem sortem cum omni sua progenie subsequente in labore et erumpna proiectus est, cumque nature sub lege per multa tempora innumerabili prole nacioneque erat solutus, tandem misericors auctor ne sua factura periret, misericordiam non iudicium pensans, legem littere prophetasque et mundo uesperascente per unigenitum filium suum incarnatum legem gracie super homines,[b] et pro multiplici hominum multitudine, humanum genus per multas gentes linguasque diuidens secundum eiusdem legis iudicium, quamuis equali origine, tamen diuina consciencia[c] et humana sollercia pro lege seruanda alios in superiori gradu consistuit, imperatores reges qui spiritu sancto gubernante subditorum causam modo disciplinaliter modo misericorditer procurarent et, diuinis legibus adherentes, militum curam munera dando, humilumque inopiam consolacia prestando sustinerent; alios in inferiori humiles subditos qui aliis gubernantibus obsequium subiectionis ministrarent. Igitur quoniam omnis[d] qui presunt propter dolorum[e] largicionem et diuiciarum impericionem[f] ab hominibus amabilem laudem et a Deo gloriam remuneracionem habent. Ideo ego Admundus, ex regali progenie Deo annuente regenteque super Angligenas aliasque multas gentes in circuitu habitantes rex ordinatus, amabili uassallo meo Adrico fidelique amico duas terre mansas in perpetuam dono hereditatem, quatinus, temporalium rerum mobili presencia utens, fidelem obedienciam ac pacem laudabilem erga regni ceptra[g] nostri et regale nostrum solium eternabiliter impetret et benigniter seruet. Et post presentis uite excessum illis quibuscumque uoluerit subsequentibus hoc donum comendet, ut in omnibus paterne obediencie exemplis circa regiam dignitatem fideles inueniantur. [h]Pro eo illam terram perhenniter ipse primus pater cum suis quibus post se comendauit a progenie in progenie,[h] in illis terminis quibus periti coloni ipsius regionis nomen proprium antiquo proposito esse dicunt[i] Stoke, dispono ut possideat et perpetua graphii custodia me largiente cum omnibus pertinentibus ipsius telluris officio, campis, pratis, pascuis, teneatur, hiis tribus exceptis ad regalem dignitatem necessariis, expedicione, pontis arcisue cooperacione. Hiis namque terminis omni parte sita terra dinoscitur esse circumgirata.

þis sand þes landes imare at Stoke. Up anlang ninge burne[j] oð ðat hrisc lad, anlang þese richtledes on þane ealde treo stede, þanan anlang weies on stanforde, þanen anlang streame on botenwelle, and of botenwelle on prestes setel, þanen anlang þeges on Wiuelesforde,[k] þanen up anlang Mercdene onne Stokebroc, þanen anlang Stocbroc on hringheburne þar it^l arest onfeng. Cuicumque^m istam terram presignatam cum mea uoluntate meaque benediccione benigniter et humaniter sub tali decreto talique graphio eternaliter custodierit et regali more terminos ipsius in ampliore telluris protentu dilatauerit, auctor donorum spiritus omnem presentem conuersacionem illius omni hilaritate et rerum omnium prosperitate magnificet et iocundet, potens in terra sit semen eius, ipsius generacio benedicatur, gloria et diuicia in domo eius et iusticia ipsius manet in seculum seculi et post hanc lucem temporalem eterno lumine cum omnibus sanctis in regno celi perfruantur. Et econtrario quisquis me nolente meque perhibente,ⁿ inuidie stimulis^o agitatus et eius execrabili liuore retortus, eiusdem terre dimensionem diminuerit et sub tali pacto non custodierit, presens conuersacio ipsius in terris ab omni bonorum pussibilitate^p diminuatur et in die futuro calamitatis collocetur a sinistris cum tartarorum demoniis, ubi erit fletus et stridor dencium, pena eterna sine prestulacione^q consolacionis, nisi digna penitencia et reconsiliacione^r pura per satisfaccionem in huius lucis spacio hoc emendauerit et amplius peccare disiuerit.^s Anno ab incarnacione Domini nostri Iesu Christi .d.cccc.xli., indiccione .xiiii., librata^t est in hoc graphio ista terra. Hec sunt nomina illorum testium graphium hoc attestancium cum nomine regis.

Ego Admundus Anglicarum aliarumque nacionum rex hanc telluris donacionem sub sigillo dominice crucis tradidi. +

Ego Adred eiusdem regis frater consignaui. +

Ego Odo Dorobernensis ecclesie archiepiscopus regis tradicionem tropheo crucis assignato benedixi. +

Ego þeodred Londoniensis episcopus consecraui. +

Ego Alphech Wintoniensis episcopus adunaui. +

Ego Cenwold^u episcopus predestinaui. +^v

Ego Eluric episcopus muniui. +

Ego Wlfhelm episcopus hoc sigillum impressi. +

Ego Burgric episcopus in hec adhesi. +

Ego Alfgar^w episcopus hec certando me esse decreui. +

Ego Þulfgar dux +

Ego Atelþold dux +

Ego Athelstan dux +

Ego Elhhelm dux +

Ego Aþelmund dux +

Ego Uhterd dux +

Ego Oda minister +

Ego Aluric minister +
Ego Admund minister +
Ego Þullaf minister +
Ego Þithgar minister +
Ego Alfred minister +
Ego Þuluric minister +
Ego Þulgar minister +
Ego Alfsige minister +
Ego Ordeah minister +
Ego Aþeric[^x] minister +
Ego Alfsige minister +
Ego Aþered minister +
Ego Þulfhelm minister +

[^a] For supernarum   *[^b] A verb is required here* (? dedit, largitus est)   *[^c]* consiencia C
[^d] For omnes   *[^e] Probably for* donorum   *[^f] For* imperticionem   *[^g] For* sceptra
[^h-h] The meaning of this passage is unclear (see commentary)   *[^i]* dimcant C
[^j] Probably for (h)ringe burne   *[^k]* -forð C   *[^l]* in C   *[^m] Error for* Quicumque
[^n] Error for prohibente   *[^o]* stumulus C   *[^p] A spelling for* possibilitate
[^q] A spelling for prestolatione   *[^r] A spelling for* reconciliatione   *[^s] A spelling for* desiuerit
[^t] For liberata   *[^u]* Cenwobo C   *[^v] The remaining subscriptions are written across the page*
[^w] For Æthelgar   *[^x] Possibly for* Eadric *(compare the order of thegns in S 476)*

12 stands out among Eadmund's charters, but there is no good reason to doubt its authenticity; it is very difficult to believe that such a document would have been fabricated at Shaftesbury or in any ecclesiastical context. The draftsman, who was probably not regularly involved in charter-production, proceeds throughout the text to explore aspects of hierarchy which bear upon the relationship between the royal donor and his thegn. It can be no coincidence that the beneficiary is here called *vassallus*, a style occasionally found in Anglo-Saxon royal charters of the tenth century (see S 369, 559, 666, 755; and discussion by Stevenson in *Asser*, p. 255 n. 2), but not elsewhere saddled with such exegesis.

The proem is the starting-point for the draftsman's theme. This is by far the longest proem in any of Eadmund's charters; it was not until Æthelred's reign that formulas comparable in length and ideological complexity were produced. The principal themes (the Creation and Fall, and the divine origin of hierarchy) are also encountered in the proems of a small number of other diplomas from the middle decades of the century (see especially S 461–4, 526, 644, 647 and 666), but they are considered in **12** at very much greater length. The draftsman is particularly interested in ideas relating to law. He begins with the Creation and the Fall, the latter being ascribed emphatically to disobedience to divine commands. Subsequently degraded mankind existed under the law of nature (*nature sub lege*), until God supplied the law of the scriptures (*lex littere*) and Christ brought the law of grace (*lex gracie*). After this the draftsman turns his attention to the relationship between ruler and ruled; his ideas are sometimes rather obscured by grammatical weakness. Mankind, divided into many peoples and tongues, is subject to the divine law. Although all are in origin equal, some are accorded a superior status, in order to preserve the law. These are emperors and kings who rule their subjects with justice and mercy, governed by the Holy Spirit; following divine commands, they take care of warriors by giving them gifts and relieve poverty. Other men, placed in a humble position, are obliged to show the obedience of subjects to those who rule them. Rulers shall receive praise from men and divine reward for their generosity.

Eadmund's extravagant royal style is pushed into prominence by the theme of the proem; he is of royal stock (*ex regali progenie*) and hence inherits both the privileges and obligations of that status. He makes the grant of land to his *amabilis vassallus* and *fidelis amicus* Eadric explicitly in return for the latter's future loyalty and service to the throne. After his death, Eadric is to 'commend' the land to any of his successors (*quibuscumque uoluerit subsequentibus*), so that they may also be faithful to the king, *in omnibus paterne obedientie exemplis*; this may imply that Eadric was expected to hand on the land to his immediate descendants (perhaps to his sons). The next sentence seems to expand upon this idea, but its meaning is very difficult to extract; there appears to be some corruption or loss of text. There is a reference to *ipse primus pater*, presumably the beneficiary (unless the draftsman's ideas have reverted back to Adam), followed by an apparent comment on his successors in future generations (*a progenie in progenie*), and at the beginning there seems to be some reference to reciprocal obligations (*pro eo*); but making sense of this passage without considerable emendation is impossible. My impression is that this is a statement to the effect that the beneficiary has committed himself and his descendants to the service of the king in return for the land, which has interesting feudal connotations, but any certainty here is impossible. It is however clear that the draftsman was trying to express some idea about the relationship of obligation between the royal donor and the beneficiary.

There are a small number of other diplomas in which the right of post-obitum alienation seems to be explicitly restricted to the beneficiary's kindred (see **11** and commentary), and there are also other charters in which the grant is linked with the continuing loyalty of the donee (see, for instance, S 508). But the expression of these conditions in **12** is completely unparalleled. The language and sentiments would be less remarkable in an eleventh-century document, but it is difficult to understand why **12** should be concocted at that date; the stress on service and loyalty to the throne are details that might be insisted on by the king, but would seem to have no place in a document forged on behalf of a layman, and would be even less relevant in a fabrication made for ecclesiastical ends. It seems that **12** must be accepted on its own terms as a contemporary production. The draftsman does not appear to have been familiar with the mainstream of contemporary diplomatic, or else did not feel constrained to produce a conventional text; he made no use of standard formulas or wording in the business clauses of the dispositive section, and he has allowed himself great licence in the immensely long proem and in the lengthy sanction. The dating clause is also unconventional, but the formulation of the witness-list is closely comparable to that in other contemporary charters (compare S 475 from the same year). It is probable that the charter was produced in two stages, the text as far as the dating clause being drafted by a scribe who was not usually involved in charter-production, with the witness-list being added by a royal scribe (or from a memorandum prepared by a royal scribe) during or after the ratification of the grant by King Eadmund. The witnesses are generally compatible with the date, but there may be a problem with the subscription of Archbishop Oda. This is the only diploma of 941 which he attests, and there is some possibility that his predecessor, Wulfhelm, in fact survived until 942; but the evidence is far from secure, and recent commentators have concluded that **12** is sufficiently trustworthy to tip the balance towards 941 for the date of Oda's succession (see O'Donovan 1972, pp. 36–7; Brooks, *Church of Canterbury*, pp. 221–2, 371 n. 46).

Beechingstoke lies in central Wiltshire and was, like Liddington (see **11**), an isolated Shaftesbury manor at the time of the Domesday survey, with an assessment of five hides (GDB 67v). (It is possible that a copyist of **12** has at some stage confused *v* with *ii.*) The Domesday entry for Beechingstoke gives a hint of some recent dispute over the estate. We are told that a tenant named Thurstan held the manor from the abbess in 1086, and that the pre-Conquest tenant had been Harding, who should have held the land for his lifetime but had returned it voluntarily to Shaftesbury. This implies that the problem was solved, but a list of donors to the abbey compiled between 1089 and 1121 mentions that Harding fitz Alnoth and the abbess were in dispute over the manor of *Estokes*, which is probably Beechingstoke: 'que fuit de dominico abbatie ubi habentur .v. hidas et valet .lx. s. sicut homines eiusdem ville dicunt, set abbatissa et conventus dicunt quod ipse deberet inde dare centum s. et ipse negat set dicit se tenere in feudo' (BL Harley 61, 54r; see discussion by Cooke 1982, pp. 53–4). It is tempting to think that the terms of this dispute may have some bearing on the unique qualities of **12**, but it is difficult to see how this can be so, since the document does not seem in any way to support Shaftesbury's position.

The land called *Stoke* in **12** was already known as *Bichenestoch* in 1086; the first element is perhaps *bicca* (gen pl. *bic(c)ena*,) 'bitch' (*PN Wilts.*, pp. 318–19; compare *bicendich* in the Liddington bounds in **11**). The boundary clause appears to describe the whole of the later parish (see Grundy 1919, pp. 269–71); it has some details in common with the bounds of North Newton (S 348) and Patney (S 715). The survey begins and ends at a stream called *ningeburne* in the first instance and *hringeburne* in the second. The second spelling is to be preferred (the first being perhaps the result of a misreading of insular *r*); the first element would then be OE *hring*, 'ring, circle', and would presumably have a topographical sense. The stream in question is apparently that which forms the western part of the northern boundary of Beechingstoke parish. The next boundary mark appears to be 'rush stream' (*hrisc, lad*). It should be noticed that the North Newton bounds mention a 'rush valley' (*risc slæd*), which is remembered as a field-name Russlett (*PN Wilts.*, p. 502); but this cannot be the same feature as the *hrisc lad* of **12**, for it seems to lie in the southern part of North Newton parish, nowhere near Beechingstoke. It is possible that *hrisc lad* was the name of the stream which branches from the *hring-burna* at SU 090595, and which was followed by the later parish boundary. The next feature to be mentioned is 'the old tree place' (*eald, treow, stede*), which was perhaps a clump of trees or a similar feature; there may well be a connection with Woodborough, through which the boundary now passes. The survey proceeds along a 'way' (probably the street runing west-east through Woodborough) to 'stony ford' (*stan, ford*); the ford was probably at SU 109599, where the road crosses a stream. The boundary then followed the stream south to 'Bota's spring or stream' (pers. n. *Bota, wella*), which also occurs in the North Newnton bounds, and is remembered in the names of Bottle Farm and nearby Bottlesford (see *PN Wilts.*, pp. 319, 321); it would seem to have been in the vicinity of SU 112592. This probably marked the south-eastern angle of the estate. The next boundary mark is a 'priest's dwelling' (*preost, setl*), which may be linked with the field name Press Land (*PN Wilts.*, p. 501), and probably lay just to the west, in the area of Gores. From here the boundary followed a 'way' to *Wiuelesford*, which gave rise to modern Wilsford; the first element is probably *wifel*, 'beetle' (M. Gelling. pers. comm), although it has also been held to be a personal name *Wifel* (*PN Wilts.*, p. 326). This ford, also mentioned in the bounds of S 348, was situated at SU 096579. *Mercdene* is the *merh dæne* of the Patney bounds (S 715); the first element is apparently OE *mærh, mærg*, 'marrow, fat', so the name probably means 'fertile valley' (*PN Wilts.*, p. 321–2). The name is now applied to the nearby village of Marden, but originally referred to the valley of the river Avon, which the boundary follows west for almost a mile, before turning into *Stoc broc*, which is evidently the stream flowing through Beechingstoke village; the brook formed the western boundary of Beechingstoke parish and the eastern boundary of Patney. It joins the *hring-burna* just west of Beechingstoke village.

13

King Eadmund restores and confirms seven hides (mansae) *at Cheselbourne, Dorset, to Wynflæd, a nun, and grants her a further eight hides in the same place.* A.D. 942

C. BL Harley 61, 7r–8r: copy, s. xv
    Rubric: Admundus rex dedit .vii. mansas que a suis antecessoribus prius date fuerunt ut presens testatur inscriptio ecclesie de Shaftesbury roborauit.
D. Bodleian, Dodsworth 38, 6v–7v: copy of C, s. xvii (bounds omitted)
Ed.: a. Hutchins, *Dorset*, ii. 510 (in part, bounds omitted)
    b. Kemble 392 (with the bounds in vol. iii, p. 417)
    c. Birch 775
    d. Pierquin, *Recueil*, pt 2, no. 75
Listed: Sawyer 485; Finberg, *ECW*, no. 585

Regnante imperpetuum Domino nostro Iesu Christo. Sacre autem scripture edicta fona catholicorum patrum nos admonet ut cum hiis fugitiuis et sine dubio transitoriis possessiunculis iugiter mansura regna Deo largiente fragilique nature consolacionis subleuamine adipiscenda sunt, quia nobis mortalibus temporalia gaza necnon et lucra possessionum inaniter fruentibus facescunt ac defluunt. Quapropter ego Admundus, desiderio regni celestis exardens, fauente superno numine basyleos industrius*ª* Anglorum rex ceterarumque gencium in circuitu persistencium, cuidam religiose sancte conuersacionis monialis femine uocitate nomine Wenflede .vii. mansas, que fuerunt a meis antecessoribus prius date, firmiter recuperando roboraui.

Insuper et hereditatis mee .viii. mansas ad augmentum perhenniter predicte moniali concessi, ibidem ubi uulgares prisco more mobilique relacione uocitant at Cheselburne, cum pratis pascuisque necnon et siluis siluarumque densitatibus, ut hec prospere possideat ac eternaliter teneat dum huius labentis eui cursum transeat inlesus atque uitalis spiritus in coruptibili carne inhereat, post se autem ueluti affirmauimus cuicumque uoluerit heredi derelinquat. Fiat etenim prefata terra ab omni seruili iugo libera cum omnibus sibi recte pertinentibus, exceptis hiis tribus, expedicione, pontis arcisue coedificacione. Denique uero siquis nobis non optantibus nostrum hoc donum uiolari fraudulenter perpetrando consenserit, consideret hic sic[b] die ultima[c] iudicii coram Deo ⟨rationem⟩[d] redditurum atque cum reprobis[e] quibus dicitur, 'Discedite a me maledicti in ignem eternum',[1] penis atrocibus se esse passurum, si non antea corporea lamentacione emendauerit. Istis terminibus predicta terra circumgirata esse uidetur.

þis sant þa landimare to Cheselburne. Of lisebroke[f] on þane fearngaren, of þane fearngaren on þone ston istel, of þan istelle anlang ricges on þa iheafde, of þane iheafde[g] on þane forð erthe acre, of þane forerð akere on Cheselburne stream, of þane streame on þe twifelde dich, of þare dic onne flescumbe, on þane crundel, of þane crundel on Deulisc stream, of þane streame on langhelee northward, on[h] langhelee on þe blaken þorne[i] northward, of þane blake þornen anlang hricge weges to þe beorge, of þe berge on ðone crundel, of þane crundele on ða holu suthward to Deuliscstreame.

þis is þe tweire hide boch at Winterburne þe Admund king ibokede Wenflede on echenhalue[j] in to Cheselburne, þo sealde hire Alfsige .v. hiden þar to on echehalue,[j] þo ichte Admund kyng ðis[k] boc þar midde. þis sand þare .ii. hide landimare at Winterburne. Arest of Winterburne to chelfgraue, of chelfgraue one wic weie neþerward, anlang broke one mearcweie, anlang weies to widesgete, anlang Cunucces dich on þe sherd, of þene sherde [of þane shearde[l] anlang þides to nearuwan anstigan, of þan anstigan to midelgete, of midelgate þurh þane garen, anlang herepaþes on hornget, of horngetes hirne lang[m] land share to leaxen oc, anlang wdes to þane ealde seale, þanen one þo berges astward to Winterburne, of Winterburne tou[n] þares tunes hirne, onlang þane herepaþe on þene depe crundel, of dune anlang land share eft on Winterburne.

Acta est prefata donacio anno ab incarnacione Domini .d.cccc.xlii., indiccione .xv.

Ego Admundus rex Anglorum prefatam donacionem cum sigillo sancte crucis confirmaui. +

Ego Adgiue eiusdem regis mater predictum donum consensi. +

Ego Adred eiusdem regis frater consignaui. +

Ego Wlstan archiepiscopus urbis[o] Efrace metropolitana eiusdem regis donacionem cum sigillo sancte crucis subarraui. +

Ego Odo Dorobernensis ecclesie archiepiscopus eiusdem regis donacionem cum tropheo agie crucis confirmaui. +

Ego þeodred Londoniensis ecclesie episcopus consignaui. +

Ego Alphec Wintoniensis ecclesie episcopus triumphalem tropheum agie crucis impressi. +[p]

Ego Kenward episcopus consensi. +

Ego Aluric episcopus confirmaui. +

Ego Alured episcopus consignaui. +

Ego Bulgrif[q] episcopus consensi. +

Ego Aþelgar episcopus roboraui. +

Ego Wlfhelm episcopus confirmaui. +

Ego Wlgar dux +

Ego Athelstan dux +

Ego Athelwold dux +

Ego Aþelstan dux +

Ego Ealhhelm dux +

Ego Adric dux +

Ego Aþelmund dux +

Ego Uhtred dux +

Ego Odda dux[r] +

Ego Wlgar dux[r] +

Ego Admund dux[r] +

Ego Wllaf dux[r] +

Ego Alfstan minister +

Ego Aþered minister +

Ego Alsige minister +

Ego Aþered minister +

Ego Aþelgerd minister +

Ego Þithgar minister +

---

[a] indistrius C   [b] *Error for* se   [c] *Error for* ultimo
[d] *The word* rationem *has fallen out here*   [e] reprobus C   [f] *Probably for* lisc broce
[g] theafde C   [h] *Probably for* of   [i] þorne's' C
[j] *Perhaps for* on ecen yrfe (*same corruption in* 20)   [k] dis C   [l...l] *Repetition*
[m] *For* andlang   [m] *For* to   [o] urbs C
[p] *The remaining subscriptions are written across the page*   [q] *For* Burgric
[r] *Error for* minister.

[1] Matt. 25: 41

The beneficiary of this charter is probably to be identified with the woman of the same name whose grant or bequest to Shaftesbury of land at Piddletrenthide was confirmed by Edgar in 966 (26); Piddletrenthide lies just to the west of Cheselbourne. The Wynflæd of 26 was King Edgar's grandmother, presumably the mother of King Eadmund's first wife, Ælfgifu, who was buried and culted at Shaftesbury (see pp. xiii–xiv) and who was also a benefactor of the nunnery (see 28). There is some possibility of a further identification with the testator of S 1539 (a single-sheet original which may be a stray from the Shaftesbury archive; see p. xvi n. 17); this woman seems to have been a widow who had become a lay associate of a religious community, not named specifically but most probably Shaftesbury (see Whitelock, *Wills*, p. 109). Wynflæd's will cannot be dated precisely, but the script would be compatible with a date in the mid tenth century and so it is very tempting to suppose that the nun of 13 was the same woman. In this case, the possibility arises that the Beorhtwyn who was the beneficiary of a grant of land at East Orchard (see 10) could be identified with the woman of the same name mentioned in S 1539 as Wynflæd's mother. This attractive line of speculation is perhaps dampened by the fact that S 1539 does not give the impression that the testator was in any way linked with the West Saxon dynasty; if she was indeed the nun of 13 and the benefactor of 26, then she would appear to have been King Eadmund's mother-in-law and the grandmother of his sons, yet no members of the royal kindred are remembered in the will.

13 appears to be in the main authentic. The verbal invocation is one of the most common formulas in Anglo-Saxon charters, in use throughout the period. The proem is not precisely paralleled elsewhere, but several parts of it are found in contemporary charters. The first section (to *admonet ut*) appears in S 504, S (Add.) 517a (one of the newly discovered Barking charters), S 619, S 834 and S (Add.) 931a (another new Barking charter); the section from *ut cum his fugitivis* to *adipiscenda sunt* occurs in S 448; and the final part, from *nobis mortalibus*, is found in S 447 and 468. The royal style is contemporary (see, for example, S 480 from 942), as is the form of the reference to the beneficiary (compare S 465, from 940). The apologetic reference to the place-name is paralleled, for example, in S 480 from 942. The list of appurtenances, statement of powers, immunity clause and sanction are all stock formulas found in numerous charters of the 940s. The dating clause and witness-list are entirely acceptable, although in the latter four thegns are mistakenly promoted to ealdormen, presumably by a careless copyist.

Several transactions are recorded in 13. In the first place King Eadmund restores and confirms to Wynflæd seven hides, which had previously been granted by his predecessors; we are not told the circumstances which make the restoration necessary. He then grants her in addition eight hides of his own hereditary land at Cheselbourne. The boundary clause is followed by an Old English note (the language has been modernized) relating to land at *Winterburne*, which seems to be Winterborne Tomson, situated about seven miles east of Cheselbourne. The meaning is far from clear, and some sections of this passage seem to be corrupt. One difficulty is the repeated phrase *on echenhalue*. The sense seems to require a formula such as *on ecen yrfe*, 'in perpetual inheritance', which would be a plausible emendation (perhaps via a spelling *on eche(n) herue*); but it is a complication that there is a corresponding phrase *on elche(n) halue* in 6 and 20 (neither of them authentic documents). The latter reading suggests an original *on ælce healfe*, perhaps meaning 'on every side'; this formula is found elsewhere only in two documents from Old Minster, Winchester (S 536 and the vernacular version of S 817), both appearing to represent pre-Conquest fabrication on the basis of earlier material. This is a tentative translation: 'This is the landbook for the two hides at Winterborne which King Eadmund booked to Wynflæd in perpetual inheritance (on every side) to belong to Cheselbourne, (? which) Ælfsige gave her five hides belonging to it in perpetual inheritance (on every side), which King Eadmund added to (in) this book'. The following boundary clause is introduced by the phrase: 'These are the boundaries of the two hides at Winterborne'. A simple solution would be to assume that the note relating to Winterborne and the associated boundary clause represent a later addition to an existing diploma which originally related only to Cheselbourne; to see the variation between two and five hides as a product of scribal error (*v* for *ii*); and to explain the addition of this material as a consequence of the Winterborne property being an addition to the Cheselbourne estate. Two other diplomas of Eadmund, both preserved in the Winchester cathedral archive (S 463, 488), also include an added vernacular note covering secondary grants connected with the original donation. An alternative, more complex view would be that this passage formed an integral part of the original diploma, and that it related to the holding of seven hides which was restored to Wynflæd in the main part of the charter. On this reading, these seven hides would appear to have consisted of five hides at Cheselbourne itself (the land which Ælfsige had given to Wynflæd) and a detached area of two hides at Winterborne Tomson, which was 'booked' to Wynflæd by Eadmund, and was to be associated with the Cheselbourne estate.

The first boundary clause is incomplete; it starts on the western boundary and ends in the eastern part of Cheselbourne, but gives no details of the southern boundary. It seems likely that it was intended to outline only the eight hides which Eadmund was adding to Wynflæd's holding in the area, not the original seven hides; the draftsman did not think it necessary to define the common boundary of the two properties. It may have been the case that Wynflæd already had written documentation for her existing property. This has not survived – at least, not in its original form. There are two earlier charters in the archive dealing with land at Cheselbourne: a Latin diploma of *c.* 870 in favour of Ealdorman Ælfstan and covering two hides (**5**); and an undated English text which appears to be a free translation of the Latin diploma, but refers to five hides instead of two (**6**). Both documents have the same boundary clause, which covers almost the whole of Cheselbourne parish, an area roughly equivalent to the territory of the sixteen-hide estate at Cheselbourne granted to a thegn in 1019 (**30**). It seems likely that at some stage **5** and **6** were regarded (or were intended to be regarded) as the earlier documentation for the seven hides of Wynflæd's original holding at Cheselbourne, although this would be incompatible with their common boundary clause (perhaps a substitution for a more modest survey or surveys). **5** is clearly based on an authentic ninth-century diploma, but it has obviously been tampered with, and **6** has no independent authority; while it is possible that in its original form **5** was indeed a title-deed for part of Wynflæd's Cheselbourne holding, little confidence can now be placed in its details.

Although Wynflæd gave or bequeathed her estate at Piddletrenthide to Shaftesbury, her lands at Cheselbourne seem to have had a different history. In 1019 Cnut granted sixteen hides at Cheselbourne (probably approximately equivalent to Wynflæd's

estate) to his thegn Aghmundr (**30**); these sixteen hides appear to correspond to
Shaftesbury's Domesday manor (GDB 78v). The date at which the land passed into
the community's possession is unknown. At some point in the Confessor's reign,
Cheselbourne (along with a number of other Shaftesbury properties) was seized by
Earl Harold; it was restored by William on the discovery of a writ of the Confessor
supporting the nuns' claim (see further, p. xxiii). This dispute may form the background for the evident tampering with **5**, and could also provide a context for
the insertion of details about Winterborne Tomson in **13** (if this section is an
interpolation).

The bounds in **13** are discussed by Grundy (1934, pp. 120–2); see also *PN Dorset*,
iii. 202–8, for the individual boundary marks. The survey begins in the north-western
part of the later parish of Cheselbourne, at *lisc broc*, the stream which flows south
from Lyscombe Farm to the river Piddle; this is the *burnstowe* in the bounds of **5**
and **6** (*PN Dorset*, iii. 205). From here the survey appears to define the northern
and eastern boundaries of the parish; it runs eastwards to Devil's Brook, takes in
an area beyond, and then rejoins the Brook further south, at which point it ends
abruptly (apparently because the compiler was not concerned to define the boundary
with Wynflæd's existing estate at Cheselbourne; see discussion above). The next
boundary mark after *lisc broc* is a 'fern gore' (*fearn, gara*), which may have been
the sharp angle in the boundary at ST 740008. *PN Dorset* (iii. 208) translates *ston
istel* as 'stone enclosure' (*stan, st(i)ell*), but it seems more likely that this is a
corruption of the feature called *stan castel*, 'heap of stones' (*ceastel*), mentioned in
5 and **6**. From here the boundary follows a ridge (*hrycg*) to 'the headland' (*heafod*)
and 'the projecting piece of ploughland' (*forierð æcer*), before touching on the
Cheselbourne stream (apparently near its source, at ST 755014). 'The double ditch'
(*twifeald, dic*) is perhaps the earthwork at ST 758014. Next the boundary enters 'flax
combe' (*fleax, cumb*), which also occurs in the survey in **30** and appears to be the
combe on the south flank of Henning Hill, and then touches on a gully or quarry
(*crundel*), before passing east to the Devil's Brook, which it meets at ST 774013.
From here the boundary is running north-eastwards. It passes to the north of 'long
wood or clearing' (*lang, leah*) and 'the black-thorn tree' and along a ridge way to a
barrow (probably the tumulus at ST 784018, marking the north-eastern angle of the
later parish). The boundary then runs south to another gully or quarry and to a
hollow (*holh*), before rejoining Devil's Brook at ST 777000, where the survey ends.

The *Winterburne* bounds were located at Winterborne Tomson by Forsberg
(*Contribution*, p. 204); for discussion of the individual boundary marks, see *PN
Dorset*, ii. 81–2. The survey seems to describe the whole area of the later parish. It
begins on the river Winterborne itself, in the south-western part of the estate. 'Calf
grove' (*cealf, graf*) was probably located at the place where the parish boundary
crosses the river (at approximately SY 878974). The '*wic* way' seems to have been
on the line of the present road from Winterborne Tomson to Winterborne Kingston,
which the parish boundary here follows for a short distance westwards. The *broc*
was probably the northerly branch of the Winterborne, with which the boundary
coincides for a short distance before it turns abruptly north. The 'boundary way'
(*mearc, weg*) is the track marking the western boundary of the Winterborne Tomson
parish. The next boundary mark is a 'wood gate or opening' (*widu, wudu, geat*),
which probably lay at the north-western angle of the estate (at approximately ST

873006). From here the boundary runs east along *Cunucces dich*, the ancient earthwork known as Combs Ditch, also mentioned in the bounds of the neighbouring estate of Mapperton in Almer (**14**); the first element is of British origin and doubtful meaning (*PN Dorset*, ii. 70–1). The 'gap' (*sceard*) is probably the break in Combs Ditch a few hundred yards along the northern boundary of the estate. After this the boundary runs along (the edge of) a wood (Great Coll Wood) to 'the narrow paths' (*nearu, anstiga*), 'middle gate or gap' (*middel, geat*) and a 'gore' (*gara*), in this instance probably a triangular-shaped field, which survives as the minor name Gore Field (*PN Dorset*, ii. 82). The boundary then follows a highway (*herepæð*) to 'horn gate or gap' (*horn, geat*), which appears to be the *horgate* of the Mapperton bounds; the first element probably refers to the nearby hill-spur. Next comes the corner or angle (*hyrne*) of 'horn gate', after which the survey follows the boundary (*landscearu*), evidently south, to 'Leaxa's oak-tree' (OE pers. n. **Leaxa, oc*), and then passes alongside another wood to 'the old willow' (*eald, sealh*) and from a group of tumuli eastward to the Winterborne. The boundary crosses the Winterborne and runs (south) for a short distance to the 'corner' (*hyrne*) of the *tun*, which would have been the south-eastern corner of the estate. The 'highway' must have been on the line of the main road to Bere Regis, which the parish boundary follows south-west for a short distance. The 'deep gully or quarry' was probably at the place where the parish boundary branches north from the road (SY 881968). The boundary then returns to the Winterborne.

14

King Eadmund grants eleven hides (mansae) *at Mapperton in Almer, Dorset, to Eadric*, comes. A.D. 943

C. BL Harley 61, 10rv: copy, s. xv
   Rubric: + Munimine regis Admundi .xi. mansas apud Mape[. . . . . . .]ᵃ sancti Edwardi.
Ed.: a. Kemble 394 (with the bounds in vol. iii, pp. 417–18)
   b. Birch 781
   c. Pierquin, *Recueil*, pt 2, no. 76
Listed: Sawyer 490; Finberg, *ECW*, no. 586

In nomine Dei et Domini nostri Iesu Christi ueri redemptorisᵇ mundi. Anno uero dominice incarnacionis .d.cccc.xliii. Ego Admundus omnicreantisᶜ disponente clemencia Angligenarum omniumque gencium undique secus habitancium rex, .iiii. anno imperii mei, diuina Dei gracia suadente quod cogitarem quam mirabiliter et quam subtiliter omnia supernus rector celestia ⟨et⟩ᵈ terrestria firme racionis serreᵉ gubernat atque custodit. Iccirco minime in obliuione habui quod paruam partem potestatis mei Adrico meo comite, id est .xi. mansas, meorum episcoporum testimonio ceterarumqueᶠ fidelium adstipulacione, hilariter perpetuali libertate donaui, ubi iamdudum ⟨solicole illius regionis⟩ᵍ nomen imposuerunt at Mapeldertune, quatenus ille bene perfruatur ac perpetualiter pussideat[h] quamdiu istius caducis seculi uitam tenere presumet et post se cuicumque uoluerit seu[i] coroborauimus perhenniter heredi derelinquat seu[i] supradiximus in eternam hereditatem. Sit autem predictum rus liber ab omni mundiali obstaculo cum omnibus ad se rite pertinentibus, campis, pascuis, pratis, siluis diriuatisque cursibus[j] aquarum, exceptis istis tribus, expedicione, pontis arcisue construccione. Siquis uero quod non optamus hanc nostram difinicionem elacionis habitu incedens infringere temptauerit, perpessus[k] sit gelidis glaciarum flatibus et pennino excercitu[l] malignorum spiritum nisi prius inriguis penitencie gemetibus[m] et pura emendacione emendauerit. Istis terminibus predicta terra circumgerata[n] esse uidetur.

þis sanden[o] þe land imaren to Mapeldertune. Arest of Elmere up anlang streames on Winterburne on þa dich, and þanne anlang riscemeres oþ hit cumð[p] to þere alde dich, þanne andlang diche foren ongen wiþig þeuel, þanen on rupan þorn, of þane þorn on sex þorn, of sex þorne on anne þorn þiuel with Winterburne, and þanne andlang[q] Winterburne on anne water pet, of þane pitte on stanhecheres ande, of stanhecheres ande on grenenhille, of[r] þa hege reawe, onlang heie reawe on hþete cumb, anlang cumbes to wde,[s] innen wde, on anne crundel, of þane crundele on þe elþen stret, of þare streate on anne weie to horgate,[t] of horgate[t] on weritun, of wertune on limbenlee, of limbenlee on Cunnucesdic, anlang standene to molenhame, of molenhame to cellor, of cellor on windee bergh, of þane berghe anlang weies on Winterburne ford, anlang streames eft on Elmere.

Ego Admundus rex Anglorum prefatam donacionem cum sigillo sancte crucis confirmaui. +
Ego Oda Dorobernensis ecclesie archiepiscopus eiusdem regis donacionem cum sigillo sancte crucis subarraui. +
Ego þedred Londoniensis ecclesie episcopus consignaui et ceteri. +

[a] *Rubric partly illegible*   [b] remptoris C   [c] omnicreantes C
[d] *The word* et *has probably fallen out here* (*compare* S 529)
[e] *Probably for* serie (*compare* S 529)   [f] *For* ceterorumque (*same error in* S 529)
[g] *The words* solicole illius regionis *seem to have fallen out here* (*compare* S 489, 497 *etc.*)
[h] *A spelling for* possideat   [i] *For* ceu   [j] curribus C   [k] perpessis C
[l] *A spelling for* exercitu   [m] *A spelling for* gemitibus   [n] *A spelling for* circumgirata
[o] saden C   [p] cumd C   [q] andland C   [r] *For* on *or* oþ   [s] wþe C
[t] *Probably equivalent to* hornget(e) *in* **13**

There is no reason to question the authenticity of **14**. Its formulation can be precisely paralleled in other charters of the period: the section from the verbal invocation to the dispositive verb recurs verbatim in S 529 from 947 (see also S 512, 575, 585), and the statement of powers, immunity clause and anathema are all standard formulas which are found together in S 447, 449, 468, 476 and 527. The form of the subscriptions in the curtailed witness-list is contemporary (compare S 487). Ealdorman Eadric attests charters between 942 and 949. He was the brother of Ealdorman Æthelstan 'Half-King' and of Ealdorman Æthelwold; their father was an ealdorman named Æthelfrith (see Hart 1973). Æthelwold bequeathed to Eadric estates at Ogbourne in Wiltshire, Ashdown in Berkshire, Cheam in Surrey and Washington in Sussex (S 1504, A.D. 946 × 947), and in 947 Eadric secured royal charters for two of these estates, Ashdown (S 524) and Washington (S 525), presumably because because the earlier documentation was defective. It is tempting to see a link with Ealdorman Æthelfrith's much earlier loss of his hereditary landbooks in a fire (see S 367, 371 and S (Add.) 367a). There is some reason to believe that Æthelfrith, although ealdorman of part of Mercia, was of West Saxon origin, so it is not impossible that he had owned an estate in Sussex (Hart 1973, pp. 116–18; Keynes 1993, pp. 307–8). J. A. Robinson (*Dunstan*, pp. 45–50) made a spirited but unconvincing attempt to identify with the later Ealdorman Eadric the thegn of that name who received a replacement for another lost charter (for Farnborough, Warwickshire, not Berkshire as Sawyer) from Æthelflæd of Mercia in *c.* 916 (S 225), arguing that this represented the replacement of another of Æthelfrith's burnt landbooks; the argument collapses on the fact that the lost charter preceding S 225 had belonged to another thegn from whom Eadric acquired the estate.

14 is concerned with land at Mapperton in Almer, where Shaftesbury held a manor assessed at eleven hides in 1066 (GDB 78v). To the north-west the estate has a common boundary with the two hides at Winterborne Tomson which formed part of Shaftesbury's Cheselbourne estate (see **13**). Grundy (1933, pp. 224–9; 1937, pp. 100–1) located the estate at Mapperton in Almer, but was unable to identify the boundaries precisely; Forsberg (*Contribution*, p. 205) was more confident in stating that the survey probably outlined the whole of the later parish of Almer, although he did not attempt to explain the complete circuit. The survey begins at the 'eel pool' (*æl, mere*) from which Almer takes its name, apparently one of the pools in the river Winterborne to the south-east of the village (*PN Dorset*, ii. 55). From here the boundary follows the river (westwards) to a ditch or dyke, then goes along 'rush mere' (*risc*) as far as 'the old ditch'. *Risc mere* appears to be connected with *risc mor*, 'marshy ground where rushes grow', which gave its name to the tiny Rushmore Hundred, containing only Winterborne Zelstone and West Morden in Morden; *mere* may be an error for *mor*, but it is also possible that there were two similar names, referring to different features of the same marshy area (*PN Dorset*, ii. 67). This apparently lay along a small tributary of the Winterborne, rising at Botany Bay Farm, which joins the Winterborne at SY 908981. The later parish boundary certainly follows this stream south, and then cuts north again to rejoin the Winterborne, as does the survey. After 'the old ditch' the boundary marks are a willow thicket (*withig, thyfel*; identified as Winterborne Withy Bed in *PN Dorset*, ii. 69), a 'rough' thorn-tree (*ruh*, weak obl. *ruwan, rugan*), a 'dagger' thorn-tree (*seax*), which was presumably a particular variety, and a 'thorn-tree thicket' (*thyfel*) beside the Winterbourne. The parish boundary rejoins the Winterborne at approximately SY 906976, and follows it for a short distance before turning north-west; this point may have been marked by the 'water pit' of the survey (perhaps to be identified with Huish Pit in Winterborne Zelstone; *PN Dorset*, ii. 69). The meaning of *stanhecheres ande* (*ende*) is uncertain;

PN Dorset (ii. 58) suggests 'the end of the stone field', taking the first part as a misreading of *stanæceres*. But there may be a connection with the field-name Stonehayes Mead in Winterborne Zelstone (perhaps *stan* (*ge*)*hæg*, 'stone enclosure'; *PN Dorset*, ii. 70). The next boundary marks are: 'green hill' (*grene*, wk. obl., *grenan*, *hyll*), a hedge-row (*hege-ræwe*), which survives as a field-name (*PN Dorset*, ii. 57), 'wheat combe' (*hwæte*, *cumb*), a wood and a gully (*crundel*). These presumably all lay along the western boundary, but are difficult to identify. *PN Dorset* (ii. 57) suggests that the first element in *elthen stret* could be an error for *elden* (*ealden*), thus 'the old street'; it must be the Roman road from Badbury to Dorchester which the parish boundary crosses at SY 892990. From here the survey follows a 'way' to *hor geat*, which is probably the *horn geat* of the Winterborne Tomson bounds; it seems to have marked the meeting point of the later parishes of Almer, Winterborne Zelstone and Winterborne Tomson, at the southern tip of Great Coll Wood (SY 889992). The Mapperton boundary now marches for a short distance with that of Winterborne Tomson, along the western edge of Great Coll Wood. The first element of *weritun/wertune* is obscure; the suggestion in *PN Dorset* (ii. 58) that it is *wering*, 'weir, dam', seems topographically improbable. *Limbenlee* is also difficult; the second element is *leah*, 'wood, clearing', and the first may be a corruption of *linden*, 'growing with lime-trees'. The boundary now reaches Combs Ditch (*Cunnucces dic*), an ancient earthwork which also formed part of the northern boundary of Winterborne Tomson (*PN Dorset*, ii. 71). At this point the Almer parish boundary turns north-east and runs across as far as the river Stour, which it joins at ST 924020. The survey in **14** also seems to follow this line. The 'stone valley' (*stan*, *denu*) is presumably the combe through which the boundary now runs to the Stour (see *PN Dorset*, ii. 58, for a rectification of a misidentification). In *molenhame* the second element is *hamm*, 'river-meadow'; this would have been alongside the Stour. *PN Dorset* suggests *myl(e)n*, 'mill', for the first element, which would be entirely appropriate for the location (near a place where two branches of the Stour form an island). *Cellor* is obscure; *PN Dorset* (ii. 57) suggests that it may be a misspelling of OE *ceolor*, 'throat, channel, gorge'. It seems likely that this feature is in some way connected with the river Stour itself, which the later parish boundary now follows for a short distance; it may refer to the confluence near this point of the Stour and the Tarrant. *Windee bergh* is likely to be the tumulus near the river bank opposite Shapwick (ST 934017); *PN Dorset* identifies the first element as *windig*, 'windy'. From here the survey follows a 'way' to a ford on the Winterborne, and then goes west along the river back to Almer.

15

King Eadmund grants five hides (mansae) *at Hinton St Mary, Dorset, to Wulfgar,* minister. A.D. 944

C. BL Harley 61, 10v–11r: copy, s. xv
 Rubric: Hoc consecracionis dono inscripto Admundus rex Hamtune ad donacionem in-
 perpetuum conscripsit.
Ed.: a. Kemble 397 (with the bounds in vol. iii, p. 420)
    b. Birch 793
    c. Pierquin, *Recueil*, pt 2, no. 78
Listed: Sawyer 502; Finberg, *ECW*, no. 591

Regnante Domino nostro Iesu Christo. Mundi huius labentibus properanter temporibus regnaque functi*ᵃ* cum regibus uelocissimo transeuntibus cursu, licet stare firmiter a priori statu cito labi nullo sapiente ignoter*ᵇ* est, et gaudia hic fallentis uite quatiuntur et dissipantur; iccirco incertum futurorum temporum statum prouidentes posteris succidentibus*ᶜ* profuturum esse decreuimus, ut ea que communi tractu salubri consilio difiniuntur paginis saltem uilibus roborata confirmentur. Quapropter ego Admundus rex Anglorum ceterarumque gencium in circuitu persistencium cuidam fideli meo ministro uocitato nomine Wlfgario*ᵈ* ob illius amabile obsequium eiusque placabili fidelitate modicam numinis mei partem, id est .v. mansas agelluli, eternaliter tradendo concessi, ubi turbarum collacione iamdudum nomen illatum hoc adesse profertur at Hamtune, ut terram iam prefatam meo scilicet ouante concessu tramitibus sue possideat uite; deinceps namque sibi succidenti*ᵉ* cui uoluerit heredi derelinquat ceu predixi in eternam hereditatem. Maneat igitur meum hoc inmobile donum eterna liberalitate*ᶠ* iocundum cum omnibus que ad ipsum locum pertinere dinoscuntur, tam in magnis quam in modicis rebus, campis, pascuis, pratis et siluis, excepto communi labore, expedicione, pontis arcisue coedificacione. Siqui denique mihi non optanti hanc libertatis cartam liuore depressi uiolari*ᵍ* satagerint, agminibus tetre*ʰ* caliginis lapsi uocem audiant examinacionis die arbitris sibi dicentis, 'Discedite a me maledicti in ignem eternum',[1] ubi cum demonibus ferreis sartaginibus crudeli torqueantur in pena, si non ante mortem digna hoc emendauerit penitencia. Istis terminibus predicta terra circumgerata*ⁱ* esse uidetur.

þis sand þe landes imare at Hamtune. Arest of hefdeswelle on nunnenlinc, of nunnene linche on litiges heuede, of litiges heuede anlang diche on Sture at oxene bricge, unen*ʲ* up anlang Sture at suðwde, þannen of*ᵏ* þane hegen, of þane hegen to dich, þanen anlang dich ouer ciuerget mor on þane mapelder, of þane mapeldere be þane akere heueden on chelbrichtes dich, anlang cuterget mores on þane stream, anlang streames on adwines imare, up anlang imares þat eft on efdeswelle suthward.

Acta est hec prefata donacio anno ab incarnacione Domini nostri Iesu Christi .d.cccc.xliiii., indiccione .ii.

Ego Admundus rex Anglorum prefatam donacionem cum sigillo sancte crucis confirmaui. +

Ego Oda Dorobernensis ecclesie archiepiscopus eiusdem regis donacionem cum sigillo sancte crucis roboraui. +

Ego Theodred Londoniensis ecclesie episcopis consignaui, et ceteri. +

ᵃ Perhaps read regnisque functis (*but all examples of this formula have* regnaque functi)
ᵇ For ignotum (*compare S 530 etc.*)   *ᶜ A spelling for* succedentibus   *ᵈ For* Wulfgaro
ᵉ A spelling for succedenti   *ᶠ Probably for* libertate (*compare S 465 etc.*)
ᵍ For uiolare (*all examples of this formula have the same reading*)   *ʰ* terre C
ⁱ A spelling for circumgirata   *ʲ For* þanen   *ᵏ Probably for* on

¹ Matt. 25: 41

15 appears to be entirely authentic. The invocation is an occasional variant on the common formula *Regnante inperpetuum Domino nostro Iesu Christo*, often associated with dubious documents (S 281, 450, 581), but not in any way reason for suspicion (and see S 1019, 1348). The proem is an amalgam of elements from two standard formulas. The first part (to *dissipantur*) is found in S 530, 559, 604, 668 (and see S 283); the second part (from *iccirco*) derives from the proem beginning *Quamuis decreta pontificum* (see S 493, 497, 501, 506–7, 525, 528, and cf. S 783). Much of the formulation of the dispositive section and sanction is also found in S 465 and 475 (and various elements appear in S 482, 488, 493, 512). The anathema is a common formula, used regularly between 939 and 960, and occasionally revived in later years.

In 958 Wulfgar was granted three hides at Thornton (in the eastern part of Marnhull parish) and at Iwerne Courtney (**23**); the rubric to the bounds suggests that this land was to be attached to Hinton St Mary. Shaftesbury's Domesday manor at Hinton was assessed at eight hides (GDB 78v), and it is tempting to assume that this was formed from the five hides of **15** together with the three hides of **23**. But there was a separate Domesday manor at Iwerne Courtney, and it may have been the case that this land was hived off before the Conquest (see further discussion in the commentary to **23**). Wulfgar may perhaps be identified with the beneficiary of S 492 (A.D. 943), which covers land in Wiltshire. A thegn named Wulfgar attests royal diplomas regularly throughout Eadmund's reign, in a prominent position from 942. None of Eadred's charters has the subscription of a man of that name, but a Wulfgar began to attest regularly after Eadwig succeeded; possibly this was a different man, but it may also have been the case that the prominent Wulfgar of Eadmund's reign fell out of favour under Eadred and then was reinstated by Eadwig. It is perhaps no coincidence that the Wulfgar of **15** received Hinton St Mary in 944, and then had to wait until Eadwig's reign to acquire the appurtenant properties. He may possibly have held an office in the royal household; in a difficult Abingdon charter of 959 (S 658), a Wulfgar styled *custos* attests at the head of a group of thegns who seem to be household officials. The Wulfgar Leofa who acquired a small area of land in Shaftesbury itself in 958 (**22**) is evidently a different man; note that the bounds of East Orchard (**24**) refer both to 'Wulfgar's boundary' (at Thornton in Marnhull) and to 'Leofa's boundary' (perhaps at Sutton Waldron).

The original name of Hinton seems to have been *Hean-tun*, 'high farm, farm situated on high land' (from *heah, tun*), a reference to its position on a 300' hill (*PN Dorset*, iii. 159–60); the later affix, 'St Mary', refers to Shaftesbury's ownership of the estate. The spelling of the place-name in the text of **15** (and in **23**) shows the influence of the commoner *ham-tun*. The bounds have been discussed by Grundy (1936, pp. 119–21) and Forsberg (*Contribution*, pp. 143–4). The survey describes an area which was bounded to the south by the estate at Sturminster Newton which passed to Glastonbury in 968 (see S 764), to the west by the river Stour and to the east by Chivrick's Brook. The survey begins in the south-east, and describes first the common boundary with Sturminster Newton; the first five boundary marks in **15** (up to the point where the survey meets the River Stour) also occur in the Sturminster bounds. The Hinton survey begins and ends at 'the spring of the headland' (*heafod, welle*; for the sense of *heafod* here, see Forsberg, *Contribution*, p. 144); this survives in the field-name Hitsel (*PN Dorset*, iii. 162). The next boundary mark appears to read *nunnenlinc*, which *PN Dorset* (iii. 163) translates as 'ridge or bank of the nuns' (*nunne*, gen. pl. *nunnena, hlinc*), and associates with Shaftesbury's possession of Hinton St Mary. But the bounds ought to predate the nuns' acquisition of the estate, so (unless the clause is a later addition) this would have to be taken as a reference to a neighbouring estate owned by nuns, presumably Sturminster Newton, given that the two sets of bounds run together here. However, the corresponding element in the Sturminster bounds is *minnanlinche*, which *PN Dorset* regards as a corruption of *nunnanhlinc*. It may be that *minnanlinche* is the preferable reading (? from a pers. n. Mynna), the variant in **15** being the result of the same sort of scribal error that gave *scaftesbury* in place of *ceatwanberge* in **5** . The first element in *litiges heuede* is probably a personal name *Lytig*, so 'Lytig's headland' (see *PN Dorset*, iii. 199–200; Forsberg, *Contribution*, pp. 143–4). From here the survey passes along a ditch to the Stour at 'oxen bridge' (*oxa*, gen. pl. *oxena, brycg*), probably where the parish boundary meets the river at ST 782152. The boundary then follows the river northwards to 'south wood' (*suth, wudu*), which was probably situated where the parish boundary leaves the Stour and turns east (perhaps at ST 774167, where a small area of woodland is still marked on older maps). After this the survey mentions a hedge (*hege*, unless this is another instance of *hægen; see **8** and *PN Dorset*, iii. 110, but also above, p. 35) and a ditch or dyke which it followed over a marsh called *ciuerget mor*. The first part of the compound survives in the stream-name Chivrick's Brook, and is perhaps *cefer, ceafer*, 'beetle'; the second element is presumably *geat*, 'gate, gap'. The boundary proceeds past a maple-tree (*mapuldor*) and 'the ends of arable plots' (*æcer, heafod*; see *PN Dorset*, iii. 163) to 'Ceolberht's ditch' (pers. n. Ceolberht). *Cuterget mores* is presumably a misspelling of *ciuerget mores*. The boundary now follows a stream, apparently Chivrick's Brook, to 'Eadwine's bound- ary' (pers. n. Eadwine, (ge)*mære*); the brook thus defined the eastern boundary. Eadwine may have held land in the vicinity of Manston.

16

King Eadred grants eight hides (mansae) *in the Isle of Purbeck, Dorset, to Ælfthryth, a religious woman.* A.D. 948

C. BL Harley 61, 3v–4v: copy, s. xv
> Rubric: Adredus rex huius scripti testimonio .ix. mansas agelluli in loco qui a ruricolis Purbicinga nuncupatur ut in presente continetur scripto a dono suo commisit.

D. Bodleian, Dodsworth 38, 3v–4r: copy of C, s. xvii
Ed.: a. *Mon. Angl.*, i. 215
     b. Kemble 418 (with bounds in vol. iii, pp. 426–7)
     c. *Mon. Angl.* (rev. edn), ii. 478–9 (no. 5)
     d. Birch 868
     e. Pierquin, *Recueil*, pt 2, no. 90
Listed: Sawyer 534; Finberg, *ECW*, no. 593
Printed from C

In nomine Dei summi et altissimi Iesu Christi. Beantis[a] uniuersorum uoce monemur preclara, procuremus incessanter sine amaritudine mentis huius seculi ambicione integra libertate apertis ianuis intrare ad eum qui suo cruore scelera nostra detersit iniusta. Iccirco ego Ádredus rex Anglorum ceterarumque gencium in circuitu persistencium gubernator et rector, secundo anno imperii mei, litteratoriis apicibus roboraui quod cum consensu heroicorum uirorum tradidi cuidam religiose femine uocitate nomine Alfþriþ, et pro amabili peticione patris sui, .viii. mansas agelluli, necnon et pro placabili pecunia quam mihi in sue deuocionis obsequio detulit, hoc est .lx. mancusas purissimi olei,[b] in illo loco ubi turbarum collacione iamdudum nomen illatum hoc adesse profertur pars telluris Purbicinga, ut terram iam prefatam meo[c] scilicet ouante concessu tramitibus[d] sue possideat uite; deinceps namque sibi succedenti cuicumque uoluerit heredi derelinquat in eternam hereditatem. Maneat igitur meum hoc inmobile donum eterna libertate iocundum cum omnibus que ad ipsum locum pertinere dinoscuntur, campis, pascuis, pratis, siluis, excepto communi labore et[e] expedicione, pontis arcisue coedificacione. Si qui denique mihi non optanti hanc libertatis cartam liuore depressi uiolari[f] satagerunt,[g] agminibus tetre caliginis lapsi uocem audeant[h] examinacionis die arbitris sibi dicentis, 'Discedite a me maledicti in ignem eternum',[i] ubi cum demonibus ferreis sartaginibus crudeli torqueantur in pena, si non ante mortem digna hoc emendauerint penitencia. Istis terminibus predicta terra circumgerata[i] esse uidetur.

þese sanden þe land imare. Arest fram Þican forde[j] on beam broc, an[k] ðonnen anlang broke on anne wiþig þefele, þiers ouer þane merse þare weilaite, þanne on[l] anne ston, of þanne stane on alle þiscan, of alle ðiscan[m]

on anne dich, þannen suth at lang[n] dich on ðone[o] herepaþ, of þen herepaþe suth anlang dich on þanne cumb, þonne anlang cumbe on þen hirnen, onne strutheardes paþe, of þane paþe forðe anlange welles one þane westrene cumbe, þanne adun anlang cumbes on þane broc, þonne anlang stremes on þe schort mannes pol þerth ut on sce.
Þane is þis seo westere land sceare. Of sa an[p] anne stan tor, of þane tore on þane clif upward on anne dich, þanen north anlang safandune on þene richte herepath, þanen north anlang dich oþ þan ealden stodfald estward, þane forþ on ða ealden hege rewe, anlang þare hege rewe oþ þa dich, of þare dich on anne linc reawe, of þane linche on bl[. . .],[q] þanne anlang broces oþ olle discan,[m] of olle discan[m] north ouer þane [. . .][r] on scyleford, þane anlang streame þat it cometh eft to Wikenforde.
Acta est hec prefata donacio anno ab incarnacione Domini .dcccc.xlviii., indiccione .vi.

Ego Adredus rex Anglorum prefatam donacionem sub sigillo sancte crucis indeclinabiliter consensi atque roboraui. +
Ego Oda Dorobernensis ecclesie archiepiscopus eiusdem regis principatum et beniuolenciam sub sigillo sancte crucis conclusi. +
Ego Þeodred Lundoniensis episcopus coroboraui. +
Ego Alphech Wintoniensis ecclesie episcopus testitudinem sancte crucis subscripsi. +[s]
Ego Aluric episcopus consignaui. +
Ego Alfgar[t] episcopus roboraui. +
Ego Wlsige episcopus conclusi. +
Ego Alfred episcopus consensi. +
Ego Aþelstan dux +
Ego Adric dux +
Ego Ealhdem[u] dux +
Ego Admund minister +
Ego Elfstan minister +
Ego Wluric minister +
Ego Alfsige minister +
Ego Wluric minister +
Ego Aluric minister +
Ego Aþelsige minister +
Ego Alfred minister +
Ego Aþelgerd minister +

[a] Beatis C (*compare S 465 etc.*) [b] *Probably error for* aurei [c] in eo C
[d] teamitibus C [e] et *probably added by a copyist* (*compare S 465 etc.*)

[f] For uiolare (*all examples of this formula have the same reading*)
[g] For satagerint (*compare S 465 etc.*) *[h]* For audiant (*compare S 465 etc.*)
[i] A spelling for circumgirata *[j]* forð C *[k]* For and *[l]* or C
[m] Probably for piscan (*see commentary*) *[n]* Probably for andlang *[o]* done C *[p]* For on
[q] bl *followed by blank space sufficient for several words* C (*the first word was probably*
blechene *or* blechenenwelle) *[r]* Blank space, sufficient for two or three words C
[s] The remaining subscriptions are written across the page *[t]* For Æthelgar
[u] For Ealhhelm

[1] Matt. 25: 41

16 appears to be authentic. The verbal invocation is a standard type which was used regularly in the 940s (see S 470, 471 etc.), and much of the rest of the formulation is shared by a group of diplomas from between 940 and 943 (S 465, 474–5, 481, 488: see also S (Add.) 517b, and cf. S 470). The inclusion of an 'imperial' year after the royal style is a feature regularly associated with this proem (see S 465, 474–5, 481, 488; the same feature occurs in a group of charters with an incarnation date inserted after the invocation, for which see **14**). **16** diverges from this group primarily in the dispositive section, which has been distorted by the clumsy introduction of references to the beneficiary's father and to the price paid in return for the grant. On the face of it, the king received sixty mancuses of the purest oil for his generosity; *oleum* is probably a corruption of *aureum*, since gifts presented to the king in return for land are almost invariably in the form of money, bullion or precious objects. It is fairly rare at this date for a reference to be made to the price exacted for a land-grant, but there are other examples: see, for instance, S 500 and 505. The reference to *pars telluris Purbicinga*, instead of a simple place-name, is notable but not necessarily suspicious. The dating clause is consistent with the regnal year at the beginning of the charter and the witness-list seems contemporary.

It is possible that Ælfthryth was attached to the minster at Shaftesbury, although that was not necessarily the case. **16** is one of a large group of charters from the middle years of the tenth century in favour of religious women: see also **13**, **17**, S 448–9, 464–5, 474, 482, 487, 493, 535, 563, 775, 1793, and S (Add.) 517a, 517b (discussed in Dumville, *Wessex*, pp. 177–8). In only one diploma (S 563) is the beneficiary explicitly linked with a religious community (Wilton). It may have been the case that in at least some of these instances the woman in question was expected to live an independent religious life on her estate (or perhaps to gather around her a new community). The land in Purbeck covered in **16** formed part of Shaftesbury's Domesday manor of Kingston, which was assessed at sixteen hides TRE (GDB 78v); on one hide of this manor William subsequently built Wareham Castle (later Corfe Castle), giving the community in exchange the church of Gillingham with its dependencies. Also forming part of the Kingston manor was the seven-hide estate at Corfe and Blashenwell assigned to a thegn named Wihtsige in 956 (**19**). The third charter in the archive which covers land in the area (**20**) is a forgery created by the conflation of **16** and **19**, apparently intended to provide explicit title to the whole sixteen hides of the holding TRE. It is not known whether the Purbeck property descended to Shaftesbury directly from Ælfthryth or at a later date (for comparison, the Cheselbourne estate granted to Wynflæd in **13** does not seem to have passed to the abbey until after 1019). It seems significant that Corfe Gap was reputed to have been the site of the murder of King Edward the Martyr, whose remains were (allegedly) buried at Wareham and later translated to Shaftesbury. Æthelred promoted his brother's cult and gave the minster at Bradford-on-Avon to Shaftesbury as a refuge for the nuns and their relics, including those of Edward (29). It is possible that Æthelred also transferred to the nunnery the land at Corfe where his brother had been killed. Corfe was later associated with the cult of St Edward; the church there was dedicated to him, and St Edward's Bridge and St Edward's Fountain are local features, with attached legends. Corfe Gap is a highly strategic landscape feature, which we would expect to find in royal hands; it is not surprising that William was anxious to gain possession of it.

Shaftesbury's Kingston manor appears to have approximated to the later parish of Corfe Castle, which extended from Poole Harbour in the north, across the Purbeck Hills down to the Channel. The eight hides of **16** evidently lay in the south-eastern portion of the parish; their western boundary corresponds to part of the eastern boundary of the seven hides in **19** (see discussion in Grundy 1935, pp. 117–22; the separate boundary marks are considered in *PN Dorset*, i. 1–33). The survey is divided into two parts, the first outlining the eastern boundary down to the sea, the second covering the western boundary as it runs north from a point further along the coast. The starting-point is a ford over the river Wych, the old name for the river Corfe (*PN Dorset*, i. 20); the ford may have been on the site of St Edward's Bridge in Corfe Gap, where the river runs through the Purbeck Hills (SY 959824; see *PN Dorset*, i. 18). *Beam broc* ('brook with a treetrunk (*beam*) across it': *PN Dorset*, i. 31) appears to be the tributary of the river which the boundary follows south as far as a 'willow thicket' (*withig, thyfel*). The marsh (*mersc*) by 'the road-junction' (*weg, (ge)læte*) would have been located in the low-lying land directly below the Purbeck Hills. After this the boundary passes a stone and then reaches a feature which appears to have survived in the lost field-name Hollish (approximately SY 955806; see *PN Dorset*, i. 14–15). This is mentioned as *alle wiscan, alle discan* and *olle discan* in the bounds of **16**, as *olle discan* in **19** and as *holewisken* in **20**; later forms suggest that the reading *wiscan* is to be preferred for the second element (which implies that at some point a copyist of these bounds mistook *p* for *þ* and transformed it in to *ð*, later mistaken for *d*; for the significance of this, see pp. xix–xx). The first element may be the rare personal name *Olla* and the second is probably *wisce*, 'marshy meadow': so, 'Olla's marshy meadows'. From here the boundary follows a ditch south to a highway (*herepæð*), probably represented by the road from Kingston to Langton Maltravers, and then south again to 'the combe' (*cumb*); this is Coombe Bottom (SY 968785), and probably corresponds to *struthgeardes cum* in the bounds of **20** (see *PN Dorset*, i. 10). The boundary passes along Coombe Bottom to 'the bend' (*hyrne*), and then runs on to *strutheardes pathe*, where the first element is a personal name *Strutheard*; this is *struthherdes wege* in **20**. It continues along the *welle*, here 'stream' rather than 'spring' (unless this is an error for *weies, weges*), to 'the western combe' (see the adjacent West Hill), and then down along the combe to the brook, which reaches the coast at *schortmannes pol*, apparently Chapman's Pool (SY 956770; see *PN Dorset*, i. 64).

The survey resumes at a point a little further west along the coast and continues north along the western boundary (which corresponds with the eastern boundary of

19). From the sea the boundary runs to a stone crag (*torr*), to the cliff up to a ditch and then northwards along a hill called *safandune*, which may be the spur now occupied by West Hill Farm (SY 952782); the first element is possibly *safene*, 'safine', a kind of juniper (*PN Dorset*, i. 32). 'The straight highway' (*riht, herepæð*) is probably the road running directly south from Kingston. From here the boundary continues north along the line of a ditch. *PN Dorset* (i. 30) associates 'the old stud-fold' (*stodfald*) with an eighteenth-century field-name Stot Field. The next boundary marks are 'the old hedge-row' (*eald, hege-ræw*), another ditch, and a 'linchet-row' (*hlinc-ræw*) which may have been in the vicinity of Lynch Farm (SY 960800; see *PN Dorset*, i. 15–16). The scribe has left the next section of the bounds blank, probably because her source was unclear or illegible; the first word was probably Blashenwell (*ble-cenenwelle*) or *blecen*, the stream from which Blashenwell is named (see further discussion in **19**, and Blashenwell Farm, SY 952803). The boundary then runs along a brook (probably the *blecen*) back to Hollish. The following boundary mark has also been left blank, and this time there is no guide to the probable reading. Next comes a ford, presumably over another tributary of the Wych; the element *scyle* is obscure (see discussion in *PN Dorset*, i. 94). From here the boundary follows the stream back to the 'Wych ford'.

17

King Eadred grants thirty hides (mansiones) *at Felpham, Sussex, to Eadgifu, his mother.* A.D. 953

C. BL Harley 61, 12rv: copy, s. xv
> *Rubric*: Sub presentis tituli conscripcione Adredus rex .xxx. mansiones iuxta ffelcham adiacentes omni tempore dare conscripsit.

Ed.: a. Kemble 432 (with the bounds in vol. iii, p. 431)
     b. Birch 898
     c. Barker 1949, pp. 71–2, with translation
Listed: Sawyer 562

Anno ab incarnacione Domini nostri Iesu Christi .d.cccc.liii. Ego Adred rex Christo perpetualiter superni numinis intuitu subtronizato preregente et eque illo confauente tocius Albionis primecherius et*[a]* famose famuli*[b]* Dei Adgiue matri mee, sub instinctu diuini timoris, terre particulam sub estimacione .xxx. mansionum in loco qui dicitur Felhham libenter admodum imperpetuum cui sibi placuerit derelinquendi concedo, et hiis limitibus hec telluris particula, libera preter arcem, pontem, expedicionem, circumgirari uidetur.

Arest of Elmerespole on biken muþe, swo anlang brines fleotes to tilbir[. . .]*[c]* forde, swo on sa, of sa on þane stapel, of þanne stapele eft in tilbirhthes forde, of þanne forde eft þanen on stanford, of stanforde eft on Almerspol. Et hec sunt pascua porcorum: quatuor mansiones in loco qui dicitur et Boganora, at Hidhirst in silua et in communi silua pascuale quod dicitur

Palinga schittas. Et huius munificencie constipulaciones*d* sunt, nomina quorum infra conrecitari uidentur. Huius doni munificenciam signo crucis corroboro.*e*

Ego Odo Christi ecclesie archon. +

Ego Alured episcopus consensi et subscripsi. +

Ego Athelgar episcopus et ceteri multi. +

a A word such as rex *has fallen out here (unless* et *is redundant)*   *b For* famule
c MS is damaged (perhaps read tilbirhtes)
d Probably error for constipulatores *(compare S 560 etc.)*
e This sentence may belong with Archbishop Oda's subscription

17 is a representative of the group of closely related and diplomatically anomalous charters issued between 951 and 975, which have been associated with Dunstan and Glastonbury, and are generally known as 'Dunstan B' charters (see also **18** and Keynes 1994b). Symptomatic features are: the substitution of a brief dating clause for the usual protocol; a royal style including the word *primicerius*; extremely concise formulation in the dispositive section; the use of specific formulas for the statement of powers and sanction, and to introduce the boundary clause and witness-list. The diplomas in this group generally display some, but not always all of these features. **17** has an untypically elaborate royal style (which still includes the key word *primicerius*). The formulation of the dispositive section is particularly compressed, even to the point of confusion; instead of a separate statement of powers, a reference to the right of alienation is inserted before the dispositive verb (with consequent problems of syntax) and the reservation clause is combined with the introduction to the bounds. There is no sanction. In other respects, much of the formulation is closely comparable with that of other 'Dunstan B' charters: note especially the reference to the estate as *terre particulam* (in the other charters of this group the typical phrase is *ruris particulam*), the insertion of *sub estimatione* before the assessment, and the use of the phrase *libenter admodum*. For the form of the reservation clause, see **18** and S 563. The 'Dunstan B' model fell out of favour under Eadwig, but was used quite regularly in Edgar's reign (see further discussion in Keynes 1994b). In the curtailed witness-list the subscriptions are those of Oda of Canterbury, Ælfred of Selsey and Æthelgar of Crediton. There is no reason to think **17** other than authentic.

   The description of Eadgifu as *famula Dei* is probably an indication that she had taken religious vows after her husband's death; she may have become a lay associate of a female community, as had the Wynflæd of S 1539 (for other charters of this period in favour of religious women, see **16**). A connection of this kind between Eadgifu and Shaftesbury could provide the context for the community's acquisition of this distant Sussex estate, although there is no firm evidence of the date at which Felpham passed to Shaftesbury. Eadgifu survived both her sons and lived into Edgar's reign. Eadred bequeathed to his mother land at Amesbury in Wiltshire, Wantage in Berkshire and Basing in Hampshire, together with all his bookland in Sussex, Surrey and Kent (S 1515), but there is some reason to believe that his will was never implemented; moreover, Eadwig is known to have deprived his grandmother of all her property, although she regained her possessions when Edgar came to power (S 1211). Shaftesbury held Felpham in 1066, with an assessment of twenty-one hides (GDB 17v). An estate there had been bequeathed by King Alfred to his kinsman Osferth (S 1507); it had presumably found its way back to the royal patrimony by the mid tenth century.

Felpham is now an eastern suburb of Bognor Regis, but was previously a separate parish. The boundary clause is remarkably brief for an estate as large as thirty hides, and it may also be slightly corrupt; it is difficult to make sense of the boundary marks. The survey begins at *Elmerspole*, where the second element is *pol*, usually 'pool, deep place in a river', but here perhaps with the meaning 'tidal stream' (*DEPN*, p. 369). It seems almost certain that the first element is to be associated with the village of Elmer (at SU 985000), until recently represented by Elmer Farm in Middleton parish, but now the name of a Middleton suburb. The name Elmer derives from *æl-mere*, 'eel-lake' (*PN Sussex*, i. 142), so the combination with *pol* is oddly tautological. A connection with Elmer would suggest that the Felpham survey began and ended in the south-east of the estate, although this is difficult to reconcile with some of the other boundary marks. Next comes *bikenmuthe*, where the second element is probably (*ge*)*mythe*, used to describe a confluence of rivers or streams, and the first a personal name Bica. From here the boundary follows a creek called *brines fleote*, a name used in the Pagham bounds of S 230 to refer to the creek forming the boundary between Bersted and Felpham (*PN Sussex*, i. 93). If both these references are to the same waterway, then the Felpham bounds are here describing the western boundary of the estate, even though shortly before they appear to mention Elmer in the south-east. It would also seem to be the case, from the evidence of the later boundary marks, that the survey was running anticlockwise. The next boundary mark is partly damaged in the manuscript, but seems to have been *tilbirhtes ford* (pers. n. Tilbirht, *ford*), to which the survey later returns a second time (*eft*); it is difficult to understand how this boundary mark could occur twice, and this may be ground for thinking that the survey is corrupt. The survey now reaches the coast, which it probably follows for some distance before turning inland at a boundary post (*stapel*). The next two boundary marks are both fords, 'Tilbirht's ford' and 'stony ford'; in both cases the use of the word *eft* indicates that the survey is returning to the ford, although 'stony ford' at least has not previously been encountered. *Eft* may possibly be an error for *est*, 'east'.

After the boundary clause comes a description of the swine-pastures attached to Felpham; most estates in Kent and Sussex had appurtenant rights to specified swine-pastures (dens) in communal forests and particularly in the Weald, and these are frequently listed in Anglo-Saxon charters. The Felpham dens amounted to four hides and were located at *Boganora* (Little Bognor in Fittleworth: *PN Sussex*, i. 126), in the wood at *Hidhirst* (Idehurst Farm in Kirdford: *PN Sussex*, i. 105) and in the common woodland called *Palinga schittas*. This last seems to be an early name for Limbo Farm in Petworth (see *PN Sussex*, i. 117–18). A Middle English form was *Paleschudde*, where the second element derives from OE *scydd*, 'hovel, pig-sty'. The first element of *palinga schittas* is linked with Poling (*Palinge*), six miles north-east of Felpham; this is a tribal name, probably meaning 'Pal's people' (*PN Sussex*, i. 171–2; *DEPN*, p. 370). Thus *palinga schittas* would be 'the pig-sties of the *Palingas*' and would refer to an area particularly devoted to the raising of swine.

18

King Eadred grants five hides (caracti *for* cassati) *at Henstridge, Somerset, to Brihtric*, minister. A.D. 956 [? for 953 × 955]

C. BL Harley 61, 6v–7r: copy, s. xv
   Rubric: Adredus rex ruris particulam sub estimacione .v. caractorum in loco qui Hengstesreg dicitur sub munificencie sue dono inperpetuum consignavit.
D. Bodleian, Dodsworth 38, 6rv: copy of C, s. xvii
Ed.: a. Hutchins, *Dorset* (1st edn), ii. 510 (bounds omitted)
     b. Kemble 455 (with the bounds in vol. iii, p. 445)
     c. Birch 923
Listed: Sawyer 570; Finberg, *ECW*, no. 467
Edited from C

Anno ab incarnacione Domini .dcccclvi. Ego Adred diuina gracia fauente rex et primicherius tocius Albionis Brithrico ministro meo ob eius amabile et fidele obsequiolum ruris particulam sub estimacione .v. caractorum[a] ab omni seculari seruicio, diuino iure in suo statu perdurante, preter arcem, pontum,[b] expedicionem, liberam, libenter admodum concessi, in loco qui dicitur Hengstesrig, eo tenore huius munificencie donum perstringens ut post obitum suum imperpetuum ius cuicumque uoluerit heredi derelinquat. Quod si quisque quod non optamus[c] huiusmodi donacionis cartam infringere temptauerit, nisi prius in hoc seculo digne castigetur, in futuro perhenni cruciatu prematur. Et his limitibus hec telluris particula circumgirari uidetur. Arest of horspoles heauede anlang dich on ludenham, of ludenhame alang[d] streames on eldenham, þannen forð to þere ealden hege, þannen forðer[e] be hegen one stoc wey, of stok wei anlang hecgham to filed hamme, of filed hamme ut þurth þere groue, on irichte to þere eald dich, of þere eald idich on irichte to herepað, of herepaþe anlang richtes to lortenpille, on ða elden dich, of þere ealden dic on duccenhulle, of duccenhulle on Cawel, andlang dich on Wricawel,[f] þannen anlang streames on hors poles heaued. Huius doni constipulatorum nomina inferius notata uidentur.

Ego Oda archiepiscopus consensi et subscripsi. +
Ego Wlfstan archiepiscopus consensi et subscripsi . +[g]
Ego Alsige episcopus consensi et subscripsi. +
Ego Osulf episcopus consensi et subscripsi. +
Ego Wlfsige episcopus consensi et subscripsi. +
Ego Alwold episcopus consensi et subscripsi. +
Ego Brichtem[h] episcopus consensi et subscripsi. +
Ego Kenward episcopus consensi et subscripsi. +
Ego Cinsige episcopus consensi et subscripsi. +

Ego Wlfhelm episcopus consensi et subscripsi. +
Ego Leofwine episcopus consensi et subscripsi. +
Ego Adwi cliton^i consensi et subscripsi. +
Ego Adgar cliton^i +
Ego Athelstan dux +
Ego Athelstan dux +
Ego Admund dux +
Ego Birhtferd dux +
Ego Aþelsige dux +
Ego Alfsige minister +
Ego Alfech minister +

---

^{a} *For* cassatorum ^{b} *Error for* pontem (*same error in* S 676, 678 *and* S (Add.) 676a)
^{c} optam C ^{d} *For* andlang ^{e} forder C ^{f} *Probably for* Wincawel
^{g} *The remaining subscriptions are written across the page* ^{h} *For* Bricthelm ^{i} diton C

18 is another example of the anomalous diplomas issued in the last years of Eadred's reign (see 17, and Keynes 1994b). It is more typical of the standard 'Dunstan B' type than is 17, for it includes the royal style, statement of powers and anathema which are usually associated with this model and which are missing in 17, but even so it is diplomatically very similar. As is generally the case in 'Dunstan B' charters from Eadred's reign, there is no royal subscription. The remainder of the witness-list gives dating limits of between 953 and 955 or 956; Ælfwold of Crediton took office in the former year, and Wulfstan of York died either in December 955 or December 956 (see Keynes, *Diplomas*, pp. 49–50, arguing for the later date).

The principal difficulty with 18 is the incarnation year of 956, impossible for a charter of Eadred (and perhaps incompatible with Archbishop Wulfstan's subscription). This is not a charter of Eadwig with the king's name altered, for the witness-list list includes Eadwig's subscription as ætheling; any emendation must centre on the incarnation year. The simplest explanation, that 956 is a scribal error for 955, is not without its own problems. The Brihtric of this charter is almost certainly to be identified with the beneficiary of another charter of Eadred, preserved in the Winchester cathedral archive, which concerns land at Rimpton in Somerset (S 571); it has a vernacular addition (S 1512) in which Brihtric (surnamed 'Grim') bequeathes the estate to the Old Minster, and it mentions that Eadred's charter had been granted as a supplement to the old charter issued by Æthelstan (i.e. S 441). S 571 is also dated 956, and has the correct indiction for that year. The fact that another charter of Brihtric in a separate archive has the same impossible incarnation year means that the reading in 18 cannot be explained as a simple copying error by a Shaftesbury scribe. If both charters had been drawn up at the same time, then we could attribute the error to the original draftsman; but the very different witness-lists seem to rule out simultaneous production. It would appear that the corruption had crept in before the charters had left Brihtric's hands, but the explanation for this remains elusive. In the last resort, the presence of a similar charter in a different archive probably indicates that 18 is fundamentally authentic, despite this difficulty.

Brihtric would also seem to have been the beneficiary of a number of charters copied into the Glastonbury cartulary known as the *Liber Terrarum*; the cartulary has been lost, but its contents are inventoried in a surviving thirteenth-century manuscript (Cambridge, Trinity College, R. 5. 33, 77rv; printed in Hearne, *John of Glastonbury*, ii. 370–5; see Edwards, *Charters*, pp. 3–5). Brihtric was remembered as a benefactor of Glastonbury, and is said by William of Malmesbury to have been buried in the abbey (*De Ant. Glast.*, p. 120). The *Liber Terrarum* apparently included three charters in favour of Brihtric, all concerning estates in Somerset. As well as a diploma of Eadwig covering land at Yeovilton (S 1754; *LT* no. 118) and one in the name of Edgar relating to an estate at Camel (S 1764; *LT* no. 119), the cartulary also seems to have contained a charter in which Eadred granted to Brihtric land at Henstridge (*LT* no. 97). This generates considerable difficulties. Was Brihtric the beneficiary of two charters of Eadred covering land at Henstridge? Or were copies of the same diploma preserved at both Shaftesbury and Glastonbury? It has been suggested that the latter possibility might be a consequence of the supposed link between 'Dunstan B' charters and Glastonbury; if these texts were drawn up in the abbey, then drafts or copies may have been preserved there (see discussion of this aspect in Keynes 1994b). But it seems significant that the *Liber Terrarum* also contained two other diplomas covering land at Henstridge: a charter of King Æthelstan in favour of Æthelred (S 1712; *LT* no. 95), and another charter of Eadred, this time in favour of Ælfheah (S 1736; *LT* no. 96). This suggests that an explanation should probably be sought in terms of estate history.

In 1066 ten hides at Henstridge were held by Earl Harold and a further four by a certain Eadnoth (GDB 87r, 91v); there is no evidence of any Shaftesbury interest in either of these manors. However, the abbey did own property assessed at five hides TRE in Abbas Combe, the parish immediately to the north of Henstridge (GDB 91r), for which there appears to be no pre-Conquest documentation. The bounds of **18** are difficult to interpret, but a case has been made that they relate to Abbas Combe, rather than to Henstridge itself (see below). The likelihood is that **18** should be regarded as the title-deed to the abbey's estate at Abbas Combe. The charters in the Glastonbury archive, on the other hand, may have covered a separate estate or estates in Henstridge proper (representing the land later held by Earl Harold and/or Eadnoth). If this suggestion is correct, then Brihtric would indeed appear to have received two diplomas for separate estates in the Henstridge area, one that was to be preserved at Shaftesbury (**18**) and the other at Glastonbury (*LT* no. 97). The remaining Henstridge charters in the *Liber Terrarum* may represent earlier documentation which was transferred to Brihtric when he acquired the estate covered in *LT* no. 97. It is still not possible to account with entire satisfaction for the presence of these charters at Glastonbury, since that community is not known to have held land at Henstridge (Lesley Abrams, pers. comm.). Possibly the three diplomas were preserved at Glastonbury because Brihtric deposited them there for safekeeping; perhaps Glastonbury did own land at Henstridge at some stage, but lost or alienated it before 1066.

Henstridge lies just across the Dorset/Somerset border, approximately ten miles from Shaftesbury. The first element is *hengest*, 'stallion', and the place-name means 'ridge where stallions were kept'. Ekwall (*DEPN*, p. 235) draws attention to nearby Horsington. Evidently this was an area noted for horse-rearing; in this context it is significant that the first boundary mark includes a reference to a 'horse-pool'. Grundy (*Somerset*, pp. 109–12) was unable to make a satisfactory connection between the later parish boundary of Henstridge and the survey in **18**; it was left to Forsberg (1942, p. 158) to suggest that the survey was probably associated with Abbas Combe. Few of the boundary marks can be identified with any confidence. According to Forsberg's interpretation, the survey apparently begins in the south-east of the parish, between the river Cale and Bow Brook. The first boundary mark mentioned is 'the upper end' (*heafod*) of 'horse pool' (*hors, pol*), which was perhaps associated with the river Cale. From here the boundary runs along a ditch or dyke to 'Luda's river-meadow' (*hamm*). The 'stream' is likely to be Bow Brook, which the parish boundary follows for a short distance; but from this point it proves very difficult indeed to suggest identifications for the boundary marks. Next is *eldenham*, probably 'Ealda's river-meadow' (*hamm*), after which the boundary follows 'the old hedge' (*eald, hege*) to the '*stoc* way' (*stoc* here probably means 'secondary settlement, farm'). *Hecgham* appears to be 'hedge enclosure or meadow' (*hecg, ham/hamm*); it may be an error for *hecg* (*hecgan*), influenced by the next boundary mark, 'hay meadow' (*fileðe, hamm*). From here the boundary passes out through 'the grove' (*graf*) straight to 'the old ditch' and then runs directly to a highway (*herepæð*), which may be the road passing through Temple Combe. It seems likely that *anlang richtes* is a corruption of *on gerihte*, a direction used several times in this boundary-clause; alternatively, it may be *anlang ricges*, 'along the ridge' (*hrycg*). The first element of *lortenwelle* may be a personal name *Lorta*, with *welle*, 'spring' (see Forsberg, *Contribution*, pp. 158–60); an alternative possibility would be **lorte*, 'muddy place'. The boundary then meets yet another 'old ditch'. 'Ducks' hill' (*duce, hyll*) is likely to be the rising ground in the north-west of Abbas Combe parish. After this the boundary reaches the *Cawel*, follows a ditch or dyke to the *Wricawel* and then follows the stream back to its starting-point. *Wricawel* is evidently an error for *Wincawel*, which was the name of at least the upper reaches of the river Cale and was the origin of Wincanton (see Ekwall, *River-Names*, p. 63; *DEPN*, p. 522). The Abbas Combe parish is bounded to the east by the river Cale. The *Cawel* of the bounds was apparently a tributary of the river Cale; Ekwall thinks that this was probably Bow Brook, the water-course which runs parallel to the Cale on the west, and he speculates that both streams were originally called *Cawel*. In terms of the boundary itself there is some difficulty of identification. If *duccenhulle* is indeed the high ground on the north-west of the parish, then there is a considerable distance from that point to the next boundary mark, the *Cawel*, if that is indeed the stream known as Bow Brook. It is tempting to consider the possibility that in this case *Cawel* refers to the tributary of Bow Brook which rises in the north-west of Abbas Combe parish and runs east between Horsington and Abbas Combe to join the Brook at ST 725239; perhaps this stream formed the northern boundary of the pre-Conquest estate.

19

King Eadwig grants seven hides (mansae) *at Corfe and Blashenwell, Dorset,*
to Wihtsige, minister. A.D. 956

C. BL Harley 61, 16v–17v: copy, s. xv
    Rubric: Hoc est t[estament]um*ᵃ* regis supradicti de Corf et [de]*ᵃ* Blakenwelle intitulatum.
Ed.: a. Kemble vol. iii, p. 433 (bounds only)
      b. Finberg, *ECW*, p. 171 (witness-list only)
Listed: Sawyer 632; Finberg, *ECW*, no. 598

In nomine Domini nostri Iesu Christi. Apostolicis imbuti uesagiis,*ᵇ* quos
quodam olim in tempore mererentur aut*ᶜ* audire,*ᵈ* munia*ᵉ* uocis precelsa
conditoris reminiscimur proprii*ᶠ* ab ore tonantis, 'Uos qui secuti estis me
centuplum accipietis et uitam possidebitis eternam',[1] quos*ᵍ* eciam caducis
opibus implicati, tamen superno fulti amminiculo prosequi indigemus ad
alta. Cuius scilicet feruoris igne coarctus, ego Adwig basileus Anglorum
huiusque insule barbarorum ministro meo cuidam dilecto meo*ʰ* nomine
Withsige .vii. mansas gratuito datu perhenniter tribuo quodam in loco
priscorum ⟨uocabulo⟩*ⁱ* ad Corf and at Blachenwelle, cum optimatum meorum
consilio, ut ille uiuens secure possideat; in successoribus uero suis cui libuerit
sibi concedat heredi. Imminencia denique uite curricula hec nostra tradicio
illesa liberaque permaneat cum appendiciis suis, tam pascuis quam pratis,
siluis, exceptis tribus, expedicione, pontis arcisue confeccione. Nam siquis
seculorum in generacione ⟨Belial⟩*ʲ* gnatus*ᵏ* nostrum hoc uolumen inmutare
temptauerit, Iude reus scelere iudicii die magna cum turma truces trudatur
in flammas, nisi hoc in seculo penitencie prius fletu detersus*ˡ* hinc se corrigere
studuerit. Istis terminibus predicta terra circumgirata esse uidetur.

Ðis sand þa land imare to Corf and to Blechenenwelle þare .vii. hide. Arest
of Wikenforde, andlang*ᵐ* Wiken of*ⁿ* scylenford, of scylenforde on richt wege,
of þanne weie on olle discan,*ᵒ* þanen on blechene, of þanne welle on þane
hlinc, anlang hlinkes on anne dich, þanen one þo ealde rode, onlang rode
onne þo alde stodfald, of þanen falde on anne dich, suth anlang dic on þare
herepaþ, of þanne herepaþ suth anlang sapendune on anne dich, onlang
dich oþe clif, þanen ut on se.

Þanen sant þis þat westrene landimare. Of se one þe stod dic, þanen forð
be wertrumen on anne stanweal, of þanne walle þweres ouer smalencumbe,
of þa þornen upwarde, þanen forð be euisc ⟨ . . . ⟩*ᵖ* one þat northene stod
dich, of þare dich on anne stanen wal, norð*�q* onlang walles on stan þege,
anlang weies on anne dic, þanen norþ anlang dich, of þare diche on Wicean,
of Wichen on anne þorn, 7 þanen on anne diche, of þare diche on anne

þorne, 7 þanen north on iricht wege, of þane iwege on alfstanes paþ, þanen forð be eficlif on aueres[r] broc, adune anlang brokes oþ þane bige, of þane bige on anne þorn, þanne suth on irichte on anne mor, adune anlang mores on Þicean, up anlang Þicean eft on Wichenford.

Acta est hec prefata donacio anno ab incarnacione Domini nostri Iesu .dcccc.lvi., indiccione .xiiii.

+ Ego Adwig rex Anglorum prefatam donacionem sub sigillo sancte crucis indeclinabiliter consensi.

+ Ego Adgar eiusdem regis frater cum sigillo sancte crucis confirmaui.

+ Ego Oda Dorobernensis ecclesie archiepiscopus + eiusdem regis principatum et beniuolenciam cum sigillo sancte crucis subscripsi et ceteri.

[a] *Rubric partly illegible* [b] uestigiis C (*for the preferred reading, see* 20) [c] aut *seems redundant* [d] *This clause is difficult to understand. Perhaps read '(We), steeped in apostolic warnings, which we were once formerly worthy to hear . . .' (taking* mererentur *as an error for* mereremur; quos *presumably refers to* uesagiis, *although we might expect the latter to be neuter plural)* [e] *Perhaps a byform of* munera [f] *For* proprio [g] *Probably error for* nos [h] *The second* meo *seems redundant and does not occur in* 20 [i] *The word* uocabulo *has fallen out here* (*compare* 20) [j] *The word* Belial *has fallen out here* (*compare* 20 *and S 500, 504*) [k] grauatus C (*compare S 500, 504; same error in* 20) [l] deterius C (*compare S 500, 504*) [m] andland C [n] *For* oþ *or* on [o] *Probably for* þiscan (*see* 16) [p] *It is possible that part of the boundary clause has been lost at this point* (*see commentary*) [q] nord C [r] *Probably for* auenes (*compare* 20)

[1] cf. Matt. 19: 29

19 appears to be authentic. It covers land immediately to the west and north of the eight hides granted in 16; both charters were used as models by the forger of 20, which was intended to give title to the combined estates. 19 has not previously been edited, apparently because it was regarded as a duplicate of 20, to which it is very similar. There is no difficulty in accepting 19 as one of the large number of diplomatically various diplomas issued in the course of 956, although the truncated witness-list makes it impossible to allocate it to any of the four principal groups identified by Keynes (*Diplomas*, pp. 48–69). Much of the formulation of 19 appears to have been modelled on that of a charter or charters of the early 940s. The section of the proem from *uocis* to *possidebitis* is closely paralleled in S 469 (A.D. 942), which also has the same exposition, and the anathema is found elsewhere only in two charters of 944 (S 500, 504). The royal style is unique, but this is no difficulty in a diploma from Eadwig's reign, when there was evidently a good deal of experimentation in this area. The only detail of the text which does seem suspicious is the provision of two names for the estate, which is not normal practice. It may have been the case the charter originally referred only to Blashenwell, and that the reference to Corfe was added later as clarification, probably after the land had passed to Shaftesbury and perhaps at the time when 19 was used for the fabrication

of **20** (the use of the double name in **20** may have led to back-influence on **19**). The name Corfe seems initially to have referred only to Corfe Gap (*PN Dorset*, i. 5–6). On the other hand, a double name may have been thought appropriate for this particular estate, which comprised a narrow strip of land stretching south from Corfe Gap to the sea (which included Blashenwell, now represented by Blashenwell Farm at SY 952803) and also an area to the north of the Purbeck Hills. The seven hides of **19** were amalgamated with the eight hides of **16** to form Shaftesbury's manor of Kingston, assessed at sixteen hides TRE (GDB 78v); one hide of this was subsequently ceded to William the Conqueror, who built on it Wareham (later Corfe) Castle. **20** may have been forged soon after the Conquest, at the time of the negotiations with William, the intention being to create a single title-deed for the whole sixteen hides of the Shaftesbury holding in 1066.

The boundary-clause of **19** begins at the same point as that in **16**, a ford over the Corfe river (formerly known as the Wych) which may have been on the site of St Edward's Bridge in Corfe Gap (SY 959824). From here the survey runs south to the sea and resumes a little further west along the coast, then goes north beyond the Purbeck Hills before bearing east to rejoin the Corfe river, which it follows south back to Corfe Gap. The southern part of the eastern boundary corresponds to the western boundary of the eight hides of **16**, and many of the boundary marks are the same. From the ford the survey follows the river to another ford (*scyle/scylen* is obscure: see *PN Dorset*, i. 94), and then touches on 'the straight way' (*riht, weg*) and 'Olla's marshy meadows' (the lost Hollish, at about SY 955806: see *PN Dorset*, i. 14–15). The next boundary mark, corresponding to a blank in the bounds of **16**, is *blechene*, obviously to be linked with the place-name Blashenwell (*PN Dorset*, i. 8–9). In **19** Blashenwell is *Blachenwelle* in the text and *Blechenenwelle* in the introduction to the bounds; in **20** the spelling is *Blechenhamwelle*. *PN Dorset* prefers the form in **20**, and suggests that the name is formed from a hypothetical OE noun **blæcen*, 'bleaching', with *hamm* ('enclosure, river-meadow') and *well(a)* ('spring or stream'): hence 'spring or stream at the bleaching enclosure', referring to a place where cloth was bleached; on this basis, the use of *blechene* as the name of a spring or stream in the bounds of **19** would represent a back-formation. A far simpler explanation would be to dismiss the form *blechenhamwelle* in **20** as a corruption; the charter is a forgery, and later spellings of the name are more compatible with the *blechenenwelle* form in **19**. We could then take *blechene* as the name of the stream which ran from the spring called *blechenenwelle*. From here the boundary follows a linchet (*hlinc*) to a ditch and then reaches a feature called the 'old *rode*', where the second element is **rod, rodu*, found only in boundary clauses and meaning 'linear clearing' or sometimes 'road' (Smith, *EPNE*, ii. 86–7). 'The old stud-fold' is also mentioned in the bounds of **16**, as is the hill called *sawendune* (*safandune* in **16**). The boundary must have reached the sea in the region of Houns-tout Cliff.

The survey resumes a little further west along the coast, probably just south of Swyre Head (compare the western boundary in **20**) and runs north. Most of the boundary marks require no comment. The *stod-dic* was presumably a ditch associated with a field where horses were kept; 'the northern *stod-dic*' is mentioned later in the survey. From here the boundary follows a woodbank (*wyrtrume*) to a stone wall or embankment (*stan, weall*) and a 'narrow combe' (*smæl, cumb*). *Efisc* means 'an edge or escarpment'; in **20** this feature is called an *ecg*. At this point it is possible that a section has dropped out of the boundary clause of **19**. The next boundary-marks are 'the northern stud-ditch', a 'stone wall or embankment' (*stan*, *weall*) and a 'stone way'; after this the boundary joins the river Wych once more. The same sequence of features occurs in the bounds of **20**, but there it is preceded by a number of other boundary marks: 'Ælfric's spring or stream' (*welle*), a 'way' and a 'ditch', and an earlier encounter with Wych. It seems possible that a copyist of **19** was confused by the similar and repetitive boundary marks of this survey, and inadvertently omitted the intervening section. From the Wych the survey goes past a couple of thorn-trees and a ditch, and then runs further north along a 'straight way'. The boundary at this stage is probably crossing the Purbeck Hills; the corresponding section of the survey in **20** went 'straight up through the wood'. After this the boundary follows 'Ælfstan's path' and then passes an 'ivy-covered slope or cliff' (*ifig*, *clif*), which may refer to a feature on the northern escarpment (perhaps corresponding to the *crundel* mentioned in **20**). *Aueres broc* is *auenes broc* in **20**; this would seem to be another instance of the common river-name Avon, from OBrit *Abona*, 'river' (Ekwall, *River-Names*, pp. 20–3), although it does not give good sense in combination with *broc*. This stream was presumably one of the western tributaries of the river Corfe; the boundary follows it as far as 'the bend' (*byge*), then turns south after a thorn-tree and crosses a *mor* ('moor, marshland, wasteland', presumably a southerly fringe of Middlebere Heath), before rejoining the Corfe river and following it south back to Corfe Gap.

20

King Eadred grants sixteen hides (mansae) *at Corfe and Blashenwell, Dorset, to Wihtsige, minister.* A.D. 956

C. BL Harley 61, 12v–13r: copy, s. xv
    Rubric: Adredus rex .xvi. mansas apud Corf et Blakenhanwelle in donum perpetuum hic inscripto munivit.
Ed.: a. Kemble 435 (with bounds in vol. iii, p. 432)
      b. Birch 910
      c. Earle p. 428 (bounds only)
      d. Pierquin, *Recueil*, pt 2, no. 98
Listed: Sawyer 573; Finberg, *ECW*, no. 596

In nomine Domini nostri Iesu Christi. Apostolicis imbuti uesagiis, quos quondam olim in tempore mererentur aut[a] audire,[b] munia[c] uocis precelsa conditoris reminiscimur proprii[d] ab ore tonantis, 'Uos qui secuti estis me centuplum accipietis et uitam posidebitis',[1] quos[e] eciam caducis opibus implicati,[f] tamen superno[g] fulti amminiculo prosequi indigemus ad alta. Cuius scilicet feruoris igne coartus, ego Adredus basileos Anglorum huiusque insule barbarorum ministro meo cuidam dilecto nomine Wihtsige .xvi. mansas gratuito datu perhenniter tribuo quodam in loco priscorum uocabulo at Corf and at Blechenhamwelle, cum optimatum meorum consilio, ut ille uiuens[h] secure possideat; in successoribus[i] uero suis cui uoluerit sibi concedat heredi. Imminencia denique uite curricula hec nostra tradicio illesa liberaque permaneat cum appendiciis suis, tam pascuis quam pratis, siluis, exceptis tribus, expedicione, pontis arcisue confeccione. Nam siquis seculorum in generacione Belial gnatus[j] nostrum hoc uolumen inmutare temptauerit, Iude reus scelere iudicii die magna cum turma truces trudatur in flammas, nisi hoc in seculo penitencie prius fletu detersus hinc se corrigere studuerit. Istis terminibus predicta terra circumgirata esse uidetur.

þis sand þare .xvi. hyde land imare at Corf þe Adred king bokien Wihsige his þegene on elchehalue.[k] Arest of sa on anne dich, anlang dich uppe on Spuren, þþert ouer Spuran on þ þþers dich, of þare diche on ecge, forð be ecge on alfricheswelle, of þane welle on anne þeg, of þane þige on an dich, anlang dich north richte on Þicun, niþer anlang[l] Wicum streames, of þanne streame on anne þorn, north anlang dich on anne walle, onlang walles on stanwei, of þane dich on anne dich, onlang diche north irichte on Þicum, niþer anlang Þicunstreames, of þat streame on anne þorn, of þane þorne on þa holendich, anlang dich uppen iricht þurch þane wde on þare dich, on þane rupemor,[m] of þane more on þone crundel, of þane crundel up irichte on þat holenbedde, of þat holnebedde on þare holne stoke, of þane stocke on þare stream, anlang streames on auenes broc, of þane broke on þane ealde weg, andlang weies on hecgan sled, of þane slede on þare streame, anlang streames on þat stanene bregge, of þare brigge on þare wei, anlang weies of irichte on þane richt wei, of þane weie on anne stan wal, of þane walle nither irichte on Wickenford, onlang Wiken forð[n] uppen irichte on beam broc, swo up anlang streames, of þane streame on þat withi begh, of þanne wiþibedde on anne stan, of þane stane on þane oþerne, of þane stane on holewisken eft on þare stan, of þane stan on þa ealdene dich, anlang dich on þane wal,[o] anlang welles on struthgeardes cum, anlang welles on struthherdes þege, of þane wege eft on anne wal,[o] onlang welles on seuen þilles þry, anlang streames ut a irichte on seortmannes pol.

Acta est hec prefata donacio anno ab incarnacione Domini nostri Iesu Christi .dcccclvi., indiccione .xiii.

Ego Adredus rex Anglorum prefatam donacionem sub sigillo sancte crucis indeclinabiliter consensi atque roboraui. +
Ego Oda Dorobernensis ecclesie archiepiscopus eiusdem regis principatum et beniuolenciam sub sigillo sancte crucis conclusi. +
Ego Theodred Lundoniensis ecclesie testitudinem sancte crucis subscripsi et roboraui et ceteri plurimi. +

 ᵃ aut *seems redundant*

ᵇ trudire C. *This clause is difficult to understand. Perhaps read '(We), steeped in apostolic warnings, which we were once formerly worthy to hear . . .' (taking* mererentur *as an error for* mereremur; quos *presumably refers to* uesagiis, *although we might expect the latter to be neuter plural*)   *ᶜ Perhaps a byform of* munera   *ᵈ For* proprio

ᵉ Probably error for nos   *ᶠ* implicari C *(compare* **19**)   *ᵍ* superni C *(compare* **19**)

ʰ initens C *(compare* **19**)   *ⁱ* sucenssoribus C

ʲ grauatus C *(compare S 500, 504; same error in* **19**)

ᵏ Probably for on ece yrfe *(same corruption in* **13**)   *ˡ* anland C

ᵐ Probably for rupemor   *ⁿ Probably for* forde   *ᵒ Probably for* welle

---

¹ cf. Matt. 19: 29

20 is a spurious conflation of **16** and **19**. The text of **20** as far as the witness-list, including the name of the beneficiary and the date, was based on **19** (the date was slightly miscopied, so that a minim is missing from the indiction). The name of the donor (King Eadred) and the witness-list were taken from **16**. The boundary clause outlines an area which represents an amalgamation of the neighbouring estates conveyed in **16** and **19**. It seems clear that the motive for the fabrication of **20** was the desire for a title-deed for the whole of Shaftesbury's Domesday manor of Kingston, assessed at sixteen hides TRE (GDB 78v), for which **16** and **19** provide partial documentation. The context for the creation of **20** may have been King William's acquisition of one hide of the manor for the building of Wareham (later Corfe) Castle; Shaftesbury received in exchange the church at Gillingham and its dependencies. It is possible that, in the course of negotiating this exchange, the Shaftesbury community felt the lack of an overall title-deed for the Kingston manor, and decided to conflate two existing diplomas dealing with this property. The retention of the name of the lay beneficiary points to a certain amount of good faith.

The bounds are discussed by Grundy (1935, pp. 123–8), and individual boundary-marks are covered in *PN Dorset*, i. 1–33. Unlike the surveys in the two authentic diplomas, which both begin at a ford in the vicinity of Corfe Gap, the circuit in **20** starts at the south-western angle of the estate, on the coast to the south of Swyre Head, follows the line of the later parish boundary north to take in an area beyond the Purbeck Hills and then runs south through Corfe Gap and back to the sea, meeting the coast at a point near Chapman's Pool. The western boundary probably corresponded, at least approximately, to the western boundary of **19**, although the compiler of the survey has generally noted different boundary marks. From the sea the survey runs to a ditch or dyke, which is probably the *stod-dic* of **19**, and then traverses a *sweora*, 'neck of land, col': see Swyre Head (SY 935782; *PN Dorset*, i, 19). After 'the cross-wise ditch' (*ðweors* here is used as an adjective, meaning 'lying or passing across'), the boundary follows an *ecg*, 'edge or escarpment', presumably the *efisc* of **19**. Next the survey mentions 'Ælfric's spring or stream' (*welle*), and then a 'way' and a 'ditch'; after this it joins the Wych (the old name for Corfe river; see **16**) or one of its tributaries for a short distance, then goes along a 'ditch' (probably the 'northern stud-ditch' of **19**) to a wall or embankment (*stan-weall* in **19**). In both surveys the boundary now follows a 'stone way' to a 'ditch', and then goes north along the ditch to rejoin the river Wych. The next boundary marks are a thorn-tree and a ditch, identified as 'the hollow ditch' (*hol*) in **20**. From here the survey in **20** goes upwards straight through a wood (this corresponds to 'the straight way' in **19**); it is likely that this refers to the stage where the boundary crosses the Purbeck Hills. It can probably be assumed that the following boundary marks, as far as *Wickenford*, describe the area to the north of Corfe which is also covered in **19**, although far more detail is given here. The first element of *rupemor* should probably be *ruwe-* (from *ruwan*, wk. obl. of *ruh*, 'rough'): so 'rough(-surfaced) moor' (*PN Dorset*, i. 32). The gully or quarry (*crundel*) may be connected with the 'ivy-covered cliff or slope' mentioned at this point in **19**. In *holenbedde* and *holnestoke* the first element appears to be *holegn*, 'holly' (hence, 'place where holly grows' (*bedd*) and 'holly stump' (*stocc*) or 'outlying farmstead characterised by holly' (*stoc*): see *PN Dorset* i. 31). *Avenes broc* seems to be a better reading than the *aueres broc* of **19** (although the river-name Avon does not make good sense in the genitive form with *broc*); this appears to have been a western tributary of the river Wych. *Hecgan sled* is a valley (*slæd*) with a hedge (*hecg*). From here the boundary follows a 'stream', which is probably the Wych, past a stone bridge (*stanen*, *brycg*) and a series of 'walls' and 'ways' to the 'Wych ford' that was the starting point of the bounds in **16** and **19**, and probably lay on the site of St Edward's Bridge in Corfe Gap (SY 959824). From this point the survey in **20** corresponds with the eastern boundary of the Purbeck estate conveyed in **16**. *Beam broc*, 'brook with a tree-truck across it', is also mentioned in the Purbeck bounds. Shortly after this the survey in **20** encounters a feature called both *withibegh* and *withibedde*; presumably one of these is a misspelling. *Withibegh* points to *withig-beag*, 'the ring of willows', while the second element of *withibedde* looks like *bedd*, hence, 'place where willows grow'; the latter seems preferable, given the earlier reference to a 'holly-bed', and *PN Dorset* (i. 26) notes a field-name Withy Bed which occurs twice in the area. In **16** this is a *withig-thyfel*, 'willow thicket'. *Holewisken* is the lost 'Hollish' (*PN Dorset*, i. 14–15); the elements are probably a personal name Olla, with *wisce*, 'marshy meadow'. 'Strutheard's combe' is the unnamed *cumb* of **16**, and probably corresponds to Coombe Bottom (*PN Dorset*, i. 10); the next boundary mark is 'Strutheard's way' ('Strutheard's path' in **16**). *Seuen willes thry* appears to be 'the trough (*thryh*) of seven springs'. As in **16** the boundary meets the sea at Chapman's Pool.

21

King Eadwig grants eighty or ninety hides (mansae) *to the minster at Shaftesbury.* A.D. 956. *With the bounds of Donhead and Easton Bassett in Wiltshire, and of Compton Abbas, Sixpenny Handley and Iwerne Minster in Dorset.*

C. BL Harley 61, 20v–21v: copy, s. xv
   Rubric: Hec inscriptio Adwi .lxxxx. mansas ecclesie de Shaftesbury in hereditatem optulit*ᵃ* perhennem.
Ed.: a. Kemble 447 (with the bounds in vol. iii, pp. 440–1)
    b. Birch 970
Listed: Sawyer 630; Finberg, *ECW*, no. 281

Omnipotens celi terreque in principio creator, karismatum pro temporibus tributor patriarchas et prophetas sensim tangencium, at ubi messias human-iter descendere dignatur, in quo pleniter requieuit septiformis spiritus, eodem spiritu repleuit orbem terrarum, unicuique in quam diuidit kata captum*ᵇ* singulorum, ex quo preuenti ingenio fulgent, uiribus pollent, dominari iam audent, insuper uncti nomine Christi, unde uocatis*ᶜ* electi peregrini ad patriam anhelando festinant ac sua largiri aut*ᵈ* dubitant, caduca uilia deputantes comparando mansura. Quapropter ego Adwig gracia Dei rex Anglorum .lxxx.*ᵉ* mansas ad monasterium quod a ruricolis uocatur Sceaftesburi in hereditatem offero perhennem, pro Christi amore et uenerabilium sanctorum quorum reliquie ibidem uenerantur, cum omnibus ad se rite pertinentibus, pratis, siluis, pascuis. Facta est autem hec libertas telluris ab omni censu regali soluta, excepta expedicione, pontis arcisque construccione. Anno .d.cccc.lvi. ab incarnacione dominica, indiccione .xiiii., primo uero anno imperii mei, coram testibus ydoneis.

þis sent þe fiftiga hide landimare to Dunheued and to Estune and to Cumtune ðe man þa hiþen offet*ᶠ* on Sceaftesbur'.

⟨Arest on heaued stokes⟩,*ᵍ* þanen on hert mere forðer,*ʰ* on wermes hore forðward, þanen forð ⟨be bine⟩*ⁱ* on ⟨laiboc⟩*ʲ* heued, þanen on berg hore*ᵏ* uuepearde, þanen on cealuelege, þanen on stanburne, up anlang streames, þanen up on dune, þanen est be wirtrume oð bridinghe dich, þanen on þa gereðe, of þone dune forþerwarde, þanen up anlang scordene*ˡ* swo on þanne ealden hole weg to becheshlepe, þanen on mad alleres,*ᵐ* on land cumbes,*ⁿ* up on gemanen cumb, þanen on þat michle flode oð alfsiges land imare, þanen anlang cumbes hracan, þanen on watdune beorch, þanen on cheluedune, þannen eft on heued stockes.

*ᵒ*Ðis sant þe fiftiþe*ᵖ* hide þe sex hide at Estune. þane sant þis ðane sex hide landimare. Arest on offen weg, þanen on þone ellen stub, þanen on miclen diches get, þanen on esnes diges*q* get, þanen on stan scylien, þanen on elchene seað, þanen on Mapeldere cumb, þanen on empenbeorch,*r* þanen on bican pet, þanen on þornwelles, þanen onlang stret eft*s* offenweg.

*t*þis .x. hide hereð in to þanne fiftigen hiden atte Cumtune. þis sent þare .x. hide land gemare. Arest on tor scylget, þanen be wirtrume oð dollen beorge, þanen on þane imeren hole weg, þanen on holenþylle, of hollenwelle on holencumb, *u*þanen on þa lake to smale broke, þanen adun one þat lake to smale broke, þanen adun one þat lake*u* at hereweg on Stirchel, anlang streames on þat litlen lake at Meleburge imare, þanen on fernhelle forð, þanen on anne hus, þanen on Meleberig dune duneward on þat ealde ad, þonne þanen on lippen scagen, swo be wirtrume eft on torchil gat.

þanen sent at Heanlegen and at Iwern and forþe hide ða es fostodr*v* landes, and þis sent þa landimare.

*w*Arest on litlen ac lee estward, of aclee on pegan beorh, þanen on berendes beorh, þanen on þere herepað at mesdelle, þanen on þat get at seuen diche suð ende, anlang diche oþes sledes northecge, þanen on þane anlipien þorn, þanne be þane onheueden adun to wege, andlang*x* weges on þannen mylen stede, þanen on þane hege reawe oð ða furuh, on land*y* furuh on totenberg, þanen on ac hylle on tilluches lege, þanen on biken settle, þanen on mealeburg*z* norþewarde, þanen eft to aclee*a2* estward.

þanne sent þis landimare at Iwern.

*b2*Arest on Terente dene, þanen to fideriches dene uueward, þanne on þare crundel at þare weie itþislen, on þane crundel, þanen on budencumbe hracan, þanen on þung*c2* þylle, þanen on þane ealdan forde,*d2* þanen on cranmere, þanen on cing hille, þanen onne smal þornes, þanen on sþylles, þanen on lacmere, þanen anlang streames oð*e2* sand ford, þanen on ears mores heaued, þanen on styb, þanen on foxlee nortwarde, þanen on agen þorn, þanen on þere crundel northwarde, þannen on waddene uuewarde, on hlinc reawe, þanen on þone gren wai at merewege uue, þanen on þa heren apeldren, þ eft on Terente dene.

Quicumque amodo *f2* hoc priuilegii donum ecclesie Dei sic attributum conseruare uoluerit, eternam recipiat mercedem inter choros angelorum. Sin autem peruersus raptor et auarus infringere moliens, obstaculum patiatur diuinum a Deo ut non dimidiet dies suos et nequaquam uideat bona in terra uiuencium, nisi quamtocius emendet.

Ego Adþig rex Domino fauente hoc donum tropheo sancte crucis sigillo +*g2*

Ego Oda archiepiscopus corroboraui. +

Ego Adgar indolis clito annui. +

Ego Oscytil episcopus faui. +

Ego Alfsige episcopus +

Ego Wlsige episcopus +

Ego Osulf episcopus +

Ego Berthelm episcopus +

Ego Daniel episcopus +

Ego Birthelm^{h2} +

Ego Aþelstan dux +

Ego Alsige^{i2} dux +

Ego Alfhere dux +

Ego Alfgar^{j2} +

Ego Byrtferð dux^{k2} +

Ego Aþelmer^{l2} +

Ego Alfsige^{l2} +

Ego Alfech^{l2} +

Ego Ailwine^{l2} +

Ego Wlfric minister +

Ego Aþelþard minister +

Ego Alfred minister +

^{a} optuli C ^{b} Perhaps read capita or capacitatem (with Greek κατα, 'according to')
^{c} Perhaps for uocati et ^{d} For haut
^{e} Perhaps error for .lxxxx. (see rubric and commentary) ^{f} ? For offreþ
^{g} The MS is partly illegible here. Kemble and Birch read Ærest on heaued lakes, but the final boundary mark in this clause suggests that the last word should be stokes ^{h} forder C
^{i} The MS is illegible here. Kemble and Birch read be dine, but the last word looks more like bine ^{j} The MS is partly illegible here. This is the reading in Kemble and Birch.
^{k} This corresponds to beorc oran in S 582 ^{l} Perhaps for on landscor dene
^{m} This corresponds to med akeren in S 582 ^{n} Probably for anlang cumbes
^{o} Estune marginal rubric C ^{p} For fiftige ^{q} For dices
^{r} This seems to correspond with ippan beorge in S 582
^{s} A word such as on or oþ has fallen out here ^{t} Cumtune marginal rubric C
$^{u...u}$ This section of the survey appears to be corrupt ^{v} Probably for fostor
^{w} Hanlee marginal rubric C ^{x} andland C ^{y} Probably for anlang
^{z} This corresponds to michelan byrg in S 582 ^{a2} anclee C ^{b2} Iwerne marginal rubric C
^{c2} Kemble and Birch read þung (the scribe does not distinguish between p and þ)
^{d2} forð C ^{e2} od C ^{f2} amado C
^{g2} The remaining subscriptions are arranged across the page
^{h2} The word episcopus has fallen out of this subscription ^{i2} For Æthelsige
^{j2} The word minister has fallen out of this subscription ^{k2} Probably error for minister
^{l2} These witnesses are all ministri

21 is perhaps the most difficult charter in the Shaftesbury archive. There can be no doubt that underlying the present text is a genuine diploma of 956, closely linked with the earliest of the four principal groups of charters issued in that year (represented by S 589, 594, 597, 608, 614, 627, 629, 631, 637, 666; see Keynes, *Diplomas*, pp. 51–4, 62–3). The witness-lists of these charters suggest that they were issued on the same occasion, and their formulation is so similar that it seems likely that a single draftsman was responsible for all of them. **21** appears to have been issued on a separate occasion, for it has a substantially different witness-list, but it was almost certainly a product of the same draftsman. The ambitious proem is a variant of that of S 594 (and see also S 608), and is thematically linked with other proems from this group. Like them it has a rather perfunctory dispositive section (the phrase *in hereditatem . . . perhennem* also occurs in S 594, 627, 629 and 637; there is a similar immunity clause in S 594, 608, 614 and 637). The formulation of the sanction is also characteristic of this draftsman, especially the insertion of the word *amodo*, of which he was evidently fond (compare S 608, 629, 631, 637, 666). The draftsman had the unusual habit of placing the sanction after the witness-list (of the 'Group One' diplomas only S 597 does not have this feature); it is possible that a later copyist of **21** altered the text by moving the sanction to its conventional position. S 594, which survives as an apparent original, may be a guide to the physical appearance of these charters, and perhaps also of **21**; it is the earliest surviving charter written in Caroline minuscule (see Bishop, *English Caroline Minuscule*, p. xix). The witness-list of **21** seems acceptable for a document of 956, but it may have become corrupted in transmission; one of the bishops and several *ministri* are unstyled, and a witness who can be identified as a thegn is called *dux*.

Any diploma apparently conveying a very large area of land directly to a religious community must be considered with a degree of caution, since charters of this type make up a significant proportion of known fabrications. An immediately suspicious feature in **21** is the oblique reference to the land granted; the dispositive section mentions only the number of hides that were conveyed, and it is necessary to turn to the five sets of vernacular bounds to identify the properties concerned. This is untypical of Anglo-Saxon diplomatic, but perhaps explicable by the fact that the charter covered several distinct estates; it is possible that the draftsman felt that he could not elegantly include all the relevant detail in the dispositive section and so left it for the boundary clauses. A more concrete reason to reject **21** is the probability that Iwerne Minster, one of the estates which it appears to convey, did not belong to Shaftesbury in 963. A charter of that year (**24**) records the grant to a thegn of an estate at East Orchard, which had a common boundary with Iwerne Minster; at the crucial point the East Orchard bounds refer to 'the king's boundary', implying that in 963 Iwerne Minster was still part of the royal patrimony and had not yet passed to Shaftesbury. There is no comparable evidence bearing on the ownership of the other estates supposedly conveyed in **21**: all certainly belonged to Shaftesbury by the Conquest and could conceivably have been granted by Eadwig; but the contradictory information about Iwerne Minster certainly indicates that **21** should probably be regarded as spurious in its present form.

Yet the present text was apparently based on a contemporary diploma of Eadwig, and there is some evidence that the model is likely to have been in favour of Shaftesbury itself. In S 629, another of the 'Group One' charters, the king is said to have granted to Malmesbury Abbey 100 hides at Brokenborough in Wiltshire. Like many of the diplomas directly in favour of Malmesbury, S 629 may well have been tampered with, but it seems significant that its dispositive section includes a phrase also found in **21**, a reference to 'the saints whose relics are venerated there' ([*amore*] *sanctorum quorum reliquie ibidem uenerantur*). Another charter from the same period which is clearly related to **21** is S 582 in the Wilton archive, dated 955 and presumably belonging to the very end of that year. This records a grant by Eadwig to the Wilton community of 100 hides at Chalke in Wiltshire. It has a complex boundary clause which appears to cover the whole of Chalke hundred, including the detached portion at Semley; in places in the west and south-west the Wilton lands have common boundaries with estates at Donhead St Andrew and Sixpenny Handley which are supposedly conveyed to Shaftesbury in **21**. A notable component of the boundary clause in S 582 is the section which occurs after the main survey, describing six hides lying 'within these bounds' which 'belong to Donhead'. It is followed by a note stating: 'These bounds and these six hides we assign out of this landbook'. This survey is almost identical to, and covers the same area as, the survey in **21** outlining six hides at *Estune*. The area in question is Easton Bassett, a detached dependency of Shaftesbury's estate at Donhead; it lay entirely within Chalke hundred, surrounded by Wilton property, but was reckoned as part of Dunworth hundred (see maps in *VCH Wilts.* XIII, pp. 2, 90). In S 582 the boundary clause describes an internal boundary, defining an alien property within an area which otherwise belonged wholly to Wilton; in **21** essentially the same survey describes a detached portion of a Shaftesbury estate. It is clear that **21** and S 582 have to be considered together. Both relate to large neighbouring blocks of territory, with detached portions lying beyond their common boundaries (Easton Bassett is balanced by Semley, a Chalke dependency lying within Dunworth hundred and partly surrounded by Shaftesbury estates); the tenurial situation that they describe is clearly the result of a long history of acquisition and consolidation, which probably indicates that in their present form they belong to a period rather later than 956. It is possible that the two communities at some stage co-operated in defining their respective boundaries; they may have been improving genuine diplomas issued in their favour in Eadwig's reign.

It seems then that **21** cannot be regarded an authentic diploma in its received form, although it may be based upon a genuine charter of 956 in favour of Shaftesbury; at the very least it would appear to have been reworked to include property which came to the nuns at a later date. At present it covers five separate estates lying to the south-east and south of Shaftesbury itself: Donhead and its detached dependency at Easton Bassett (now part of the parish of Berwick St John); Compton Abbas; Sixpenny Handley; and Iwerne Minster. At a later date it was claimed that these estates formed part of the initial endowment given to Shaftesbury by King Alfred; the forged foundation charter in Alfred's name (**7**) refers to Donhead, Compton, Sixpenny Handley (with Gussage St Andrew) and Iwerne Minster (plus the estates at Fontmell Magna and Tarrant Hinton which are granted by Æthelstan in **8** and **9**). **7** was probably fabricated after the Conquest, and may be based in part on **21**; it is impossible to tell whether there is any truth in the claim that land in these places formed part of the early Shaftesbury endowment (see further, pp. xxiii–xxvi). In **21** Donhead, Easton Bassett and Compton Abbas are reckoned together as one unit of fifty hides (although nowhere do they have a common boundary). Shaftesbury's Donhead manor had an assessment of forty hides TRE (GDB 67v); the six hides of this manor held in 1086 by a tenant named Thurstan may represent the Easton

Bassett dependency. Shaftesbury also held a ten-hide manor at Compton Abbas (GDB 78v). The bounds of Sixpenny Handley and Iwerne Minster are introduced by a rubric to the effect that the fourth hide is *fostodr land*, presumably for *fostorland*; in this context the statement probably means that a quarter of the land was treated as demesne, and not let to tenants (which is approximately equivalent to the Domesday figures). In 1066 the community's manor at Sixpenny Handley was assessed at twenty hides, with just under four hides in lordship, and it also held eighteen hides at Iwerne Minster, of which five and a half were demesne (GDB 78v). Sixpenny Handley was sandwiched between the Wiltshire/Hampshire border, but was treated as a detached portion of Dorset, part of the hundred in which Shaftesbury itself was located (originally 'Sixpenny' Hundred, from Pen Hill (*Seaxpenn*) in Sutton Waldron, but later Sixpenny Handley Hundred, recognising the discrete portion: see *PN Dorset*, iii. 89). The total assessment of these five properties in 1066 was therefore eighty-eight hides, which suggests that the ninety hides mentioned in the rubric to 21 may be preferable to the eighty hides of the text.

Shaftsbury's Donhead manor included most of the later parishes of Donhead St Mary and Donhead St Andrew, but in Grundy's view the survey in 21 seems to describe only Donhead St Andrew, excluding a portion of Wardour Park in the north-east (see Grundy 1920, pp. 57–60). The comments by Jackson (1984, p. 168) appear to be based on the assumption that the survey relates to both Donheads (although the point is not explored in any detail). This does seem to be a strong possibility. While Grundy's explanation of the boundaries to the north and east of Donhead St Andrew is convincing, the interpretation of the boundary marks to the south and west is far less so; this would allow for the inclusion of at least part of Donhead St Mary. It is an added difficulty that some sections of the bounds are no longer legible, even under ultra-violet light; the lacunae have been supplied from the nineteenth-century editions, which are not necessarily reliable. The survey begins and ends at a feature called *heaued stokes* (*heafod, stocc*), which was probably a group of stumps pollarded at head-height (my thanks to Peter Kitson for suggesting this interpretation). Grundy places the starting-point on the boundary between Donhead St Andrew and Donhead St Mary; if the survey does include Donhead St Mary, then an alternative location for the pollards would be somewhere in the western part of that parish. The first element in *hert mere* is *heorot*, 'hart, stag' (with *mere*, 'pond'). *Wermes hore* is probably 'snake's ridge' (*wyrm, ora*); Jackson associates this with a feature called *Wearmewell* in the Gillingham Forest perambulation of 1299–1300, and places it at Little Down, just to the north of Shaftesbury. The next two boundary marks are impossible to make out, although the second was a 'headland' of some kind. The survey now reaches the upper part of *berg hore*, which corresponds with (*andlang*) *beorc oran* in the Semley bounds in S 582: the latter reading seems preferable, which would make this 'birch-tree ridge' (*beorc, ora*). This feature is associated with Barker's Hill in Semley, now known as St Bartholomew's Hill (*PN Wilts.*, p. 209); from this point Grundy's interpretation of the bounds seems more convincing. The following 'calf wood or clearing' (*cealf, leah*) also occurs in the Semley bounds, and would have been located between Barker's Hill and the river Nadder. The Donhead survey now (silently) crosses the Nadder and follows 'the stony stream' for a distance before going up on to a down. The stream is likely to be the water-course flowing south-east through a series of ponds in Wardour

Park, and the 'down' was probably White Sheet Hill; this suggests that the estate did not include the area of Wardour Park to the north-east of the stream (which probably represents the separate estate at Wardour, held by the abbess of Wilton in 1066 and assessed at a single hide: see GDB 68r and also **28**). Once up on the down, the boundary follows a wood-bank (*wyrtrume*) to *bridinghe dich*, which is the *brydinga dic* mentioned in the main survey of S 582; this is apparently the earthwork on the flank of White Sheet Hill which the parish boundary crosses at approximately ST 941241. The first element is probably a personal name Bryda, found also in Bridmore in Berwick St John (*PN Wilts.*, p. 201). The boundary, still running south, continues to a stretch of plough-land (*yrth*) and then descends from White Sheet Hill and follows 'border valley' (*landscearu, denu*), to 'the old hollow way' (*eald, holh, weg*) and 'beech-tree barrow' (*bece, hlæw*); the valley and the barrow are mentioned in the main survey of S 582, which also provides a superior reading for the next boundary mark (*mæd æceras*, 'meadow pastures'). The 'old hollow way' appears to be the track leading south to Ferne House; 'beech-tree barrow' and the 'meadow pastures' presumably lay on the slopes of the downs, south of Ferne House. Most of the remaining boundary marks seem appropriate for this downland area. *On land cumbes* is probably a mistake for *andlang cumbes* ('along the combe'). It is followed by 'shared combe' (*gemæne, cumb*), 'the great (intermittent) stream' (*micel, flode*), 'Ælfsige's boundary' (*land-(ge)mære*), the 'throat' (*hraca*) of a combe (*cumb*), a barrow (*beorg*) on *watdune* (where the first element may be *wad*, 'woad', or *waδ*, 'hunting'), and 'calf down' (*cealf, dun*). It is difficult to locate these features, and Grundy's suggestions relating them to the Donhead St Andrew parish boundary are not convincing; on the other hand, there is a string of combes and intervening hills to the south and west of Donhead St Mary, which would seem more compatible with the survey.

　The six-hide dependency at Easton Bassett remained a detached part of the parish of Donhead St Andrew until 1884, when it was transferred to Berwick St John (*VCH Wilts.* XIII, pp. 126, 128–9). The survey in **21** can be set alongside the very similar boundary clause in S 582, which defines the internal boundaries of the Chalke estate in which Easton Bassett formed an alien intrusion (see above, and discussion in Grundy 1920, pp. 32–6). The Easton Bassett survey begins and ends in the north-east of the tithing, at *offen weg*, where the first element is probably the personal name *Offa*. 'Offa's way' appears to be the track which crosses the road running east from the village of Berwick St John at approximately ST 951223. The boundary follows the track south to 'the elder-tree stump' (*ellen, stybb*) and then encounters 'the gap in the great ditch' (*great, micel, dic*), which corresponds with *winterburge geate* in S 582. At this point the boundary is running through the hillfort known as Winkelbury Camp (*PN Wilts.*, p. 202). 'The gap in Esne's (or the servant's) ditch' (*esne, dic, geat*) refers to a break in the earthwork south of the camp. The next boundary mark, *stan scylien*, may be a substantive use of the adjective *stan-scylig*, 'stony'; the corresponding section of the Donhead bounds in S 582 refers to 'the stone which lies on the street' (*þan stane þe ligδ on þære stræte*; the street is the east-west ridge way known as Ox Drove) and 'the heap of stones' (*ceastel*). *Elchene seath* is *ealcan seath* in S 582 (which makes Grundy's emendation of the latter to *cealcan seath* unlikely); the second element is *seath*, 'pit, hole', but the first is obscure. 'Maple-tree combe' (*mapulder, cumb*) is Malacombe Bottom, between Berwick Down and Rotherley Down; the slightly more detailed survey in S 582 notes that the boundary goes to the 'head' of the combe. Next comes *empenbeorch*, which corresponds to *ippan beorge* in S 582: probably 'Ippa's barrow' (*beorg*). The final boundary marks, which must have been located on the western boundary, are 'Bica's pit' (*pyt*) and 'thorn-tree springs' (*thorn, welle*), after which the boundary follows a street (evidently Water Street in Berwick St John) back to 'Offa's way'.

The southern boundary of the ten hides at Compton Abbas corresponds with the eastern part of the northern boundary of Shaftesbury's estate at Fontmell (**8**): see discussion in Grundy 1935, pp. 114–17, and remarks in *PN Dorset*, iii. 99–102. The survey begins and ends in the north-east of the estate, at *torscylget* (*torchil gat*); the first element is *torr*, 'rock, rocky peak', the second probably *scylf*, 'shelf, ledge', and the third *geat*, 'gap, opening', and the reference appears to be to the place where the road to Ashmore Down passes through an earthwork (ST 901189). The boundary then follows a wood-bank (*wyrtrume*) to 'Dolla's hill or tumulus', which is also mentioned in the Fontmell bounds (ST 888183). The first element of *imeren hole weg* is apparently a corruption of (*ge*)*mære*: thus, 'the hollow way on the boundary (i.e. the boundary between Compton Abbas and Fontmell Magna)' (*hol, weg*). The 'way' must have passed west across Fontmell Down. *Holenwylle* is 'the hollow spring' or 'the spring in a hollow', and *holencumbe* is 'hollow combe'; the latter also appears in the Fontmell bounds, and survives as the field-name Hawkcombe Lane (*PN Dorset*, iii. 99–100). The next section of the bounds is repetitive and obviously corrupt; the 'narrow brook' (*smæl, broc*) is perhaps the tributary of Fontmell Brook which the parish boundary touches on at ST 856179, and the *hereweg* is probably the road running through Twyford and Bedchester. The next certain point is the *Stirchel*, the stream flowing through Woodbridge which the parish boundary reaches at ST 846184 (see Ekwall, *River-Names*, p. 382, Sturkel). The boundary now follows the *Stirchel* north, to 'the small pool or stream on the boundary of Melbury (Abbas)' (*lytel, lacu*); this would have marked the north-western corner of the estate. The remaining features define the northern boundary: 'fern-hill' (*fearn, hyll*), a house (*hus*), Melbury Hill, 'the old beacon' (*eald, ad*) and 'Lippa's copse' (probably a pers. n. Lippa, *sceaga*). (For the *eald ad*, see discussion in Forsberg 1970, pp. 41–2, 72.) From the copse the boundary follows a wood-bank (*wyrtrume*) back to its starting-point.

The Sixpenny Handley survey clearly follows the boundary of the later parish (see Grundy 1936, pp. 116–18; *PN Dorset*, iii. 113–23). It begins in the north-eastern corner, at approximately SU 004196. From 'the small oak-wood' (*lytel, ac, leah*) it proceeds to 'Pæga's barrow' (pers. n. Pæga, *beorg*), which is probably to be identified with Wor Barrow just east of the village (SU 012174). The next boundary mark is another barrow, apparently the tumulus at SU 014163 . *PN Dorset*, iii. 122, suggests the first element may derive from *bere-ærn, beren*, 'barn'; alternatively, this may be a corrupt personal name, or the word *berend*, 'carrier', noted in *BTSuppl*. The 'highway' is the road running south from the village which the boundary crosses at SU 002155. In *mesdelle*, the first element is *meos*, meaning either 'moss, lichen' or 'bog, swamp', and the second is *dell*, 'hollow'; the reference could be to the landscape feature named Endless Pit (*PN Dorset*, iii. 117). The next boundary mark is associated with the sequence of earthworks on Gussage Hill which the boundary meets at ST 992147; it is 'the gap' (*geat*) at the 'south end of seven ditches' The boundary follows the line of the earthworks for some distance south and west, then runs along 'the north edge of the valley' (*slæd*), which may have been near Cashmoor, to 'the solitary thorn-tree' (*anlipig, thorn*), and past a headland (*andheafod*) to a 'way'; the last is the road going north towards Farnham. 'The mill-site' (*myln, stede*) may have been on the stream between Farnham and Minchington. Beyond a hedgerow (*hege-ræwe*) and a furrow or trench (*furh*) was *totenberg*, either 'Tota's barrow' (*beorg*) or 'the barrow of the look-out' (*tote*); this was perhaps the earthwork at ST 960160. 'Oak Hill' (*ac, hyll*) survives in the name of Oakley Lane, which follows the later parish boundary (*PN Dorset*, iii. 119), and *tilluches lege* (probably a personal name Tilluc, with *leah*, 'wood, clearing') is preserved in the names of Tinkley Down, Wood and Coppice in Tollard Royal (*PN Dorset*, iii. 123; *PN Wilts.*, p. 202). From this point the boundary is running north-east, and corresponds to part of the main survey in the Chalke charter, S 582. *Bican settle* is 'Bica's dwelling' (*setl*). In *mealeburg* the first element appears to be *mæle*, 'variegated, multicoloured' (with *burh*, 'fortified place'), but the corresponding boundary-mark in S 582 is (*to*) *micelan byrg*, 'the great *burh*' (*micel*), which may represent a superior reading, rather than an alternative name for the same feature; both surveys seem to be referring to the earthwork which also gave its name to Mistleberry Wood in Sixpenny Handley, and Mistleberry is probably derived from *micel burh* (see *PN Dorset*, iii. 116).

The bounds of Iwerne Minster are discussed by Grundy (1936, pp. 131–4); see also *PN Dorset*, iii. 123–9. The survey begins in the north-east, in the valley (*denu*) of the river Tarrant (in fact the upper part of the valley further down which the river begins to flow); the starting-point was probably around ST 905148. From here the boundary goes south and west across the downs to the river Iwerne, which it meets a mile south of Iwerne Minster itself; the intervening boundary marks are 'the upper part of Frithuric's valley' (pers. n. Frithuric, *denu, ufanweard*), a gully (*crundel*) at a fork in the road (*weg, twisla*), 'the throat of the tub-shaped combe' (if the first element is *byden*, 'tub, vessel'; with *cumb, hraca*) and 'the spring or stream (*welle*) of the *thung* (a poisonous plant, such as aconite)'. 'The old ford' was probably at the place where the later parish boundary crossed the Iwerne (ST 861130). From here the boundary corresponds with that of Iwerne Courtney (**23**) for some distance. *Cranmere* is a pool frequented by cranes or herons (*cran, mere*). In *cing hille* the first element appears to be an uninflected form of *cyning*, 'king'. *Smal thornes* means 'the narrow (belt of) thorn-trees' (*smæl, þorn*). *PN Dorset* (iii. 129) accepts the reading *swylles* and suggests it is OE *swylle*, 'sloppy mess, place where water flows freely' and that it refers to a tributary of Fontmell Brook at ST 846150. *Lac mere* is a pool from which a small stream flows (*lacu, mere*); it is also mentioned in the Iwerne Courtney bounds, and so was presumably still on the western boundary. The survey now follows the stream (north) to 'the sandy ford' (*sand, ford*), which Grundy locates at the site of Farrington Bridge (ST 841155). The remaining boundary marks lay on the northern boundary: 'the upper end of arse moor' (*ears, mor, heafod*), a tree-stump (*stybb*), 'fox wood or clearing' (*fox, leah*), which may have survived into the fifteenth century as a field-name *Voxle* in Sutton Waldron (*PN Dorset*, iii. 82), *agen thorn* (perhaps *hægthorn* or *haguthorn*, 'hawthorn': *PN Dorset*, iii. 128), a gully or quarry (*crundel*), 'the upper part of woad-valley' (*wad, denu*), a 'linchet-row' (*hlinc, ræw*) 'the green way' (*grene, weg*), '*mere* way' (the first element is either (*ge*)*mære*,

'boundary', or *mere*, 'pool') and 'the hoary apple-tree' (*har, apuldor*). The '*mere* way'
is probably the track leading south-east through Stubhampton Bottom.

22

King Eadwig grants land at Shaftesbury, Dorset, to Wulfgar Leofa.
A.D. 958

C. BL Harley 61, 16v: copy, s. xv
  Rubric: Hec est inscripcio Aduig Regis de [ ]*ª* cassatis apud Shaftesbury.
Ed.: a. Kemble 470 (with the bounds in vol iii, p. 452)
     b. Birch 1026
Listed: Sawyer 655; Finberg, *ECW*, no. 602

Domino dominorum dominante in secula seculorum. Regna regnorum huius
presentis seculi transeant sicut ignominica et locus*ᵇ* huius mundi peribit et
⟨non⟩*ᶜ* sunt eterna sed superna eterna sunt. Quam ob rem ego Adwig rex
Anglorum gubernator et rector uni meorum karorum quem cordetenus
diligo uocitato nomine Wlgar Leofa modicam partem terre id est [ ]*ª* cassatos
perpetualiter concedo in illo loco ubi Anglica more appellacione dicitur at
Sceaftesberi, ⟨ut⟩*ᵈ* habeat ac possideat quamdiu uiuat et post se cuicumque
uoluerit heredi derelinquat in eternam hereditatem. Maneat igitur meum
hoc inmobile donum eterna libertate iocundum cum omnibus que ad ipsum
locum pertinere dinoscuntur, tam in magnis quam in modicis rebus, campis,
pascuis, pratis, siluis, exceptis istis tribus, expedicione, pontis arcisue construccione. Siquis uero hoc nostrum karisma aliqua machinacione infringere
conatus fuerit, ueniam non hic mereatur nec in futuro regni celestis clauigerum propicium habeat, nisi prius hic ad satisfaccionem uenire maluerit.
Predicta siquidem tellus hiis terminis circumcincta clarescit.
Ðis sant þe landimare at Scaftesberi. Arest of bogen pylle on brandes hricg,
⁊lang hrichtes on bytelesmor, of bitelesmore on þyndrede dic, of þare diche
on bokenwelle.
Hec carta scripta est anno dominice incarnacionis .dcccclviii., indiccione .i.

Ego Adwig rex Anglorum indeclinabiliter concessi. +
Ego Alfsinus presul sigillum agie crucis impressi. +
Ego Byrhtelm*ᵉ* consignaui. +
Ego Osulf*ᵉ* confirmaui et ceteri. +

  ª Blank space left in MS
  ᵇ For iocus (*most examples of this formula have the same error*)
  ᶜ The word non *has fallen out here* (*same error in* **25**)

^d *The word* ut *has probably fallen out here* (*compare* **23**, **25**)
^e *These two witnesses are bishops*

22 appears to be an authentic charter. Its formulation is entirely compatible with the date. The verbal invocation and proem are found together in a number of diplomas between 951 and 988 (see also **25**, and S 554, 577, 642, 800, 872); the same royal style is used in two of these (S 554, 577) and recurs in three other charters of 958 (see **23**, and S 653, 657); the formulation of the dispositive section, statement of powers and immunity clause is contemporary (for the statement of powers, see also **23**, **25**); the anathema was used in **23**, also from 958, in three charters of 957 (S 641, 643, 1291) and in **25** from 964. What remains of the witness-list seems contemporary The beneficiary is probably to be identified with the thegn named Leofa who regularly attested diplomas of Eadwig and Edgar between 958 and 975; in S 577 (a charter in the name of Eadred which has a witness-list appropriate for 958) he is explicitly Wulfgar Leofa. His byname was probably stressed in order to distinguish him from the other prominent thegn of this period who was called Wulfgar. In 963 he appears to have owned an estate at Sutton Waldron (see commentary to **24**).

A peculiarity of **22** is the blank space left by the scribe, in both text and rubric, in place of the numeral for the hide-assessment. A few diplomas in other archives have the same deficiency (see, for instance, S 681, 727, 750), and it is not necessarily suspicious; it may have been the case that the assessment was left blank in the original diploma because the scribe did not yet have the requisite information. The charter probably covers the area to the east of the abbey which formed the later parish of St Peter's (see Rutter 1989). The survey begins and ends at *bogen wylle* (*bokenwelle*), which survived into the early modern period as a street-name, Bowell Lane (now lost). *PN Dorset* (iii. 148) suggests that the first element is likely to be *boga*, 'bow, arch', here with the sense 'curving hillside' (with *wella*, 'spring, stream'); alternatively, *boga* may be a personal name or byname (see Tengvik, *Bynames*, pp. 238–9). The next boundary mark is probably 'Brant's ridge' (pers. n. Brant, *hrycg*: see *PN Dorset*, iii. 156), unless it is 'ridge of burning' (*brand*), perhaps referring to a beacon. The boundary follows the ridge to *bytelesmor*, apparently 'Bytel's marshy ground' (although an alternative source for the first element may be (*ge*)*bytlu*, 'building, house': see Smith, *EPNE*, i. 74); this was Bittlesmore, now lost, near Holyrood Farm (*PN Dorset*, iii. 153). The meaning of *wyndrede* is obscure (*PN Dorset*, iii. 159).

23

King Eadric (for Eadwig) grants three hides (mansae) *at Thornton in Marnhull and at Iwerne Courtney, Dorset, to Wulfgar, minister.* A.D. 958

C. BL Harley 61, 6rv: copy, s. xv
  Rubric: Istius donacionis notamine Edricus .iii. terre mansas ad þortun perpetuo dono sub deputa forma condonavit.
D. Bodleian, Dodsworth 38, 5v–6r: copy of C, s. xvii
Ed.: a. Hutchins, *Dorset*, ii. 509 (bounds omitted)

b. Kemble 474 (with the bounds in vol. iii, p. 453)
c. Birch 1033
d. Pierquin, *Recueil*, pt 2, no. 114
Listed: Sawyer 656; Finberg, *ECW*, no. 603
Edited from C

In nomine Domini nostri Iesu Christi saluatoris. Ea*[a]* que secundum legem canonicam ac disposicionem ordinantur ac constituantur, licet solus sermo concludat, tamen fidelissimis scripturis et documentis sunt commendanda ne in obliuione succidencium fiat aliqua ignauia torpitudinis priorum constitucionum. Quam ob rem ego Adric*[b]* rex Anglorum gubernator et rector cuidam meo fideli ministro quem nonnulli uocitant noto uocamine Wlfgar modicam partem terre, id est tres mansas, duobus in locis illic ubi Anglica more appellacione dicitur at þorntune,*[c]* ut habeat ac possideat quamdiu uiuat et post se cuicumque uoluerit heredi derelinquat in eternam hereditatem. Maneat autem predictum rus liberum ab omni mundiali obstaculo, cum omnibus ad se rite pertinentibus, campis, pratis, pascuis, siluis, exceptis istis tribus, expedicione, pontis arcisue construccione. Siquis uero hoc nostrum icarisma aliqua machinacione infringere conatus fuerit, ueniam non hic mereatur nec in futuro regni celestis clauigerum propitium habeat, nisi prius hic ad satisfaccionem emendare maluerit. Istis terminis hec tellus ambita uidetur.

þis sant ða land imare at þortune þe ierð in to Hamtune. Arest on Arcetham, of Archethamme on rumanhelle, þanen of breþling made, þ on pigerðes stapel, þanen to tudesleghe,*[d]* of þere lege be kinges imare on blinnesfeld,*[e]* þanen be wde on þere hina*[f]* imare, anlang mares þ on ealdmannes pyerðe, þanan on þa seales, of þan sealen þat eft on Arcetham.

And þis sent þe tweire hide land imare þe Cyna achte þe ealde. Arest on Ipernbroc, of pane broke on þe lang dich, þan on þene weie, anlang weies to lace*[g]* mere, þane onlang sledes on ða smale þornes, þanen on ða dich, þanen swo be diche on cranemere, of cranemere eft on Ipernbroc.*[h]*

Hec carta scripta est anno dominice incarnacionis .dcccclviii., indiccione .i.

Ego Adþid*[b]* rex Anglorum indeclinabiliter concessi. +
Ego Alfinus*[i]* presul sigillum agie crucis impressi. +*[j]*
Ego Berhtelm episcopus adquieui. +
Ego Osulf episcopus confirmaui. +
Ego Berhtelm episcopus consignaui. +
Ego Alwold episcopus subscripsi. +
Ego Admund dux +
Ego Aethelside*[k]* dux +

Ego Aluric dux +
Ego Alfech minister +
Ego Alfgar minister +
Ego Bierferþ minister +
Ego Alfred minister +
Ego Alfsige minister +
Ego Alfwig minister +
Ego Leofa minister +
Ego Adric minister +
Ego Wluric minister +

a Christi. S; ea C (*see commentary*)   *b For* Adwig (Eadwig)
c A dispositive verb is required (*perhaps* concedo, *as in* **22**)
d Perhaps the same feature as cludesleghe *in* **8**   *e* blinchesfeld *in* **8**   *f* hinc C
g late C   *h* Ipernbroc C   *i For* Alfsinus (Ælfsige)
j The remaining subscriptions are written across the page   *k For* Aethelsige

There can be little doubt that **23** is an authentic charter of Eadwig. The beneficiary
had previously been granted land at Hinton St Mary (*Hamtun*) by Eadmund (**15**).
A thegn named Wulfgar attests prominently under Eadmund and regularly in
Eadwig's reign; if these are the subscriptions of the same individual, it would appear
that he was out of favour while Eadred was king (see commentary to **15**). The
formulation of **23** seems entirely acceptable. The proem is a variation on a formula
that was used in some very early charters (see **1** and S 248, 1248 etc.); it was also
revived in S 715 from 963 (and it appears in several forgeries from St Paul's and
Chertsey: S 453, 752, 1035). This proem was used regularly with the verbal invocation
In nomine Domini nostri Iesu Christi saluatoris; the abbeviation (*s;*) at the beginning
of the proem in **23** (interpreted by Kemble and Birch as *scilicet*) is probably for
saluatoris. The royal style is contemporary (see also **22**), and there is no difficulty
with the wording of the dispositive section; the statement of powers is a standard
formula found also in **22** and **25**, as is the anathema. The immunity clause is a
variant on a common formula beginning *Sit autem* (see **25**), and the subscriptions
are entirely appropriate for the date.

   The charter is said to cover three hides in two places at *Thorntune* or *Thortune*;
the name survives as Thorton (also Thornton) Farm in Marnhull (ST 805180: see
PN Dorset, iii. 171). There is a double boundary clause, the first part apparently
describing the eastern part of the parish of Marnhull and the whole of the parish of
Margaret Marsh (Grundy 1937, p. 129–31), the second relating to an estate on the
river Iwerne which was probably located in the northern part of Iwerne Courtney
and thus some four miles distant from Thornton (Grundy 1936, pp. 129–31). The
first survey is prefaced by a statement: 'These are the bounds of the land at Thornton
which belongs to Hinton (St Mary)'; while the second is introduced by the rubric:
'These are the bounds of the two hides which Cyna the Old possessed'. It is possible
that these rubrics were added or adapted by a later Shaftesbury copist, but there is
no way of proving this. Both pieces of information are mildly problematic. **23** is

supposed to be a grant of three hides in two places at Thornton, but two of the three hides appear to have been located several miles away at Iwerne Courtney. Thus there was only a single hide at Thornton itself; yet the bounds seem to cover an area rather larger than a single hide. Did the three hides at Thornton and Iwerne Courtney already have some association with each other and with Wulfgar's existing estate at Hinton St Mary, or did the connection begin only when he acquired these two separate areas? There seems to be no straightforward answer to any of these problems. The total of eight hides conveyed in **15** and **23** is equivalent to the assessment TRE of Shaftesbury's Domesday manor at Hinton St Mary (GDB 78v). However, there was a separate Domesday manor at Iwerne Courtney, assessed at eight hides; it was held by Siward TRE, and by Baldwin the Sheriff from King William in 1086 (GDB 81r). It is possible that the two hides at Iwerne Courtney were detached from Wulfgar's former holding at some stage, and that the extra two hides of Shaftesbury's Hinton manor resulted from the acquisition of the territory separating the Hinton property of **15** from the Thornton estate proper as defined in **23** (that is, the western part of Marnhull parish).

The first survey in **23**, apparently describing the eastern part of Marnhull parish and the whole of the parish of Margaret Marsh, begins and ends at *Archet hamm*, which is also mentioned in the bounds of West Orchard (**10**); this was evidently an area of river-meadow (*hamm*) on the Key Brook which was associated with the settlement at Orchard. The starting-point of the survey would therefore be about a mile east of Thorton Farm. The name *rumanhelle*, 'roomy or spacious hill' (*rum*, wk obl. *ruman*, *hyll*) seems to be preserved in Rams Hill Farm (ST 813170; *PN Dorset*, iii. 171); Grundy identifies the hill itself with the raised ground just north of the farm. The first part of *brepling made* seems corrupt, but it may be an personal name *Be(o)rhtel*, with *-ing*: 'Beorhtel's meadow' (*PN Dorset*, iii. 178); this was probably a river-meadow on the tributary of Key Brook which lies just north of 'Ram's Hill'. The two following boundary-marks are difficult to interpret. The first appears to correspond to 'Wigheard's boundary-post' (*stapel*) in the Fontmell bounds (**8**), and *tudesleghe* may be a miscopying of the *cludesleghe* mentioned in the same charter: 'wood or clearing (*leah*) of the rocky outcrop (*clud*)'. But the bounds of Thornton should not correspond with the Fontmell survey at this point, although the two do meet a little later, when the Thornton bounds refer to *higna (ge)mære*. Grundy seeks an explanation in the fact that the northern part of the parish of Margaret Marsh is only about 100 yards wide at this point; thus a feature like a *leah* might cover both the eastern and western boundaries here, while the boundary-post of **23** might be separate marker for Wigheard's estate. This is ingenious, but still not entirely satisfactory. Nevertheless, it does seem that by this point the survey has reached the northern part of Margaret Marsh. Next comes a boundary with a royal estate (*cyning*, (*ge*)*mære*, 'the king's boundary'), probably at Stour Provost. *Blinnesfeld* is *blinchesfeld* in **8**, and the latter spelling is preferable; the feature was a tract of open land associated with *Blinc* brook, and it is remembered in the name of Blynfield Farm, located further up the brook (see p. 35, and *PN Dorset*, iii. 91–3). After this the boundary (now running south) passes a wood and reaches 'the boundary of the religious community' (*hiwan*, gen. *hi(g)na*, (*ge*)mære), that is, the boundary of Shaftesbury's Fontmell estate, which it follows back to 'Ealdmann's enclosure', also mentioned in the separate surveys of West Orchard (**10**) and East Orchard (**23**); this was located at about ST 822182. The boundary then meets 'the willows' (*sealh*), before returning to its starting-point in the Orchard meadow on Key Brook.

The two hides in the second part of the boundary evidently lay on the river Iwerne and, since they shared a boundary with the Iwerne Minster estate outlined in **21**, Grundy is surely correct in locating them in the north-western part of Iwerne Courtney parish (see also the comments in *PN Dorset*, iii. 37–41). The survey begins in the east at the river Iwerne. From here the boundary (running west and north) followed 'the long ditch' and a 'way' to a 'pool in a stream' (*lacu, mere*); this last feature is also mentioned in the Iwerne Minster bounds, where it lay close to the extreme westerly point of the survey and was associated with Fontmell Brook or a tributary (see *PN Dorset*, iii. 128–9). From this point the survey in **23** corresponds with the Iwerne Minster boundary as it runs south and east back to the Iwerne. The common boundary was marked by a valley (*slæd*), 'the narrow (belt of) thorn-trees' (*smæl, thorn*), a ditch or dyke, and a 'pond with cranes or herons' (*cran, mere*).

24

King Edgar grants five hides (cassati) *at East Orchard, Dorset, to Ælfsige, minister.* A.D. 963

C. BL Harley 61, 14rv: copy, s. xv
    Rubric: Istius graphii assignacione Adgar rex quandam telluris ad Archet particulam imperpetuum ut presens manifestatur scriptum dono assignavit.
Ed.: a. Kemble 501 (with the bounds in vol. iii, p. 459)
      b. Birch 1115
      c. Pierquin, *Recueil*, pt 2, no. 125
Listed: Sawyer 710; Finberg, *ECW*, no. 604

Altitrono in eternum regnante. Uniuersis sophie studium intento mentis conamine sedulo[a] rimantibus liquido patescit quod huius uite periculis immo[b] ingruentibus terrore recidiui[c] terminus[d] cosmi appropinquare dinoscitur, ut ueridica Christi promulgat sentencia qua dicit, 'Surget gens contra gentem et regnum aduersus regnum'[1] et reliqua. Quapropter ego Adgar tocius Britannie basilius quandam telluris particulam, quinque uidelicet cassatos loco qui celibri at Archet nuncupatur uocabulo, cuidam ministro michi ualde fideli qui ab huiusmodi patrie cognosticis[e] nobili Alsige appellatur uocabulo pro obsequio eius deuotissimo perpetua largitus sum hereditate, ut ipse uita comite cum omnibus utensilibus, pratis uidelicet, pascuis, siluis, uoti compos habeat et post uite sue terminum quibuscumque uoluerit cleronomis inmunem derelinquat. Sit autem predictus[f] rus omni terrene seruitutis iugo liberum, tribus exceptis, rata uidelicet expedicione, pontis arcisue restauracione. Siquis igitur hanc nostram donacionem in aliud quam constituimus transferre uoluerit, priuatus consorcio sancte Dei ecclesie eternis baratri incendiis lugubris iugiter cum Iuda Christi proditore eiusque complicibus puniatur, si non satisfaccione emendauerit congrua quod contra nostrum deliquit^g decretum. Hiis metis prefatum rus hinc inde giratur.

Ðis sant þe landimare to Archet. Of eldmannes wrthe on irichte anlang hina imares to þan scamelen, fram þanne scamelen anlang hine imares oð Wdebrige, of Þudebricge adune anlang streames oð land scorforde,^{h} of þane forde anlang leouen imare oð kinghes imare, ⟨andlang⟩^{i} gemare oð Funtemel forde,^{h} of þanne forde^h adune mid streame oþes bissopes imare ut sceoþaþ,^{j} þanen on irichte to þan lipgete, fram þane gete on irichte to anne ponalre,^{k} of þane alre on irichte to sucgimade^l hauede, of þane hauede on irichte þurch ðene^m holt to wlgares imaren, of þan imaren eft on eldemannes wyrðe.^{n} Anno dominice incarnacionis .dcccclxiii. scripta ⟨est⟩^{o} hec carta, hiis testibus consencientibus quorum inferius nomina caraxantur.

Ego Adgar rex Anglorum concessi. +
Ego Dunstan archiepiscopus corroboraui. +
Ego Oscytelin archiepiscopus confirmaui. +
Ego Osulf episcopus consolidaui et ceteri. +

^{a} scedulo C ^{b} *Probably for* nimio (*compare* S 700 etc.) ^{c} recidui C ^{d} terminis C
^{e} *Error for* gnosticis C ^{f} *For* predictum
^{g} dereliquid C (*the form* deliquid *is often used in this formula*) ^{h} -forð C ^{i} and C
^{j} *For* sceotaþ ^{k} ponalre C ^{l} sugging made *in* 10 ^{m} *For* dene *or* ðone
^{n} wyrde C ^{o} *The word* est *has fallen out here*

[1] Luc. 21: 10

24 was probably the work of the scribe and draftsman known as 'Edgar A', who seems to have been responsible for most of the royal diplomas issued between 960 and 963 (see Keynes, *Diplomas*, pp. 70–6). It incorporates many of the standard formulas characteristic of the diplomas of 'Edgar A', in particular the statement of powers, immunity clause and sanction (see also **26**, **27**), and can be considered as part of a subgroup belonging to the years 962 and 963, which have the same verbal invocation and proem and almost identical formulation (see S 700, 702, 706, 711, 714, 716, and also 767 from 968). The form of the surviving subscriptions, with varied and alliterating verbs of attestation, is also typical of 'Edgar A'. **24** certainly appears to be authentic.

The beneficiary cannot be identified; at least three thegns named Ælfsige attested Edgar's diplomas, and he may have been one of these. The five hides of his estate lay in East Orchard, to the north and east of the West Orchard property covered in **10**; the survey appears to outline the whole of the later parish (see discussion by Grundy 1937, pp. 101–4, and also *PN Dorset*, iii. 134–7). Neither East nor West Orchard is mentioned in the Domesday survey, but it seems possible that the land covered in **10** and **24** was reckoned under one or more of the neighbouring Shaftesbury manors. Just as West Orchard was later a chapelry of Fontmell Magna, so East Orchard is known to have had a connection with the parish of Iwerne Minster (Hutchins, *Dorset* (3rd edn), ii. 550); it is possible that the nuns' eighteen-hide Domesday manor at Iwerne Minster (GDB 78v) included a dependency at East Orchard. The survey in **24** begins in the north-west part of the estate, at 'Ealdman's enclosure' (pers. n. Ealdmann, *wyrth*), also the starting-point for the West Orchard survey and mentioned in the bounds of Fontmell (**8**) and Thornton in Marnhull (**23**); this feature was located at approximately ST 822182. From this point the East Orchard boundary (now running east) corresponds for some distance with the boundary of Shaftesbury's estate at Fontmell Magna, referred to here as 'the boundary of the members of the religious community' (*hiwan*, gen. *higna*, (*ge*)*mære*). 'The shelf of land' (*sceamol*) is also mentioned in the Fontmell survey. At Woodbridge (ST 847183) the boundary turns south and follows the brook called *Stirchel* to 'boundary ford' (*landscearu, ford*), which was probably at the point where the parish boundary leaves the stream (ST 840166). From here the boundary ran along 'Leofa's boundary' and 'the king's boundary' to a ford over Fontmell Brook. Leofa is probably to be identified with the beneficiary of **22**; his estate must have been located in Sutton Waldron. 'The king's boundary' apparently refers to the boundary between Iwerne Minster and East Orchard; this implies that Iwerne Minster was in the king's possession in 963, and throws doubt on the claim in **21** that it was given to Shaftesbury in 956. The ford over Fontmell Brook seems to have been situated at ST 841156. The boundary follows the brook west to the point where 'the bishop's boundary shoots out'. This seems to refer to the place where the boundaries of East and West Orchard meet (at ST 834155), so it can probably be assumed that the bishop's estate was at West Orchard. This is a problem, for **10** appears to indicate that West Orchard was given to a Bishop Ælfred in 939 and subsequently transferred by him to a woman named Beorhtwyn; if Ælfred is correctly identified as the contemporary bishop of Sherborne, the transfer must have taken place before his death in 939 × 943. West Orchard could only be an episcopal estate in 963 if the five hides had subsequently passed into the possession of another bishop (or if the transaction in **10** was more complicated than it appears). A possible explanation is that the boundary clause in **24** was slightly out of date, because it had been copied from an earlier East Orchard diploma (this might also account for the implication that Iwerne Minster was still a royal estate). But in that case the reference to (Wulfgar) Leofa as a local landowner would be unexpected, since his attestations to royal charters do not begin until 958. The next boundary marks are a 'leap-gate' (*hlip-geat*), which was a low point or gate in a fence over which animals could pass, a 'crooked alder-tree' (*woh*, wk obl. *won*, *alor*) and 'the upper end' (*heafod*) of a meadow (*mæd*) called *sucgimade*, the *sugging made* of **10**, which gave rise to the field-name Sow Mead in West Orchard (see *PN Dorset*, iii. 138). The next boundary mark may be 'valley wood' (*denu, holt*). From here the survey follows 'Wulfgar's boundary' (at Thornton) back to its starting-point.

25

King Edgar grants five hides (cassati) *at Teffont, Wiltshire, to Sigestan,* minister. A.D. 964

C. BL Harley 61, 13rv: copy, s. xv
  Rubric: + Adgar rex .v. cassatos ad Teofuntem ut in subsequente continetur carta im-perpetuum commissum perpetualiter commisit.
Ed.: a. Kemble 513
  b. Birch 1138
Listed: Sawyer 730; Finberg, *ECW*, no. 299

Domino dominorum dominante in secula seculorum. Regna regnorum huius presentis seculi transeant sicut ignominica*a* et omnis gloria et iocus peribit huius mundi et ⟨non⟩*b* sunt eterna sed superna eterna sunt. Unde ego Adgar rex Anglorum ceterarumque gencium in circuitu persistencium gubernator et rector cuidam meo fideli ministro quem nonnulli uocant noto uocamine Sigestan pro eius beniuolo obsequio aliquam porcionem terre perhenniter mente deuota concedo, id est quinque cassatos in illo loco ubi Anglica ⟨more⟩*c* appellacione dicitur at Teofunten, ut habeat ac possideat quamdiu uiuat*d* et post se cuicumque uoluerit heredi derelinquat in eternam here-ditatem. Sit autem predictum rus liberum ab omni mundiali obstaculo cum omnibus que ad ipsum locum pertinere dinoscuntur, tam in magnis quam in modicis rebus, campis, pascuis, pratis, siluis, excepto communi labore, expedicione, pontis et arcis coedificacione. Siquis uero hoc nostrum ikarisma aliqua machinacione infringere conatus fuerit, ueniam non hic mereatur nec in futuro regni celestis clauigerum*e* propicium habeat, nisi prius hic ad satisfaccionem emendare maluerit.*f* Nullis*g* certis terminis sed iugera iacent ad iugeribus.*h* Hec carta scripta est anno dominice incarnacionis .dcccclxiiii.

Ego Adgar*i* rex Anglorum indeclinabiliter concessi. +
Ego Dunstanus archiepiscopus regie roborator donacionis agie triumphale crucis signaculum depinxi. +
Ego Athelwold Wintoniensis ecclesie episcopus hanc cartam dictitans rege suisque precipientibus perscribere iussi et ceteri plurimi. +

  a ignominia C (*compare* **22**)   *b* *The word* non *has fallen out here* (*same error in* **22**)
  c *The word* more *has fallen out here* (*compare* **23**)   *d* uiuati C
  e clauig'er C (*compare* **22**, **23**)   *f* emaluerit C   *g* Nullus C   *h* lugeribus C
  i Agar C

25 can be accepted as an authentic diploma. Its formulation is clearly contemporary: the verbal invocation and proem also occur together in **22** and in five other diplomas dated between 951 and 988 (S 554, 577, 642, 800, 872); the royal style was common in the middle years of the tenth century, and the wording of the dispositive section is also acceptable for the period (compare, for instance, **23** and S 736); the statement of powers, immunity clause and anathema are all common formulas (for the first and last see **22** and **23**; the immunity clause is the standard version of which that in **23** is a variant); and, finally, the elaborate form of the subscriptions can be paralleled in a number of other charters from Edgar's reign (compare S 712, in which Dunstan's subscription is the same and Æthulf of Elmham attests in the same words as does Æthelwold in **25**; see also S 668, 701, 705, 725 etc.). Bishop Æthelwold's subscription implies that he was responsible for the drafting of the diploma, but this is more likely to be a formulaic declaration than a realistic reflection of the documentary process (see the discussion of episcopal subscriptions of this type by Keynes, *Diplomas*, pp. 26–8). Sigestan does not occur elsewhere.

In place of the boundary clause there is a cryptic sentence, to the effect that there are no fixed bounds, but instead 'the *iugera* lie by the *iugera*'. In other words, the five hides were not enclosed, but were scattered in strips in the common land. This is one of a number of tenth-century diplomas giving title to or mentioning common land (see also S 560, 634, 650, 668, 691, 700, 711, 828, 839, 851, 856, 867, 886, 901, 1311, 1329; and discussion of the terminology in Finberg, *Agrarian History*, pp. 487–94). The formula in **25** appears in a rather longer and more comprehensible form in S 634 ('Nam prefatum rus nullis certis terminis dirimitur set iugera adiacent iugeribus'). Elsewhere the draftsmen could be more explicit. S 719 (A.D. 963), concerned with land in Wiltshire, refers to 'tres ... cassatos singulis iugeribus mixtum in communi rure huc illacque dispersis'. In S 691 (A.D. 961) a grant of nine hides in the common land at Ardington in Berkshire is clearly stated to be composed of communal meadow, pasture and arable.

The five hides covered in **25** are likely to have formed part of Shaftesbury's Domesday manor of Dinton, which was assessed at twenty hides TRE (GDB 67v) and which is known to have included Teffont Magna (see further discussion in the commentary to **3**).

26

King Edgar confirms ten hides (cassati) *at* Uppidelen (*Piddletrenthide*), *Dorset, to the church of Shaftesbury.* A.D. 966

C. BL Harley 61, 13v–14r: copy, s. xv
  Rubric: + Istius presentis graphii intitulacione Deo et ecclesie sancti Adwardi Adgar rex .x. cassatos scilicet ad Uppidelen omni tempore suo intitulat dono.
Ed.: a. Kemble 522 (with bounds in vol. iii, p. 465)
    b. Birch 1186
    c. Earle p. 429 (bounds only)
    d. Pierquin, *Recueil*, pt 2, no. 132
Listed: Sawyer 744; Finberg, *ECW*, no. 607

Cuncta seculorum patrimonia incertis nepotum heredibus*ᵃ* derelinquuntur*ᵇ* et omnis mundi gloria apropinquante uite mortis*ᶜ* termino ad nichillum reducta fatescit. Iccirco terrenis caducarum ⟨rerum⟩[d] possessionibus semper mansura superne patrie emolumenta adipiscentes Domino patrocinante lucrenda[e] decernimus.[f] Quam ob rem ego Adgar tocius Britannie basileus quandam telluris particulam, .x. uidelicet cassatos loco qui celebri at Uppidelen nuncupatur uocabulo, cuidam ecclesie in omni sanctorum ueneracione dicate loco qui celebri Schaftesbury uocatur onomate ad usus monialium inibi degencium, ut aua mea Winfled ante concesserat, eterna largitus sum hereditate. Uetus etenim prefati teritorii carta per incuriam[g] quondam perdita fuerat atque ideo hanc nouam ob firmitatis munimen scribere iussi. Si quopiam uetus reperta fuerat, uel monasterio restituatur uel eius possessor furti crimine reus iudicetur. Sit autem predictum rus cum omnibus utensilibus, pratis uidelicet et pascuis, siluis, omni terrene seruitutis iugo liberum, tribus exceptis, rata uidelicet expedicione, pontis arcisue restauracione. Siquis igitur hanc nostram donacionem in aliud quam constituimus transferre uoluerit, priuatus consorcio sancte Dei ecclesie eternis baratri incendiis lugubris iugiter cum Iuda Christi proditore eiusque complicibus puniatur, si non satisfaccione emendauerit congrua quod contra nostrum deliquit[h] decretum. Hiis metis prefatum rus hinc inde giratur.

Ðis sanden þe land imaren at Uppidele. Of Pidelen streame on hlosstedes crundles suð ecge, of þane crundle on þat mere sled, of þat mere slede on ðes herepaþe, anlang herepaþes on mearhhilde mere, of mearhhilde mere on þane haþene berielese, on midde þane punfald,[i] of þanne punfalde on Pidelenstream, of Pidelenstreme anlang burnstowe on greten linkes suth ecge, of þane gretenlinke on chellenberghe, þ eft on Pidelen streame, and se made be Frome þat to þanne tune ibereth.

Anno dominice incarnacionis .d.cccc.lxvi. scripta est hec carta, hiis testibus consencientibus quorum inferius nomina caraxantur.

Ego Adgar rex Anglorum corroboraui.
Ego Dunstan archiepiscopus consensi.
Ego Oscytel archiepiscopus confirmaui.
Ego Aþelþold episcopus consolidaui et ceteri.

[a] hered C   [b] *Probably for* relinquuntur (*see* S 701, 708 etc.)
[c] *Probably for* debite mortis (*as* S 584, 708 etc.) *or* uite huius (*as* S 701)
[d] *The word* rerum *has probably fallen out here (see* S 584, 708 etc.; *same omission in*
S 701)   [e] *For* lucranda   [f] *Or perhaps* decreuimus   [g] incurriam C
[h] reliquid C (*the form* deliquid *is often used in this formula*)   [i] punfabo C; *for* pundfald

There is no reason to think **26** other than authentic. The proem is a slight variant on a standard formula, also found in S 701 from 962 (and see S 584, 708, 846, 848,

993, 1025). The basic formulation of the rest of the document (the main dispositive section, the immunity clause, anathema, introduction to the bounds, the dating clause and the subscriptions) is typical of the majority of the diplomas issued in Edgar's name in the 960s, many of which may have been the work of the draftsman/ scribe known as 'Edgar A' (see **24**, **27** and Keynes, *Diplomas*, pp. 70–6). **26** has an additional section explaining that the diploma was issued because the old landbook for the estate had been lost; it is presumably a confirmation of an estate which already belonged to the community. The original donor was the king's grandmother, Wynflæd, the mother of Eadmund's first wife, Ælfgifu, who was buried and culted at Shaftesbury and who was herself a benefactor of the nunnery (see pp. xiii–xiv, and **28**). Wynflæd can almost certainly be identified with the nun of that name who held land at Cheselbourne and Winterborne Tomson in Eadmund's reign (**13**); Cheselbourne lies almost immediately to the east of the estate at *Uppidelen*.

Uppidelen was one of a number of settlements in Dorset named from the river Piddle. The ten hides covered in **26** appear to have been located in the northern part of the later parish of Piddletrenthide, which straddles the river Piddle. Until modern times this parish was divided into three units of a similar size, which retained their separate common-field systems until 1817; on the enclosure map these are called the Upper, Middle and Lower Tithings (see Taylor, *Dorset*, pp. **51–3**). It appears that the long, sprawling village of Piddletrenthide was originally three separate settlements, of which the most northerly was the ten hides at 'Up Piddle' covered in **26**; the name Piddletrenthide means 'Piddle of the thirty hides' (*DEPN*, p. 366), which agrees well with the suggestion that it was made up of three areas of ten hides each. Domesday Book notes that an estate at *Pidele* had been seized from the Shaftesbury by Harold, along with land at Melcombe Horsey and Stour; it was not recovered and is said to have been held by the Count of Mortain in 1086 (GDB 78v). It would seem logical to equate this lost property with the ten hides given to the abbey by Wynflæd, but the Domesday account of the history of land in this area is incompatible with this simple conclusion. Three manors called simply 'Piddle' are listed among the lands of the Count of Mortain (GDB 79rv). Two of them were tiny, with respective assessments of only $1\frac{1}{2}$ and $2\frac{1}{2}$ hides; they are said to have been held by unnamed thegns before 1066. The only sizeable 'Piddle' among the Count's manors is definitely Piddlehinton, located directly south of Piddletrenthide, which was held as two manors by two thegns TRE, with an assessment of ten hides. The similar hidage has encouraged the identification of the Piddlehinton manor with the estate covered in **26** (see *VCH Dorset* II, p. 43), but this seems unlikely to be correct; the boundary clause, although difficult to interpret, fits the northern part of Piddle-trenthide reasonably well and seems inappropriate for Piddlehinton. In 1086 Piddle-trenthide itself was a thirty-hide manor belonging to the New Minster in Winchester; before 1066 it had been held by men named Ælmær and Æthelfrith as two manors from King Edward, and after the Conquest it had briefly been held by Roger Arundel from King William (GDB 77v). The New Minster community later claimed that it had been granted Piddletrenthide by Queen Emma (see *Mon. Angl.* (rev. edn), ii. 436), but this seems to be contradicted by the Domesday account. If, as seems likely, the ten hides of **26** formed the northern third of the thirty-hide manor of Piddletrenthide, then it would appear that this was not the land at *Pidele* seized by Harold which passed to the Count of Mortain; it must have been a separate estate, lost or alienated at some point in the century between 966 and 1066. The difficulty may well arise from the confusion generated by the large number of places in Dorset that are named 'Piddle' (see further, p. xxiii).

The boundary clause has been discussed by Grundy (1937, pp. 107–12), who decided that the grant probably covered the whole of the Upper Tithing of Piddletrenthide; this conclusion was based largely on the apparent size of the estate, relative to the size of the later parish, but is difficult to reconcile with the details of the boundary clause, which appear to indicate that the estate included only a small part of the eastern half of the tithing. Few of the boundary marks can be identified with confidence, and the key to understanding the survey is Grundy's observation that the penultimate feature, *chellenberghe*, is almost certainly to be identified with *shilleburghe* in the bounds of the estate at Plush in Buckland Newton described in a charter of Alfred (S 347). Plush lies immediately north of the eastern part of the Upper Tithing of Piddletrenthide, so this feature must have been located on the north-eastern part of the *Uppidelen* boundary. Immediately after touching on *chellenberghe*, the survey returns to its starting-point on the river Piddle. This indicates, firstly, that the survey began on the northern boundary of the estate, and, secondly, that it would appear to be one of the very few Anglo-Saxon surveys which run anticlockwise. It can probably be assumed that the starting-point was where the later parish boundary crossed the river Piddle north of Piddletrenthide village (ST 703012). After this the boundary, going west, passes by the south edge of a gully or quarry (*crundel*) which was used for pig-keeping (*hlosstede*, 'place where there is a pig-sty'); it is tempting to identify this feature with the ring earthwork marked at ST 693011 (but if the boundary went south of this it did not follow the line of the later parish boundary). *Mere slæd* is probably 'valley which formed a boundary' ((ge)*mære*, *slæd*) rather than 'valley with a pool' (*mere*). The highway (*herepæð*) is apparently the north-south ridgeway running to Dorchester, which forms part of the western boundary of the parish. 'Mearhhild's boundary' (fem. pers. n. Mearhhild, (ge)*mære*) or perhaps 'pool' (*mere*) would probably have marked the place where the boundary turned east from the ridgeway, back towards the Piddle; the intervening boundary marks were 'heathen burials' (*hæðen*, *byrgels*) and a 'pin-fold' or pound (*pundfald*; see S 689 for another occurrence in a boundary clause). The boundary may have recrossed the Piddle on the line of the southern boundary of the Upper Tithing, which would have been about a mile south of its starting-point, probably close to the manor house in Piddletrenthide village. Up to this point the survey has described only the western half of the Upper Tithing, and it is difficult to see how the few remaining boundary marks could possibly describe the whole of the eastern half, which extended beyond the Piddle to the boundary with Cheselbourne. Grundy prefers to think that the survey in its present form is defective, but he does suggest an alternative interpretation which has many points in its favour. According to this the *burnstow* which the boundary now follows would be the Plush brook; here the word probably means 'the channel or bed of an intermittent stream', the sense which it has in the Cheselbourne bounds (see *PN Dorset*, iii. 205). The brook would take the boundary directly northeast from the Piddle. The next boundary mark mentioned is the southern edge of 'the great linchet' (*great*, *hlinc*); this can perhaps be connected with the field system marked on Plush Hill at ST 714015. *Chellenberghe* was probably a tumulus (*beorg*); the first element may be a personal name Ceola, or *ceole*, meaning 'gully, throat' or 'beak of ship' (the form in **26** seems preferable to the *shilleburghe* of S 347). The boundary now returns to the river Piddle. The estate had appurtenant meadow by the river Frome.

27

King Edgar grants three iugera *of farmland and twenty* iugera *of woodland at* Ealderes cumbe *to Brihtgifu.* A.D. 968

C. BL Harley 61, 14v–15r: copy, s. xv
    Rubric: Hanc suam Adgar rex terre donacionem ad Alderescumbe adiacentem sub notata forma scribere iussit.
Ed.: a. Kemble 547
    b. Birch 1218
Listed: Sawyer 762; Finberg, *ECW*, no. 653

Omnium iura regnorum celestium atque terrestrium, claustra quoque infernalium, dumtaxat diuinis Dei nutibus subiecta sunt. Quapropter cunctis sanum sapientibus satagendum est toto mentis conamine, ut preuideant qualiter tormenta ualeant euadere infernalia et celestis uite gaudia, concedente Christo Iesu, conscendere. Hinc[a] Adgar tocius Britannie basileus quandam[b] telluris particulam, .iii. uidelicet campi iugera ac silue .xx. uel paulo plura at Ealderes cumbe, cuidam femine mihi oppido fideli qui[c] ab[d] huiusmodi patrie gnosticis nobili Birthgiue appellatur uocabulo pro obsequio eam[e] deuotissimo et perpetua largitus sum hereditate, ut ipsa uita comite cum omnibus utensilibus, pratis uidelicet, pascuis, siluis, uoti compos habeat et post uite sue exitum quibuscumque uoluerit cleronomis inmunem derelinquere.[f] Sit autem predictum rus omni terrene seruitutis iugo liberum, tribus exceptis, rata uidelicet expedicione, pontis arcisue restauracione. Siquis igitur hanc nostram donacionem in aliud quam constituimus transferre uoluerit, priuatus consorcio Dei ecclesie eternis baratri incendiis lugubris iugiter cum Iuda Christi proditore eiusque complicibus puniatur, si non satisfaccione emendauerit congrua quod contra nostrum deliquit[g] decretum. Hiis metis prefatum rus hinc inde giratur.

Ðis sant þa land imare to Aldderescumbe. Arest of langan riple up be wirtrume on wlfgedyce, of wlfgedyce be wirtrume on deodepoldding lege suþeward, of teoþewolding lege adune be dich, of þat dich forðe be wirtrune on heahstanes quabben, forð be wirtrune and[h] lang riple, at[i] twelf akeres yrð landes be þe hege wege went on putel made.

Anno dominice incarnacionis .dcccclxviii. scripta est hec carticula, hiis testibus.[j]

Ego Adgar rex Anglorum concessi. +
Ego Dunstan archiepiscopus corroboraui. +
Ego Oscytel archiepiscopus confirmaui. +
Ego Aþelwold episcopus consolidaui et ceteri. +

a The word ego *may have fallen out here (but compare S 766)*   *b* quondam C
c For que   *d* ad C   *e For* eius   *f For* derelinquat
g dereliquid C *(the form* deliquid *is often used in this formula)*
h Probably for on   *i Probably for* and   *j The subscriptions are written across the page*

27 is probably authentic. The proem recurs in a diploma of the same year in favour of the Wilton community (S 766), while the rest of the formulation follows the popular model devised by 'Edgar A' in the early 960s (see **24**, **26**). The beneficiary cannot be identified, and neither can the location of the land-grant, 'Ealdhere's combe', which seems to have been a heavily wooded area. The terms of reference to the assessment of the estate are unconventional, but this could well have been a feature of the original diploma. The survey begins and ends at 'the long strip (of woodland)' (*lang, ripel*; for *ripel* see Smith, *EPNE*, ii. 84) The boundary follows a wood-bank (*wyrtrume*) to *wlfgedyce*, perhaps 'wolf-enclosure ditch' (*wulf, hege, dic*), and then proceeds along the wood-bank to the south of 'Theodwold's clearing or wood' (pers. n. Theodwold, *ing, leah*). After a ditch and another wood-bank the boundary reaches 'Heahstan's marsh' (*cwabba*, 'marsh, bog', here in the Middle English spelling), and then continues along a wood-bank back to its starting-point. The final part of the boundary clause seems to refer to an appurtenance to the estate, twelve acres of plough-land by 'the hedge way' (*hege, weg*). The last part of this passage is difficult to understand, and may be slightly corrupt. *Putel made* is probably 'hawk meadow' (*pyttel, mæd*).

28

King Æthelred confirms Shaftesbury's possession of twenty hides (mansae) *at Tisbury, Wiltshire.* A.D. 984 (before 1 August)

C. BL Harley 61, 2v–3v: copy, s. xv
  Rubric: Aeþeldredus rex istius inscriptionis [.. .. ..]*a* in loco noto nuncupatur Tissebiri .xx. mansas ecclesie sancti Edwardi inperpetuum.
D. Bodleian, Dodsworth 38, 2v–3v: copy of C, s. xvii
Ed.: a. *Mon. Angl.*, i. 215–16
    b. Hoare, *Wilts.*, Vale of Noddre and Hundred of Dunworth, pp. 236–7
    c. Kemble 641
    d. *Mon. Angl.* (rev. edn), ii. 479 (no. 6)
    e. Earle, pp. 429–30 (bounds only)
    f. Pierquin, *Recueil*, pt 4, no. 58
Listed: Sawyer 850; Finberg, *ECW*, no. 318
Edited from C

O altithroni genitoris ingeniti eiusdemque natiui[b] diuinitus unici cum sancti unione paracliti monarchia, rebus essendi facultatem ac illis ne adnullentur suauem impertiente[c] gubernacionem. 'Filiis adopcionis non iam uetuste configuratis ignorancie desideriis, sed secundum eum', ut ait beatus apostolus Petrus, 'qui uocauit nos sanctum, ipsis quoque in omni sancta conuersacione fundatis'[1] commutacione temporalium spes futurorum ac eternaliter possidendorum conceditur fiducia bonorum.[d] Huius michi gratuito uti ceteris allubescente gracia, ego Aþeldred regionis Angligenarum rex monasterio sanctimonialium quod insulani usitato Schaftesbiri appellant onomate .xx. mansas illo in loco qui noto et Tissebiri uocatur uocamine sitas, quas sicut antiquis diebus omnis antecessores mei illuc donauerunt, ita ego quoque hiis regni mei temporibus eandem donacionem cum optimatum meorum consultu renouando in hereditatem concedo perhenne. Nam et uicinis ante me temporibus auus meus Admund scilicet rex idem pro commutacione Butticanlea adquisitum coniugi sue Algife ius eternaliter habendum concessit et ipsa quoque illud ad laudem Domini et saluatoris nostri Iesu Christi eiusque genetricis semperque uirginis Marie adque eternam sui liberacionem prefato studuit attribuere loco. Sed patruus meus Adwith[e] uidelicet rex post obitum Alfgife[f] supradicte ius mutauit, hoc ipsum sibi uidelicet Butticanlea accipiens sanctoque cenobio prefatam terram et Tisseburi perpetualiter attribuens. Quod iccirco cum optimatibus meis renouare studui,[g] ut omnibus mihi hanc uoluntatem inesse manifeste eandem porcionem cum omnibus ad se rite pertinentibus ab omni mundana seruitute sicut antiquitus liberam fore, tribus exceptis, rata expedicione, pontis arcisue recuperacione.[h] Siluam sane Sfgcnyllebar[i] appellatam quam meorum quidam prepositorum ausu diripere conabantur in festo idem monasterio totam integramque restituo, ut nullus hanc inuadere, nullus unquam sibi aliquatenus audeat usurpare, sed uti olim ceu predixi ita nunc et in posterum ad inibi Deo famulancium usum quamdiu rota uoluitur huius seculi libera perpetualiter existat. Siquis igitur hanc meam cum Dei uoluntate renouatam presumpserit infringere[j] donacionem, eternis baratri incendiis cum diabolo sine fine crucietur, nisi in hac prius emendauerit uita quod contra nostrum deliquit decretum. Rus uero prefatum hiis metis in circo rotatur.

Ðis sant þa landimare þare tþentiþe hiþe[k] at Tisseburi. Arest þe Cigelmarc[l] scheth on Nodre, andlang stremes oð[m] gofesdene, þannen to þere twichenen, of þere twichene on wilburge imare, on þane grene wei, on wermundes treþ, of wermundes tre adun richt inne þe imade,[n] of þane miþon anlang stremes on þane ealde wdeforde, on þare grene wei, onne þe heued stokes, of þanne heued stocken forþ be tþelf aceron þat it comet to þealþege, þanen to hig þege, þannen to wdesfloda, þannen to suthames forde, anlange hege reawe þat it comet to Nodre, anlang Nodre on Semene, anlang Semene to rodelee, þanen oń þere hƿiten mercs,[o] þannen on mapeldere hille, þannen on þa stigele, þannen on sapcumbe, þannen forðer[p] west on cures rigt,[q] þanne cyrder it[q] north on poles leage, þannen on mane broc, þanen on wiþig broch, þanen on sidinic mor, þannen forð on Cnugel lege and on hiclesham, þannen on mearc wei, of þane wege anlang hrigces to nipedeforde,[r] anlang weges þat it cumet to Funtgeal, on þone herpoð, þannen to gificancumbe, anlang cumbe to stanweie, anlang hrygges to þere litden[s] lege, þannen on leofriches imare, forð be gemare eft on Funtal, of fintes brigce[t] anlang hrigces to alfgares imare, forðer[p] be his imare oþ heued stoccas, þanen to Cigel merc broke, anlang stremes eft on Nodre.

Anno dominice incarnacionis .dcccc.lxxxiiii. scripta est hec donacionis mee cartula, testibus hiis omnibus unanimiter adquiescentibus quorum inferius onomatum stigmata secundum competentem unicuique dignitatem caraxantur.

Ego Aþeldred rex Anglorum prefatam donacionem renouando cum sacre crucis impressione Deo omnibusque sanctis eius eternaliter concessi. +
Ego Dunstanus archiepiscopus concedendo adquieui. +
Ego Osþold[u] archiepiscopus consensi. +[v]
Ego Athelþold episcopus consolidaui. +
Ego Alfstan episcopus coroboraui. +
Ego Alfstan episcopus conscripsi. +
Ego Aþulf[w] episcopus consignaui. +
Ego Alfech episcopus consigillaui. +
Ego Asþig episcopus consensi. +
Ego Alfric episcopus coroboraui. +
Ego Aþelsige episcopus consignaui. +
Ego Wlgar episcopus conclusi. +
Ego Aþelgar episcopus confirmaui. +
Ego Alwine[x] dux +
Ego Beornoð dux +
Ego Athelþerd dux +
Ego Alfric dux +
Ego Ordulf minister +[y]
Ego Godþine minister +[y]
Ego Alfric dux +[z]
Ego Alfþarð minister +
Ego Alfsige minister +
Ego Wlsige minister +

Ego Alfric minister +
Ego Beorthƿold minister +
Ego Leofric minister +
Ego Aþelmer minister +
Ego Alfƿine minister +
Ego Aþelsige minister +
Ego Aþelƿeard minister +
Ego Alfgar minister +
Ego Wlsge minister +
Ego Wlfric minister +
Ego Leofric minister +
Ego Leofƿine minister. +

[a] *Rubric partly illegible* (Mon. Angl., *ii. 215, reads* firmitate) [b] *Probably for* nati
[c] imperiente C
[d] *Perhaps read* spes ... ac ... fiducia ... conceditur ... filiis adoptionis ... (*the scriptural quotation is freely adapted*) [e] *For* Adwig (Eadwig) [f] Alfigife C [g] studuit C
[h] *The syntax of the immunity clause seems confused* (*a verb may have fallen out*)
[i] *Corrupt, probably for* Secghyll bær [j] infingere C [k] *For* tƿentige hide
[l] *The word* broc *may have fallen out here* [m] od C [n] *For* imuðe (gemyðe)
[o] *A spelling for* mersc [p] forder C
[q] cures rigt *and* cyrder it *are the same corrupt boundary mark* (*probably* cuna (h)rycg, *'cows' ridge'*); *the word* of *may have fallen out before* cyrder it
[r] *Probably for* nipredeforde (*Kemble has* inpedeforde) [s] *Probably for* litlen
[t] *Probably for* funtes hricge [u] Osƿodo C
[v] *The remaining subscriptions are in two columns, with this subscription heading the first column* [w] *For* Æthelwulf [x] *For* Æthelwine
[y] *For the correct positions of these two subscriptions, see commentary*
[z] *This subscription heads the second column*

[1] cf. I Pet. 1: 15 (and for *filii adoptionis*, cf. Rom. 8: 15, 23; 9: 4 etc.)

In common with a number of other diplomas from the very late tenth century, **28** includes details of the earlier history of the estate with which it is concerned. The account is not entirely clear, but it appears that land at Tisbury had been an early possession of the Shaftesbury community ('.xx. mansas ... quas sicut antiquis diebus omnis antecessores mei illuc donauerunt'). The estate seems to have been exchanged with King Eadmund for another property at an unidentified place named *Butticanlea*. Eadmund transferred Tisbury to his wife, Ælfgifu, who intended to give it, or perhaps bequeath it, to Shaftesbury. Ælfgifu may already have had a family connection with the nunnery through her mother, Wynflæd (see **13**, **26**), and she herself was buried and later culted there (see pp. xiii–xiv). But Ælfgifu's intention was thwarted after her death by her son Eadwig, who seems to have permitted the transfer of Tisbury to the community only on condition that the estate at *Butticanlea* was given up to him. Ælfgifu died in 944 (*Æthelweard*, p. 54). Eadwig became king in 955, and it was apparently not until this stage that he impeded his mother's intentions with regard to Tisbury. It may have been the case that Ælfgifu did not leave the land directly to Shaftesbury, but instead bequeathed the reversion of the estate after the lifetimes of one or more intervening heirs (a common type of bequest in Anglo-Saxon wills); perhaps Eadwig himself was the intermediate heir, which would have put him in a position to interfere with the reversion (he may simply have agreed to cede Tisbury immediately, if the other estate was returned to the royal patrimony). It is likely to have been the complication of these transactions which led the Shaftesbury community to seek to acquire a new diploma from Æthelred; this would forestall future royal claims on the estate made on the basis of the exchange in Eadmund's reign. Another motive for producing the charter was to record the restitution of a wood, which certain of the king's reeves had tried to confiscate; the name of this wood is now ludicrously corrupt, but was probably *Secghyll bær* (Sedgehill is the name of a settlement immediately west of Tisbury, and *bær* means 'swine-pasture').

There is no reason to question the authenticity of **28**. The formulation cannot be paralleled, but this is not unusual in Æthelred's reign, when charter-scribes gradually abandoned the regular use of repetitive standard formulation that had been characteristic of the central decades of the tenth century. Instead they tended to produce much longer and more literary compositions, with far less repetition; when they used standard formulas, they often reworked them and significantly altered their wording (thus in **28** the anathema and the introduction to the bounds are adaptations of standard 'Edgar A' formulas: compare **24, 26, 27**). This development is not incompatible with the continued production of royal diplomas primarily by a central agency (see Keynes, *Diplomas*, pp. 84–153), but it does imply a fundamental change of policy; there is presumably a connection with the apparent decline in the rate of production of formal diplomas which is first noticeable in Æthelred's reign and increasingly evident in the eleventh century. Although **28** lies outside the diplomatic mainstream as defined by Keynes, it seems acceptable as a charter of the given date. The witness-list is certainly contemporary; it has links with the witness-list of S 852, a charter in favour of a thegn preserved at Abingdon, and may have been drawn up on the same occasion (Keynes, *Diplomas*, pp. 90–1). The order of the subscriptions has been slightly corrupted in the course of transmission (*ibid.*, p. 243). In the manuscript the subscriptions, after those of the king and Archbishop Dunstan, are arranged in two columns. The first column lists the episcopal witnesses, four ealdormen and two thegns, while the second column begins with an ealdorman but otherwise contains only thegns. Keynes suggests that the subscriptions of the two thegns which appear at the bottom of the first column were inserted by the scribe to balance the two columns, thus separating one ealdorman from his peers; these particular thegns do not usually appear in a prominent position and were perhaps originally fourteenth and sixteenth, or sixteenth and seventeenth (Keynes follows the first alternative in his own table).

Tisbury was the site of the early minster whose possession of land at Fontmell was confirmed by the production of **1** in 759. It seems likely that the minster had been disbanded by the beginning of the tenth century. The celebrated Fonthill Letter (Whitelock, *EHD*, no. 102), which describes a complicated dispute over forfeited land and its resolution in the reign of Edward the Elder, indicates that Tisbury was then in the possession of the unruly Helmstan, one of the central protagonists, and that his repeated thefts led to its forfeiture to the king (see Keynes 1992, especially pp. 80–3). It is possible that Helmstan's holdings at Tisbury represented the central part of the former endowment of the ancient minster, and that this was passed on to Shaftesbury either by King Edward or in the reign of Æthelstan or Eadmund. Shaftesbury's manor at Tisbury was reckoned at twenty hides in 1066; this is likely to be a considerable underassessment, since the Domesday entry notes that there was capacity for forty ploughs (GDB 67v). Estimates of the extent of the manor depend upon disputed interpretations of the bounds of **28**. It was the opinion of Grundy (1920, pp. 90–6) that the survey outlined the later parishes of Tisbury and West Tisbury, with part of Wardour, but a more recent discussion (Jackson 1984) has indicated that the estate may also have included additional land to the west and north, comprising the later parishes of Sedgehill and Berwick St Leonard, and also part of Semley, Hindon and Chicklade. It may be significant that there is no separate Domesday entry for either Sedgehill or Berwick, although both certainly belonged to Shaftesbury in the early twelfth century; and the fact that the Shaftesbury community apparently had rights in 'Sedgehill swine-pasture' in connection with its Tisbury holdings reinforces the suggestion that its lands extended further west than Grundy believed. The details of Jackson's interpretation may need to be refined in places, but the argument that the survey includes land beyond the boundaries of Tisbury and West Tisbury is likely to be correct. For further discussion of the history of Tisbury and the extent of the manor, see *VCH Wilts.* XIII, pp. 195–248 (especially pp. 195, 208).

The survey begins in the south-eastern corner of the estate, where Chilmark brook 'shoots' to the river Nadder (ST 986300); the word *broc* has fallen out but can be supplied from the final boundary mark in the survey (see *PN Wilts.*, p. 186 n. 1). The boundary follows the course of the Nadder west to *gofesdene* (first element obscure, with *denu* 'valley'); this is likely to have been where the later parish boundary left the Nadder, to the north-west of Sutton Mandeville (approximately ST 981294). The survey now takes in an area to the south of the Nadder which formed part of Tisbury parish. The 'road-junction' (*twichen*) was at ST 976285, where Lagpond Lane meets Sutton Row. *Wilburge imare* is likely to be 'Wilburh's boundary' (fem. pers. n. Wilburh, (*ge*)*mære*), although Jackson has also suggested that *Wilburg* may have been an earlier name of Castle Ditches hill-fort, which the boundary now skirts to the south (with *burh*, 'fortified place'). From this point the boundary coincides for a short distance with the northern boundary of the Swallowcliffe estate conveyed in S 468. The two surveys have in common 'the green way' (*grene, weg*), 'Wærmund's tree' (pers. n. Wærmund, *treow*), 'the place where two streams meet' ((*ge*)*mythe*; *mythford* in S 468), a stream and 'the old wood ford' (*eald, wudu, ford*; *wida ford* in S 468). The 'green way' appears to be the track bounding Swallowcliffe Wood to the north, and the stream-junction occurs at ST 956277; the boundary stream was the westerly branch, and 'the old wood ford' was probably at the place where the later parish boundary left it and turned due west (ST 954273). The Tisbury boundary now parts company wth Swallowcliffe and proceeds past a group of pollarded trees, 'the head(-high) stumps' (*heafod, stocc*) and along 'the twelve plots of land' (*twelf, æcer*), probably a furlong containing twelve strips; the latter is remembered in Twelve Acre Copse in the woodland to the west of Squalls Farm (ST 955265; see *PN Wilts.*, p. 198). In *wealwege* the first element may be *wealh*, 'Briton' (but this could also be *weall-weg*, 'embankment way'). From here the survey passes along a 'hay-path' (*heg, hig, weg*) to an 'intermittent stream in a wood' (*wudu, flode*) and the 'ford of the southern pasture' (*suth, hamm, ford*), and then follows a hedgerow (*hege-ræwe*) back to the river Nadder. Grundy and Jackson confidently place these features along the line of the later parish boundary, which bisects the site of Old Wardour Castle and runs north-west and west through Wardour Park to join the Nadder at ST 922265. However, there is some suggestion that the Tisbury parish boundary may have been subject to later adjustment in the Wardour area (see *VCH Wilts.* XIII, p. 195). In 1086 the abbess of Wilton held a small estate at Wardour, assessed at a single hide (GDB 68r). This is difficult to identify, but presumably lay between the Shaftesbury estate of Donhead, the northern boundary of which ran through the southern part of Wardour Park (see **21**), and the Tisbury estate to the north or north-east.

After rejoining the Nadder, the boundary follows the river to its confluence with the river Sem (ST 924273) and then runs along the Sem itself (westwards). *Rodelee* is probably 'linear clearing or wood' (**rod, leah*); it seems to be equivalent to *radeleage* on the northern boundary of Semley (S 582), which presumably points to an instance of **rod* interchanging with *rad*, 'riding', in the sense 'road' (see discussion of these elements in Smith, *EPNE*, ii. 78, 86–7; *DEPN*, p. 378). It is from this point that the interpretations of Grundy and Jackson diverge. In Grundy's view the survey now describes the western boundary of West Tisbury, though he finds some difficulty because the boundary marks appear to be very close together. Jackson argues that the estate boundary in fact goes further west, to take in Semley Common and Sedgehill parish. The next boundary mark certainly supports his case: 'the white marsh' (*hwit, mersc*) is remembered in the name of Whitemarsh Farm in Sedgehill (*PN Wilts.*, p. 192). The next features mentioned are, 'maple-tree hill' (*mapuldor, hyll*), a stile (*stigel*) and *sapcumbe* (perhaps from *sæp*, 'sap, juice', with *cumb*). These are followed by a corrupt boundary mark, given as *cures rigt* and *cyrder it*; Jackson points to a corresponding *cowrige* in the thirteenth-century bounds of Gillingham Forest, which suggests that this feature was probably *cuna* (*h*)*rycg*, 'cows' ridge' (*cu*, gen. pl. *cuna*). After this the boundary touches on 'the wood or clearing with a pool' (*pol, leah*), the 'shared or common brook' ((*ge*)*mæne, broc*), 'willow brook' (*wiðig, broc*) and a moor or wasteland called *sidinic mor*, where the first word is obscure (perhaps *sidung*, 'extension'). Next comes 'knuckle wood or clearing' (**cnugel* or **cnuwel, leah*); the 'knuckle' was a prominent local ridge which gave its name to East and West Knoyle (*PN Wilts.*, pp. 175–6; *DEPN*, p. 283). In *hiclesham* the first element seems likely to be a personal name Hicel, so 'Hicel's enclosure or meadow' (*hamm*), although it might also be a word meaning 'green woodpecker', which occurs in later dialects as 'hickwall' (*BTSuppl.*). By this stage the boundary was probably running east of East Knoyle, at or near the north-western corner of West Tisbury parish (ST 897306). The 'boundary way' (*mearc, weg*) may be the track running east from here to Ruddlemoor Farm. The first part of *nipedeforde* is likely to be *Niprede* or Nippard, a place in Fonthill Old Park (*PN Wilts.*, p. 195); 'Nippard ford' seems to have been the stream-crossing at ST 923301. From here the boundary follows a 'way' until it reaches Fonthill. The name Fonthill is apparently composed of a British river-name *Font* with a second element corresponding to Welsh *ïal*, 'fertile upland region' (*PN Wilts.*, p. 190; *DEPN*, p. 183); it is now associated with two neighbouring villages, Fonthill Bishop and Fonthill Gifford. It seems likely that 'way' followed by the estate boundary from 'Nippard Ford' to 'Fonthill' was on the line of the road going north-east towards Fonthill Bishop. This was the path of the later parish boundary, which turned east just short of the village and then ran back towards Chilmark brook. Jackson argues that the survey in fact turns west from a point near Fonthill Bishop and takes in a separate area to the north, comprising Berwick St Leonard and perhaps part of Hindon. Some support for this suggestion comes in the fact that the survey at a later stage returns to 'Fonthill' (*eft on Funtal*). The intervening boundary marks are a highway (*here-pæð*), a combe called *gificancumbe*, where the first element may be *gifete*, 'plover' (Smith, *EPNE*, i. 200), a 'stone way' (*stan, weg*), a ridge, 'the little wood' (*lytel, wudu*) and 'Leofric's boundary' (*(ge)mære*). *Fintes bricge* is probably *funtes hricge*, referring to the prominent ridge south-east of Fonthill Bishop, which has a hamlet named Ridge at its eastern end; the first element may be a district-name *Funt* or *Font* (see discussion on p. 19). From here the survey proceeds along 'Æthelgar's (or Ælfgar's) boundary' (*(ge)mære*) to another group of pollards and back to Chilmark brook and its junction with the Nadder.

29

King Æthelred grants the cenobium of Bradford-on-Avon, Wiltshire, and its appurtenant lands to the nuns of Shaftesbury. A.D. 1001

C. BL Harley 61, 1r–2v: copy, s. xv
  Rubric: Hec est carta Aetheldredi regis de Bradeforda quam in perpetuum succedens testatur transcriptum ecclesie sancti Edwardi de Shaftisbury.
D. Bodleian, Dodsworth 38, 1r–2v: copy of C, s. xvii
E. Lawrence, Kansas, University of Kansas, Kenneth Spenser Research Library, Dept of Special Collections, MS E. 107, pp. 13–14; copy of C, s. xvii
Ed.: a. *Mon. Angl.*, i. 216–17
    b. Kemble 706
    c. *Mon. Angl.* (rev. edn), ii. 479–80 (no. 7)
    d. Pierquin, *Recueil*, pt 4, no. 74
    e. Pafford 1952, pp. 212–13 (bounds only, with translation and facsimile)
Listed: Sawyer 899; Finberg, *ECW*, no. 330
Edited from C

Conditore creaturarum uniuersalium, seu que in secretis celestibus ocellis hactenus latent humanis, seu que in terris uisibiliter patent, seu que in profundis gurgitibus fluctiuagis circumquaque trahuntur[a] discursibus, in sue incommutabilitatis firmissima eternaliter regnante stabilitate, cuncta que ab ipso et per ipsum et in ipso condita, redempta, uiuificata sunt, ineffabili sue magestatis regente priuilegio. Huius erumpnose ac miserime uite instabilitas flebilibus querimoniis sue defectionis iam iamque superuenientis laboriosum prenunciat terminum, quippe cum ueritatis preconium que[b] se, post uitam[c] protoplasti preuaricacionem, carnem nostre mortalitatis ut eam inmortalem

postmodum redderet ex intemerato semper uirginis utero pro salute tocius
humani generis induere dignata est, nostra suscipiens suaque haut[d] relinquens,
inter cetera sue ammonicionis eloquia ita dicendo omnibus proclamarat,[e]
'Cum uideritis hec fieri, scitote quoniam prope est regnum Dei. Amen dico
uobis quia non preteribit generacio hec, donec omnia fiant. Celum et terra
transibunt, uerba autem mea non transibunt'.[1] Attamen alicubi fidelium
undique consulendo saluti lucrumque requirens quas proprio liuore redemit
animarum,[f] saluberimum ut ita dixerim subministrauit antidotum, taliter
uniuersos commonens, 'Uendite que possidetis et date elemosinam',[2] 'et ecce
omnia munda sunt uobis'.[3] Talibus mandatorum Christi sentenciis a meis
frequencius premonitus consiliariis et ab ipso summo omnium largitore bonorum, dirissimis hostium grauiter nos depopulancium criberrime[g] angustiatus
flagellis, ego Aetheldredus rex Anglorum, ut supradicte merear particeps
fore promissionis, quoddam Christo ⟨et⟩[h] sancto suo, germano scilicet meo
Edwardo, quem proprio cruore perfusum per multiplicia uirtutum signa ipse
Dominus nostris mirificare dignatus est temporibus, cum adiacente undique
uilla humili deuocione offero cenobium[i] quod uulgariter et Bradeforda co-
gnominatur,[j] hoc mecum sub sapientum meorum testimonio tacite preiudicans,
ut supradictum donum sancto semper subiaceat monasterio et[k] Sceftesbirio
uocitato ac dicioni uenerabilis familie sanctimonialium inibi degencium, quatenus aduersus barbarorum insidias ipsa religiosa congregacio cum beati
martiris ceterorumque sanctorum reliquiis ibidem Deo seruiendi impenetrabile
optineat confugium et, adepto postmodum (si Dei misericordia ita preuiderit)
pacis tempore, rursus ad pristinum reuertantur[l] statum, ea tamen racione ut
in loco quem Domino optuli pars aliquantula ex ipsa[m] remaneat familia, que
diuini operis sedula[n] inibi iugiter expleat officia, hocque ut fieri[o] possit sapienti
consilio, prioris premeditetur industria; sin alias preuideat rectoris examinacio,
unde ibidem continue exerceatur ordo psalmodie, ut autem ista nostra donacio
incommutabilem capiat stabilitatem, et ut presentes quid obseruent uel quid
subsequantur certius agnoscant futuri, hoc interea hac scedula annotari dignum
duxi, quatinus prescripta uilla cum omnibus ad se rite pertinentibus, campis,
siluis, pascuis, pratis, ita sane ut ego ipse illam in usus pussederam[p] proprios,
uenerabili supradicte familie Christo sanctoque martiri incessanter famulanti
semper subiugetur liberrima, tribus tantummodo exceptis, communium
laborum utilitatibus, si contingat expedicionem promoueri, arcem pontemque
construi. Hocque regia precipimus auctoritate ut nullus[q] elacio uel musitacio[r]
altioris aut inferioris persone hanc nostram donacionem euertere seu minorare
presumat, hoc solummodo aduersus omnia contradicencium machinamenta
nostre dapsilitatis preualente priuilegio, presertim cum ego hoc, non priuatim
pro remedio anime mee, sed pro tocius nostre genealogie qui uel olim

preterierunt uel in posterum forte uenturi sunt generali salute^s dictauerim, nec istud decretum nostris tantum temporibus perduret inmutabile, uerum eciam et successorum meorum diebus, quos, quales, qui seu quoti futuri sunt^t Dei prescit eterna predestinacio. Quisquis autem hanc nostram munificenciam amplificare studuerit, augeatur ei in presenti temporis quieti longeuitas^u et in futuro centuplicate retribucionis celeste premium. Qui uero euertere aut in aliud quis^v transferre satagerit, adbreuientur hic dies uite ipsius, ut cum hiis qui Christo resistere^w nituntur in inferiori prolongentur inferno, ni uelocius recedat a peruersa meditacione et eum quem offendere non metuit dignis penitencie lamentis placare festinauerit. Hiis confiniis prescripta circumcingitur tellus.

Arest of seuen pipien^x on þere herepai þe schet suthþard withuten acceslegle,^{y} þurth ut wrindesholt, and swa anlang herepaies to alwines hlip gate, fram þane hlipgate forð be is landschare inne Auene, spa forð be streme inne Byssi, spa uppe Bissy on wret,^{z} spa on[. . .]ghes^{a2} wret^z þat it comet to brisnodes land share scu[.]can,^{b2} forð be his land share inne Spinbroch, forð be broke inne Pumberig, ut þurh Pumberig inne Tefleforde,^{c2} forð mid streme þat it cumet to alfperdes land imare at Þutenham, þannes of pigeþen^{d2} broke forð be lefpines imare innen Auene, forð be Auene þat it cumet to Ferseforde^{c2} þes abbotes imare innen Mitford, of þanne forde gyet be þes abbotes imare eft in to Auene, spo niþer be Auene þat it cumet eft to þes abbotes imare to Þerleghe, spa be þes abbotes imare to alfgares imare at Farnleghe, forð be is imare oð þat it cumet to þe kinges imare at Heselberi, forð be þes kinges imare þat it cumet to alfgares imare at Attenwrthe, forð be is imare þat it cumet to lefpines land imare at Coseham, of þan imare to þes aldremannes imare at Witlege, forð be þanne imare þat it comet to elfpiges imare at Broctune, to þanne þude þe ieraþ in to Broctune, eft at seuen pirien, forð be alnoþes imare innen aþelþines imare at Chaldfelde, of his imare innen alfþines imare þe horderes, forð be his imare innen alphwines imare at Broctune, eft^{e2} in to þe pyrien.

Scripta est siquidem hec cartula anno dominice incarnacionis millesimo primo, indiccione .xiiii., horum testimonio sapientum quorum onomata inferius descripta esse cernuntur.

Ego Atheldredus rex hanc largitatem Christo sanctoque martiri Edwardo humili optuli deuocione et ne nostra oblacio obliuionem forsan in posterum sortiretur omnia prout gesta sunt hac in scedula exprimi mandaui. +

Ego Alric Dorobernensis ecclesie archiepiscopus confirmaui. +

Ego Ealdpit^{f2} Eboracensis ecclesie archiepiscopus condixi. +

Ego Alestan^{g2} Uuentane ecclesie episcopus conscripsi. +

Ego Wlfstan London' ecclesie episcopus conclusi. +
Ego Ordbricht Australium Saxonum episcopus consigillaui. +
Ego Alphech Licetfeldensis ecclesie episcopus conquieui. +
Ego Liefwine^{h2} Fontane ecclesie episcopus coadunaui. +
Ego Wlsige Scirburnensis^{i2} ecclesie episcopus consensi. +
Ego Athelstan filius regis +^{j2}
Ego Ecgebirht filius regis +
Ego Edmund filius regis +
Ego Adred filius regis +
Ego Adwig filius regis +
Ego Adgar filius regis +
Ego Aþulf Herefordensis ecclesie episcopus +
Ego Alwoto^{k2} Cridiensis ecclesie episcopus +
Ego Godþine Rouecensis ecclesie episcopus +
Ego Algar^{l2} Orientalium Anglorum episcopus +
Ego Ascpig Dorcensis ecclesie episcopus +^{m2}
Ego Atheldred^{n2} Cornubensis ecclesie episcopus +
Ego Sigeferð Lindissi ecclesie episcopus +
Ego Alþerd abbas +
Ego Alfsige abbas +
Ego Wlfgar abbas +
Ego Alfuere abbas +
Ego Alfsige abbas +
Ego Leofric abbas +
Ego Godþuine abbas +
Ego Alfric dux +
Ego Alfhelm dux +
Ego Lefsige dux +
Ego Leofþne dux +
Ego Athelmar minister +^{o2}
Ego Ordulf minister +
Ego Wlfheah minister +
Ego Adric minister +
Ego Wluric minister +
Ego Athelric minister +
Ego Siþerd^{p2} minister +
Ego Sired minister. +
Ego Wlgar minister +
Ego Leofþine minister +

a trahant C   *b* *The subject of the clause* que ... dignata est *is* ueritas
c *This should probably be an adjective (Kemble silently emends to* notam; *perhaps read*
uitiosam)   *d* aut C   *e* *The subject of* proclamarat *is* ueritatis preconium
f ' ... *and seeking the profit of the souls which he redeemed with his own blood* ...'
g *A spelling for* creberrime   *h* a C (*for the emendation, compare the king's subscription*)
i ' ... *I present to Christ and to his saint, my brother Edward (whom, steeped in his own
gore, the Lord has seen fit to exalt in the present time with manifold miracles) a certain
monastery* (quoddam ... cenobium) *with the appurtenant vill in all directions* ...'
j cogminatur C   *k* OE æt
l *? For* reuertatur (*but the draftsman may have been thinking of* congregacio *as a
plurality*)   *m* ipa C   *n* seedula C   *o* aufieri C   *p* *A spelling for* possederam
q *Error for* nulla   *r* *A spelling for* mussitatio
s ' ... *not personally for the remedy of my own soul, but also for the general salvation of
our entire family, both those who have formerly lived and died and those who may come in
the future* ...' (*the scribe shifts from the collective noun* genealogia *to the distributive plural
in the relative clause*)   *t* *For* sint   *u* *Perhaps read* in presenti tempore quieta
longeuitas
v *Perhaps read* aliquid   *w* recistere C   *x* *Or* piþen; *read* pirien   *y* *For* accesleghe
z *Possibly for* were (*see commentary*)
a2 *Word partly illegible; probably* onlonghes (*for* andlang)   *b2* *Word partly illegible*
c2 -forð C   *d2* *Or* pigepen *or* þigepen, *etc.* (*probably for* piþigen)   *e2* ef C
f2 *For* Ealdpulf   *g2* *For* Ælfheah   *h2* *For* Lyfing   *i2* Seirburnensis C
j2 *This and the following nine subscriptions are arranged in two columns, to be read across
the page*   *k2* *For* Ælfwold   *l2* *For* Ælfgar
m2 *The subscriptions on 2v are arranged in two columns, to be read down the page. This
subscription is at the head of the first column*   *n2* *For* Ealdred
o2 *This subscription is at the head of the second column on 2v*   *p2* Siwerto C

¹ Luc. 21: 31–3
² Luc. 12: 33
³ Luc. 11: 41

29 stands at the very beginning of the Shaftesbury cartulary, a position which
indicates that it may well have been regarded as the most important of the abbey's
pre-Conquest diplomas. Not only was it the title-deed for the abbey's largest and
most valuable Domesday manor; it also contained material relating to the beginning
of the cult of Edward the Martyr, which was no doubt of considerable interest to
the later medieval community. This hagiographic dimension invites a degree of
caution, and it has indeed been suggested that the references to Edward may be the
result of interpolation or revision of a less fulsome charter (Patrick Wormald,
personal comment). **29** certainly presents considerable difficulties of interpretation,
both in relation to its language and syntax and also to what is known of the historical
background. Yet there seems to be no decisive argument for concluding that it is
other than an authentic and contemporary document.

In terms of its general formulation **29** seems fundamentally acceptable. As tended
to be the case in this period, the draftsman has avoided the use of standardized
formulas and has instead been at pains to compose a unique and highly literary text
(compare also **28** and **30**); the long and turgid proem is typical of those produced
at the turn of the tenth century. Keynes (*Diplomas*, pp. 104–7) points to small details

of formulation which link **29** with contemporary diplomas, especially S 904 (A.D. 1002) from Wherwell and S 906 (A.D. 1004) from Burton, and which would be compatible with the continued influence of a royal secretariat. **29** shares with S 904 and S 906 the dispositive verb *offerro*, not found in any other charter of Æthelred. The proems of **29** and S 904 have related themes, and both end with paired scriptural quotations; there are also points of comparison in the wording of the exposition, the main dispositive section, the reservation clause and the sanction, dating clause and royal subscription. It is unlikely to be a coincidence that both diplomas are in favour of nunneries; in addition, it would appear that the female community at Amesbury also had a similar diploma of approximately the same date (see Finberg, *ECW*, pp. 103–4; Keynes, *Diplomas*, p. 107 n. 66). Keynes further argues that elements of the formulas used in the group formed by **29**, S 904 and S 906 recur in two other charters issued in 1002 (S 900, 901). In the witness-list of **29** the verbs of attestation alliterate in *c*, a feature which is also found in S 906 (in S 904 the alliteration is in *a*). The grouping of a number of apparently Kentish thegns at the end of the witness-lists of both **29** and S 904 probably indicates that they were issued in Kent (Keynes, *Diplomas*, pp. 133–4). The names of several of the bishops are corrupt: 'Ælfstan' of Winchester is Ælfheah; 'Liefwine' of Wells is Lyfing; 'Alwoto' of Crediton is Ælfwold; 'Atheldred' of Cornwall is Ealdred. See also Keynes (*Diplomas*, p. 257) for discussion of the order of the witness-list.

The origins of the cult of Edward King and Martyr are obscured by the political reverberations of the murder in 978, but the indications are that it was already being promoted by King Æthelred and his advisors by the turn of the tenth century; in 1008 it was decreed that his feastday should be celebrated throughout England (see above, pp. xiv–xv; and Keynes, *Diplomas*, pp. 169–71). In **29** the king makes the grant 'to Christ and his saint, my brother Edward' and refers to the occurrence of miracles. The theme is hammered home throughout the text. Edward's relics are specified along with those of 'other saints'. Reference is made to the service offered by the Shaftesbury community to Christ 'and the holy martyr', and in his subscription Æthelred repeats that he has made this grant with humble devotion to Christ and 'the holy martyr Edward'. The stress on Edward's sanctity was calculated to enhance the position of Æthelred and succeeding members of the dynasty; so Æthelred states that he is acting, not only for his own salvation, but for that of 'our' lineage (*genealogia*) past and future (for the significance of this, see Ridyard, *Royal Saints*, pp. 165–6). The immediate context for **29** is provided by the events of 20 June 1001, when Edward's remains (or what were claimed to be Edward's remains) are said to have been translated on the king's orders from the churchyard of the minster to a safer location within the nunnery itself (see p. xiv). **29** dates from later in the year, after 7 October, for it includes the subscription of Ælfgar, bishop of Elmham, whose predecessor died on that date (Keynes, *Diplomas*, p. 257).

It is easy to see why Æthelred should have wished to make a major donation to the abbey which was the focus of the new cult, but much harder to explain why the grant should be presented as the establishment of a refuge for the community and its relics. The south of England certainly experienced devastating Viking attacks in 1001, most of them striking north from the Channel coast. However, the Shaftesbury burh lies on a highly defensible upland site, while Bradford-on-Avon is located on a navigable river within easy access of the Bristol Channel, and would presumably have been vulnerable to sea-borne invaders; it was hardly an *impenetrabile* ... *confugium* (for further discussion of Bradford's situation and history, see Haslam 1982, pp. 90–4). There is no obvious answer to this problem. One possibility is that an otherwise unrecorded disaster at Shaftesbury (perhaps a successful Viking attack or perhaps a simple domestic conflagration) had made it necessarily for the community to relocate on a temporary basis. The diploma appears to assume that the nuns will definitely move to their 'refuge', for it alludes to the possibility that the community might return to Shaftesbury at some point in the future; in this case some of the nuns were to remain at Bradford to ensure continuity of worship, or some other arrangements were to be made. If some catastrophe had forced the community to flee Shaftesbury, then it presumably took place after the translation of Edward's relics into the abbey church on 20 June. Alternatively, it could be argued that the idea of the refuge for the nuns and their relics was a smokescreen, introduced in order to justify a large land-grant to Shaftesbury by connecting the transaction with the requirements of the martyr's cult (for Shaftesbury's possible exploitation of its possession of Edward's relics, see Ridyard, *Royal Saints*, p. 170).

Bradford-on-Avon was traditionally the site of an early minster founded by Aldhelm; a spurious privilege in Aldhelm's name which is preserved in the Malmesbury archive (BCS 114) grants freedom of election to three monasteries, among them Bradford (see Edwards, *Charters*, pp. 115–16). William of Malmesbury's comments (*GP*, p. 346) seem in the main to represent extrapolation from the privilege, but he does mention that, while the monastery itself had vanished by his own day, there still existed on the site a small church (*ecclesiola*) dedicated to St Laurence. The latter is the chapel rediscovered in the nineteenth century and originally believed to date from Aldhelm's time; later examination revealed tenth-century architectural details, leading to suggestions that the present building is a total or partial re-construction of Aldhelm's church (Taylor and Taylor, *Anglo-Saxon Architecture*, i. 87). More recently it has been argued that Aldhelm's church was probably on the site of the present parish church, and that St Laurence's chapel was built on a separate site in the early eleventh century, perhaps specifically in connection with the transfer of the Shaftesbury community and its relics to Bradford (Haslam 1982, pp. 92–3). The description of Bradford in **29** as a *cenobium* appears to indicate that organised religious life of some kind existed there in 1001, but there seems little possibility of establishing continuity or lack of it with Aldhelm's monastery The territory or *uilla* attached to the *cenobium* may represent the residual endowment of the seventh-century minster; it is largely defined by rivers and streams, which would be appropriate boundaries for an early land-unit. In **29** Bradford is treated as a royal estate (Æthelred grants it 'ita sane ut ego ipse illam in usus pussederam proprios'), so the *cenobium* there was presumably a royal minster. Some years before King Eadred had made known his intention to bequeath Bradford to the community of Nunnaminster in Winchester (S 1515); none of the Eadred's other bequests can be shown to have been fulfilled, and there is some suspicion that the will was never implemented.

Bradford-on-Avon was Shaftesbury's largest Domesday manor, assessed at forty-two hides hides TRE, with an additional seven hides at an unidentified place called *Alvestone* (GDB 67v). The details of the lengthy boundary clause are sometimes difficult to explain on a map, but the general sweep is easily recognised because so many of the places mentioned are surviving settlements (see earlier discussions in Pafford 1952 and Grundy 1920, pp. 101–6). The bounds begin at the 'seven pear-trees' (*pirig*); these would have been located on the eastern boundary, probably somewhere to the west of Broughton Gifford. From here the boundary follows a road (*here-weg*) which ran south 'outside' of *accesleghe*, apparently 'Æcci's wood or clearing'; it is very tempting to connect this with the name of nearby Oxen Leaze Farm (ST 873626), although the latter is not recorded until very late (see *PN Wilts.*, p. 121) and the forms seem incompatible. *Wrindesholt* is almost certainly to be connected with the village of Holt; the first element is obscure and probably corrupt. The next boundary mark is 'Alwine's leap-gate' (pers. n. Ælfwine or Æthelwine or Ealhwine, *hliep-geat*), a gap or low part in a hedge or fence which permitted animals to cross; from this point the boundary corresponds with Alwine's boundary (*landscearu*) as far as the river Avon, which it follows to its confluence with the river Biss (ST 851597). The *wret* is evidently the brook joining the Biss near Trowbridge (ST 847583). There is some possibility that *wret* is a corruption or earlier form of *Were*, mentioned in certain contexts in the seventeenth and eighteenth centuries and apparently the origin of the place-name Warminster; but there is a degree of confusion as to whether the *Were* was a tributary of the Biss or the Biss itself (Ekwall, *River-Names*, pp. 449–50; *PN Wilts.*, pp. 10–11; Pafford 1952, pp. 215–16). The boundary follows the *wret* to Brisnoth's boundary (the meaning of the next word, damaged in the manuscript, is difficult to determine), and then passes on to 'swine brook', which survives in a prettified form in the name of Swansbrook Farm (ST 822562; *PN Wilts.*, p. 124); the brook itself is the stream joining the *Were* at ST 837566 and flowing south of the farm. *Pumberig* may have given its name to Pomeroy Wood (ST 808565) and Farm (ST 816568); *PN Wilts.* (p. 123) suggests that the original form was *plumberig* with later loss of *l* (as in Puncknowle, Dorset, for which see *DEPN*, p. 375), which would mean 'the *burh* marked by a plum-tree'. *Tefleforde* is Tellisford, Somerset; the first element appears to derive from OE *tæfl*, 'gaming board'. The ford was over the river Frome, which the boundary now follows northwards as far as the boundary of Ælfweard's estate at *Wutenham*; this was Wittenham, also known as Rowley, a lost place in Farleigh Hungerford (*PN Wilts.*, pp. 123–4). The stream called *wigepen* (or *wigewen* etc.) brook has not been identified; the first part of the compound is likely to be a corruption of *wipigen*, from *wipig*, 'willow-tree'. The survey passes along the boundary of Leofwine, the royal huntsman granted land at Westwood and Farleigh Hungerford in 987 (S 867), back to the river Avon, and then along the river to Freshford. At this point the meaning of the survey is not entirely clear and a word or two may have been lost; probably the boundary then ran along 'the abbot's boundary' to Midford. The abbot was Ælfhere of Bath, who was bequeathed an estate at Freshford by Wulfwaru at some point between 984 and 1016 (S 1538). The boundary presumably passed from Freshford to Midford, and then went up Midford Brook back to the Avon. After this the survey proceeds along the respective boundaries of an estate held by an abbot at Warleigh, Ælfgar's estate at (Monkton) Farleigh, a royal estate at Hazelbury (Manor, ST 835685), Ælfgar's estate at Atworth, Leofwine's land at Corsham, the ealdorman's estate at Whitley, and Ælfwig's estate at Broughton (Gifford), before passing on to a wood that was appurtenant to Broughton Gifford. The interpretation of the next section is difficult. Ostensibly the the survey returns to 'the seven pear-trees' and then follows

'Alnoth's boundary' (pers. n. Ælfnoth or Æthelnoth or Ealhnoth), Æthelwine's boundary at (Great or Little) Chalfield, the boundary of Ælfwine the 'hoarder', and Ælfwine's boundary at Broughton Gifford, before once more reaching the pear-trees for the third time. One possibility is that the second of the three references to the pear-trees is a mistake, but an alternative and preferable explanation is that the intervening section of the survey describes an internal boundary, defining a group of small estates in the vicinity of the Chalfields which were surrounded on all sides by the Bradford territory but were not reckoned as part of it.

30

King Cnut grants sixteen hides (cassati) *at Cheselbourne, Dorset, to* Agemund (*Aghmundr*), minister. A.D. 1019

C. BL Harley 61, 8r–9r: copy, s. xv
   Rubric: Hec est largicionis cartula regis Knut de Cheleburna.
D. Bodleian, Dodsworth 38, 7v–8r: copy of C, s. xvii
Ed.: a. Hutchins, *Dorset*, ii. 511 (in part, bounds omitted)
      b. Kemble 730
      c. Pierquin, *Recueil*, pt 6, no. 3
Listed: Sawyer 955; Finberg, *ECW*, no. 619
Printed from C

In trino superne deitatis nomine. Uniuersarum conditor gubernatorque rerum ex nichillo cuncta quicquid usquam est aut in superis summum quodue ceteris*a* amenum ineffabili magestatis sue imperio facta fore fecit, 'celum quippe' ut ueridici stoma prophete perite profert 'Domino, tellurem scilicet filiis hominum diuisit'.[1] Postquam uero protoplaustus*b* amaro uetiti gustamine mali preceptum hiriale*c* in obliuionis transgressum preteriens negligenter floccipendit felicemque paradisiace iocunditatis uetustatis*d* lugubriter amisit, ignoratur hucusque quid pro dolor mali, quid mesticie, quid meroris, quid angoris, quidue doloris humanum perpessum sit genus, ob illud quod antecessores fecerant scelus. Sed tandem omnicreantis pia Domini clemencia mortalibus benigniter misericorditerque permisit, quatinus terrenis mundi pragmatibus celica mercari ualeant tripudia, atque qui per boni operis fructum peruenerit*e* et in euum felices sine fine manebit.*e* Huius amande felicitatis gloria cordetenus ineffabili delectatus, ego Knut telluris Britannie tocius largiflua Dei gracia subpetente subtronizatus rex ac rector cuidam meo ministro appellamine Agemund eternam in hereditatem, sub potestatis mee regimine, aliquam impendo terene particulam mansionis, scilicet .xvi. cassatos ab incolis estimatam, in loci ipsius habitamine quod regionis illius accole Cheselburne nomine solito nuncupant in cosmo, scedulamque istam illi adnotare*f* mandaui quatinus calcetenus prefatum rus possideat postque

PLATE 1

her est una uel ... Regis ... ...
... ... cue se ... e Scæftesburi...

Conditore creaturarum universarum seu que in secretis celestib; ocu-
lis hactenus latent humanis seu que in terris insibilit' patent
seu que in profundis gurgitib; fluctinagis circumquaq; trahant' discursib;
In sue incomutabilitatis firmissima eternalit' regnante stabilitate suc-
taq; ab ipo et p ipm et in ipo condita redempta unificata sunt ineffabili
sue magestatis regente privilegio huius erumpnose ac miserrime uite instabilitas flebilib; querimoniis siue defectonis iam iamq; superuenientis
laboriosii pminat' finiu quippe cu ueritatis peronuit sz se post uitam protoplasti preuaricationem carnem uite mortalitatis ut eam immortalem
postmodu redderet ex intemerato semp uirginis utero pro salute totius
humani generis induere dignata est tua suscipiens suaq; aut reliques
Int cetera sue ammonitionis eloquia ita dicendo omnib; proclamarat Cum
inderitis hec fieri scitote sp ppe est regnu dei Amen dico uobis quia non
preteribit generatio hec doner omia fiant Celum et terra transibict uerba
aut mea no transibunt At tu alicubi fidelii indiq; consulendo saluti
lucrumq; requirens quas pprio liuore redemit animaq; saluberrimu ut ita dixerim subministrauit antidotu taliter uniuos commonens Vendite que possidetis et date elemosinam et ecce omia munda sunt uobis Talib; mandá-
tory xpi sentenciis a meis frequencius pmonitus consiliariis et ab ipo
summo omniu largitore bonoy diuissimis hostiu grauiter nos depopulancium eriberimur angustiatus flagellis ego Aetheldredus Rex angloy ut
supradicte merear particeps fore pmissionis qddam xpo a fro suo germano
scilicet meo Edwardo quem pprio cruore pfusu p multiplicia uirtutu signa
ipe dominus nris mirificare dignatus est temporib; Cum adiacente undiq;
nulla humili deuotione offero cenobii qd uulgarit' et Braffordia cognminat'
hoc meii sub sapientu meoy testimonio tuere peindicans ut supradicte
domu sco semp subiaceat monasterio et Scæftesburio nocitato ac dicioni uenera-
uil familie scimonialiu ubi degetuat quatenus aduisus barbaroy insidias
ipa religiosa congregatio cu bti martiris cetroy q stoy reliquiis ibidem dco
seruiendi impenetrabile optineat confugiu Et adepto postmodu si dei

PLATE 2

inio gratur·

Þis sint þa land mare to Aldeirsþumbe mest· of laugan riple up be Wurtru
ine on wlfgedytr · of wlfgedytr be wurtrinne · on dodeyoldding lege superbard
of troyewolding lege adune be dich· of yat dich : ford be wurtrinne on heahstu
nes quabben : ford be wurtrinne and lang riple at twelf akeres yrd landes be
þe heye wege went on pirtel made · :

Anno dniee Incarnacoinis D ccc lxvm· Scripta est her articula· hiis testibz
Ego Adgar Rex anglon concelli · Ego dunstan archiepc coroborani · ✝
Ego oscytrl archiepc confirmani · Ego Aþelwold epc confolidani· ꝛc ✝

Aþelstanus Rex hec inscripto uis sex manentes ad Tarentam
deo ꝛ ecclie sci Edwardi roboratum : ꝛ

Regem regum dnoꝰ dnoy regnoy regnum sublimiꝯ regente cunctoꝛ g
creaturaꝛ quas ipe ante scla et in scło ecłoꝛ meffabiliꝯ porduxmatos
moderanio condicoinis statu regulauit; uliuꝗ terregeno meffabiliꝯ creata
prolataꝗ ad antropon falutem concellit dnouice quibz tunc; humanoy g stat
effectus attini uoluntas atꝗ potestas · Iauro ille duncie cu mentis intencoine
diligenie funt; g nuꝗm deapimt· habentem ñ in ipa morte admittuntur· ꝓ
plus habuidant du cunt qd anat" · Qua ipr ego Aþelstanus nodante dei gra
bafileos angloy ꝛ eiue totius britannie orbis dei colariiꝗ tylos atꝗ auramul;
eoy ñ innocent diuinam amonicoinem obanidiens ꝓtem ruris ꝓꝗ inris mei
dicione fibattum in fernore amoris illius ein dixit· date et dabit" nobis·

libeus ꝓetuali libertate rbnenio conuono xpicolis uirginibz etare matris ihu
feruientibz in loco celebri at scþaftesburi uis sex manenciu in loco ein uulgari
dicoine · et apellatiua relacoine mcupat; ad trecentu feu fupꝛadicun eatenus
ut stis conanimbz mellita affistentina oꝛanina catꝗnatim inportinus
ꝓnbz ꝓetrata crnnina abitihnunt archointe ꝓetna impetrent; omnim inter
dicimus · ita ut her mn donaco in fempitino gꝓhio cu signuaculo sce crucis
confirmata sit· etiam si quiliber alius luteray distrepoines g fexat · ut antiqua
cartulam mdyl adiisu hanr ꝓtitulant; constitucoine · ꝯ mn indiaiꝗ a signo ste
cruas egetcoine contempta fiant et ad michillu ualeant· Sit aut ꝓdem Rus
cu omnbz ad fe rite ꝓtinentibz campis pratis liber excepto hiis tribz pontis
et artis constructoine expedicoinisꝗ aduunanine in cunctis futtectoxibz hor
ius donacoins augento consuantibz feliut ꝓuenuint mr celibes celestium

se cuicumque uoluerit liberaliter iure relinquat hereditario. Maneat igitur hoc meum inmobile donum eterna libertate iocundum cum omnibus que ad ipsa loca pertinere dinoscuntur, tam in notis causis quam ignotis, in magnis et in modicis, campis, pratis, pascuis, communi labore excepto, expedicione, pontis arcisue municione. Sed tamen torpentes auaricie incessus omnimodo in nomine agii saluatoris ab omnibus interdico,[g] eo uidelicet tenore ut meum donum corroboratum sit, eciam siquis alium antiquum libellum in propatulo protulerit, nec sibi nec aliis proficiat sed in sempiterno graphio deleatur et cum iustis non scribatur. Si qui denique mihi non optanti hanc libertatis cartam philargirie liuore depressi uiolari[h] satagerint, cum tetre tortionis agminibus delapsi uocem examinacionis ymera districti arbitris sibi horribiliter dicentis, 'Discedite a me maledicti in ignem eternum',[2] ubi cum zabulicis gehennarum parasitis ferreis sartaginibus crudeli torqueantur in pena, si non ante mortem digna hoc emendauerit penitencia. Prefata igitur tellus undique hiis limitibus circumgirari uidetur.

Arest of berteswelle on þare ealde diches heued, of þare dich on flexcumbes heuede, on þane ealde paþe, of þane paþe on þa ellen þirnen, of þare þirnen on Deueliscstream, anlang streames on þone hwitenwelle, of þane welle on þane bergh uppen morhelle, of þane berghe on þa ealde berig, of þane bery on þane rugen bergh, of þane bergh on se bergh, of seberghe on þorþiuel, of horþiuele onne þan pol, of þane pole inne þa þornen, of þare þyrnen on þane þorn up an gretindune, of þane þorne on þo stancysten on holencumbe, of þane stancyste on blacmanne bergh, of þanne berghe be anne hefden on hippepad,[i] of þane pade[i] on Cheselburne on shete bergh, of þane berghe on bradenbergh, of bradeberghe on þare diches hirne, of þere hirne on þorndunes cnep, of þane cneppe[j] on þane greate hlinc, of þare linke on burnestowe[k] on þat ealden reshbed, of þane bedde bi streame in þane miliere, of þane miliere on þo apeltreu, of þare apeltreu on þare haren torre on hipiscbergh, of þane berghe on liscbroc, uppe be broke on þa sticelen lane, of þare lane on þo tweie pettes, of þonne petten on þane hord þiuel, of þane þiuel on þane bergh, of þane bergh on anne þorn stub, of þane stubbe on þane imeren fyrs garan, of þan garan eft on berteswelle.

Scripta uero est hec cartula anno dominice incarnacionis .mxix. indiccione .ii., hiis testibus consencientibus quorum nomina infra cerraxantur.[l]

Ego Knut gracia Dei prestante rex hoc donum firmaui sigilloque agie crucis impressi. +
Ego Leuuig[m] archiepiscopus regis munificenciam Christi crucis uexillo pretitulaui. +
Elgiue thoro consecrata regio hanc donacionem sublimaui. +[n]

Ego Alfsige episcopus confirmaui. +
Ego Brihtƿine episcopus conscripsi. +
Ego Brithwold episcopus corroboraui. +
Ego Athelwine episcopus consolidaui. +
Ego Wine episcopus consensi. +
Ego Buruhwold episcopus non renui. +
Ego þurkil dux +
Ego Godwine dux +
Ego Yrc[o] dux +
Ego þelred[p] dux +
Ego Eilaf dux +
Ego Hacun dux +
Ego þrihƿig[q] abbas +
Ego Brithtmer abbas +
Ego Alfuere abbas +
Ego Arfnoð[r] abbas +
Ego Alfstan abbas +
Ego Brichnod abbas +
Ego Athelƿold abbas +
Ego Acun minister +
Ego Hastin minister +
Ego Aslac minister +
Ego Toga minister +
Ego Boui minister +
Ego Toui minister +
Ego Kaerl minister +
Ego Aþelmer minister +
Ego Alfget minister +
Ego Brichtric minister +
Ego Siward minister +
Ego Admund minister +
Ego Brichtrich minister. +

[a] *Probably for* in terris [b] protoplaustis C [c] *Probably for* kiriale
[d] *For* uetustatem [e] *These verbs should be in the plural* [f] *Probably for* illo adnotari
[g] intdico C [h] *For* uiolare (*all examples of this formula have the same reading*)
[i] *Probably for* pað(e) [j] sneppe C [k] burestowe C [l] *A spelling for* carraxantur
[m] *For* Leuing (Lyfing) [n] *The remaining subscriptions are written across the page*
[o] *For* Yric (Eiríkr) [p] *For* Æþelred [q] *For* Brihtƿig [r] *For* Ælfnoð

[1] cf. Ps. 113: 16
[2] Matt. 25: 41

There is no reason to think **30** other than authentic. The formulation represents a development of trends apparent in the diplomas of Æthelred, towards literary elaboration and the rejection of standardization (see also **28, 29**). The diploma was conceived as a unique production, rather than a concoction of recycled formulas. The draftsman has exercised himself with a long literary proem on the theme of the Creation and Fall, which is not found elsewhere and was probably devised specifically for this text. The royal style, while not particularly extravagant, cannot be precisely paralleled and is probably a new coinage. The conventional patterns of the dispositive section are sometimes upset by the use of unusual vocabulary (for example, *habitamen*) and the introduction of novel phrases (such as *solito . . . in cosmo*). In the business section the draftsman has been rather less self-indulgent; the immunity clause is a standard formula, as is the proscription of any earlier charter. But the anathema is a subversive elaboration of a standard formula devised at the end of Æthelstan's reign and in regular use from 939 until 960 (see also **15, 16**). Comparing **30** with other diplomas of Cnut is problematic, since relatively few authentic texts survive; this seems to reflect an acceleration of the decline in charter-production which began under Æthelred (see **28**, and Keynes, *Diplomas*, pp. 140–5). The extant diplomas are very various. Some, like **30**, can be considered as the descendants of the lengthy literary productions so common in Æthelred's reign; others are more modest texts, using standard formulas, which look back to the diplomas produced in the central decades of the tenth century. It is difficult to decide whether the evidence of the surviving charters is compatible with the continued existence of a central agency responsible for the greater part of charter-production (see discussion by Lawson, *Cnut*, pp. 236–43; Keynes 1994a, pp. 48–52).

The witness-list seems to have been preserved in full. Six bishops attest, apart from Archbishop Lyfing of Canterbury: Ælfsige of Winchester, Brihtwine of Sherborne, Brihtwold of Ramsbury, Æthelwine of Wells, Buruhwold of Cornwall and an inconveniently abbreviated Wine (the candidates for identification are Ælfwine of Elmham, Godwine of Lichfield and Godwine of Rochester). There are also subscriptions of six ealdormen, four Scandinavian (Thorkell the Tall of East Anglia, Eiríkr of Northumbria, Eilífr of Mercia, and Hákon, the location of whose earldom is unclear) and two Englishmen (Godwine of Wessex and a certain Æthelred): for their careers and other attestations, see Keynes 1994a. The majority of Cnut's charters are attested by a number of abbots; here the list is headed by Brihtwig of Glastonbury and Brihtmær of Old Minster, Winchester. The first seven thegns in the witness-list have Scandinavian names; the Anglo-Saxons are grouped at the end.

The beneficiary of **30** appears to have been a Danish follower of Cnut named Aghmundr, who was being rewarded with an estate in Dorset. His subscription appears in the witness-list of S 961 (A.D. 1024), another Dorset charter, and also in S 959, a spurious charter in the archive of Christ Church, Canterbury, which is partly based on a genuine document from Cnut's reign. *Agemund* was one of a number of Scandinavian thegns whom Cnut established in the south-west. Orc, remembered as the founder of Abbotsbury minster, was given seven hides at Portesham in Dorset in 1024 (S 961), and seventeen hides at Abbotsbury itself at some point in Cnut's reign (S (Add.) 1602d; see Keynes 1989, pp. 229–31); he was later granted another Dorset estate by King Edward (S 1004). A third thegn, Bovi, received seven hides at Horton in Dorset (S 969; O'Donovan, *Sherborne*, no. 20); he was one of the witnesses of **30**. For the background, see Stenton, *ASE*, pp. 413–14; Keynes 1989, pp. 230–1; and Lawson, *Cnut*, pp. 163–74.

Aghmundr's Cheselbourne estate was transferred to Shaftesbury at some point before King Edward's death in 1066. According to the Domesday entry Earl Harold seized Cheselbourne from the community, along with other estates at Stour, Melcombe Horsey and *Pidele*; after the Conquest a writ of the Confessor was discovered in the abbey church ordering their restitution, and this was implemented (at least with regard to Cheselbourne and Stour) by King William (GDB 78v; see p. xxiii). Shaftesbury's Domesday manor at Cheselbourne was assessed at sixteen hides, and presumably represents the same land that was granted to Aghmundr. Fifteen hides of this land had belonged in 942 to a nun named Wynflæd, who was probably the mother of Ælfgifu, first wife of King Eadmund (**13**). Supposedly earlier documentation for the estate exists in the form of **5** and **6**, which are not acceptable in their present form.

The survey in **30** appears to describe the whole of the modern parish of Cheselbourne, with the exception of an area in the north-west around Lyscombe Bottom which was a relatively recent addition (see Grundy 1934, pp. 115–20, and discussion of individual boundary marks in *PN Dorset*, iii. 202–8). The survey begins on the north boundary at 'Beorht's spring' (pers. n. Beorht, *welle*), probably a reference to the source of the Cheselbourne stream at ST 755014. Next comes 'the upper end (*heafod*) of the old ditch (*eald, dic*)' which is equivalent to the *twifeald dic* of **13**; this appears to be the earthwork at ST 758014. 'Flax combe' (*fleax, cumb*) also occurs in the earlier survey. From here the boundary follows 'the old path' (*eald, pæð*) to 'the elder thorn-bush' (*ellen, ðyrne*). It then reaches Devil's Brook, probably at ST 774013, and follows it for a short distance before turning east, to take in an area to the east of the Brook. (It is here that the boundary clause in **5** and **6** diverges from the surveys in **13** and **30**; the 'earlier' circuit omits the area east of Devil's Brook, possibly because it is defective.) In **30** the boundary follows the stream to 'the white spring or stream' (*hwit, wella*) and then proceeds to the barrow (*beorg*) on 'moor hill' (*mor, hyll*), 'the old fortified place' (*eald, burh*), 'the rough(-surfaced) barrow' (*ruh*, wk obl. *ruwan, beorg*) and 'the sea barrow' (*sæ, beorg*), which was perhaps used as a sea-mark (see *PN Dorset*, iii. 207). The next boundary mark is a thicket (*pyfel*). The first element is given as both *þor* and *hor*; this could be a mistake for *thorn*, 'thorn-tree', but *hor*, 'muddy', would also be acceptable. The 'pool' (*pol*) was probably at the place where the later parish boundary recrossed Devil's Brook (ST 777000). On the western bank was a thorn-bush (*ðyrne*), and a thorn-tree on 'the great hill' (*great, dun*); the hill would have been that between Devil's Brook and the Cheselbourne stream. The *stancysten* must be equivalent to the *stan castel*, 'heap of stones', referred to at this point in **5** and **6**; this was located in 'hollow combe' (*hol*, wk obl. *holan, cumb*). The next boundary marks are 'Blæcmann's barrow', also mentioned in the bounds of **5** and **6**, a 'headland' (*heafod*) and *hippe pad* (perhaps an unrecorded pers. n. *Hippa*, with *pæð*, 'path'; see *PN Dorset*, iii. 206). At this point the survey reaches the Cheselbourne stream, which it follows for a very short distance before striking west again. *Shete bergh* is probably the same feature as *ceatwan bergh*, 'Ceatwa's barrow', mentioned in **6**. Next come 'wide or spacious hill or tumulus' (*brad, beorg*), the angle or corner (*hyrne*) of a ditch, the top (*cnæpp*) of 'thorn hill' (*ðorn, dun*) and 'the great linchet' (*great, hlinc*). At this point the boundary meets the brook flowing south from Lyscombe Bottom; in this case *burnstowe* appears to mean 'channel or bed of an intermittent stream' (see *PN Dorset*, iii. 205–6). 'The old rush-bed' (*eald, risc-bedd*) would be associated with such a feature. The boundary then follows the stream to the *myln-gear*, an enclosure for catching fish ('yair') located by a mill. From here the survey takes in an area to the west of the brook. The next boundary marks are an apple-tree (*æppel-treow*), 'the hoary crag' (*har, torr*) and a barrow or hill (*beorg*) known as *hiwiscbergh*, where the first element is apparently *hiwisc*, 'hide' or perhaps 'homestead'. The boundary rejoins the brook, now referred to as *liscbroc* (see *PN Dorset*, iii. 203) and follows it upstream to 'the steep lane' (*sticol, lane*) and 'the two pits' (*pyt*). By this point the survey must be describing the northern boundary. *Hord þivel* is another thicket (*þyfel*); the first element appears to be *hord*, 'treasure'. The boundary continues past an unnamed barrow (*beorg*), the stump (*stybb*) of a thorn-tree, and 'the furze-covered gore (triangular plot) on the boundary' ((*ge*)*mære, fyrs, gara*) back to its starting-point.

INDEXES

In these indexes *w* is substituted for *p* and *uu* is alphabetized as *w*. *Th* is substituted for *ð* and *þ*, except in index 3. Square brackets [ ] contain editorial comments. Charters are referred to by their numbers, in bold type; other references are to the pages of the introduction and the commentaries.

1. INDEX OF PERSONAL NAMES

This is an index of names and titles rather than individuals. References to those with the same name and rank are grouped together. Ecclesiastics have been identified as far as possible, and where two or more bishops of a see had the same name, they have been distinguished by the numbers conventionally assigned to them. Those names which occur in more than one variant form, or which figure in discussion in the commentaries, are given in normalized form, with the variants noted in brackets.

Acun *see* Hakon
Adelstan, bishop, *see* Ealhstan, bishop [of Sherborne]
Adgiue *see* Eadgifu
Adgar *see* Edgar
Admund *see* Eadmund
Adred *see* Eadred
Adric *see* Eadric
Adric, king, *see* Eadwig
Adulf *see* Eadwulf
Adward *see* Edward
Adwi(g) *see* Eadwig
Adwid, king, *see* Eadwig
Adwlf *see* Eadwulf
Ælfflæd (Alfled), **2**; 12–13, 16
Ælfgar (Alfgar), bishop [of Elmham], **29**; 119
—minister **23**, **28**
—**21**

Ælfgifu (Alfgiue, Alfgife, Algife, Algiue, Elgiue), wife of King Eadmund, **28**; xiii–xiv, xxvii; 56, 104, 110–11, 126
—wife of King Cnut (Emma), **30**
Ælfheah (Alestan, Alfech, Alfeth, Alpech, Alphec, Alphech), bishop [of Lichfield], **28**, **29**
—(I) bishop [of Winchester], **9**, **10**, **11**, **12**, **13**, **16**
—(II) bishop of Winchester, **29**; 119
—*minister*, **18**, **23**
—**21**
—**75**

Ælfhere (Alfhere, Alfuere), abbot [of Bath], **29**, **30**; 121
—*dux*, **21**; xiv
Ælfnoth (Arfnoth), abbot, **30**
Ælfred, bishop (Alfred, Alfricus, Alfridus, Alured), **7** [*see also* Alfred, Ealhferth]
—bishop [of Sherborne], **10**, **13**; 41–2, 100
—bishop [of Selsey], **16**, **17**; 71
—ealdorman, 46
—minister, **12**, **16**, **21**, **23**
Ælfric (Alfric, Alric, Aluric, Eluric), archbishop of Canterbury, **29**
—*minister* and bishop, **10**; 41 (? *for* Alfred)
—bishop [of Ramsbury], **12**, **13**, **16**
—bishop [of Crediton], **28**
—*dux*, **23**, **28** (*bis*), **29**
—*minister*, **12**, **16**, **28**
Ælfsige (Alfinus, Alfsige, Alfsinus, Alsige), (I) bishop [of Winchester] **18**, **21**, **22**, **23**
—(II) bishop of Winchester, **30**; 125
—abbot [of New Minster, Winchester], **29**
—abbot [of Ely], **29**
—*minister*, **12** (*bis*), **13**, **16**, **18**, **23**, **24**, **28**; 99
—**13**, **21**; 26, 57
Ælfstan (Alfstan, Elfstan), bishop [of London or Rochester], **28** (*bis*)
—abbot, **30**
—*princeps*, **5**; 24–6, 57
—alderman, **6**

129

—*minister*, **13**, **16**

Ælfthryth (Alfthrith), religious woman, **16**; xxvii; 68

Ælfweard (Alfwarth, Alwerd), abbot [of Glastonbury], **29**
—minister, **28**

Ælfwold (Alwold, Alwoto), bishop [of Crediton], (I) **18**, **23**; 74
—bishop of Crediton (II), **29**; 119

Ælmær, 104

Æscwig (Ascwig, Aswig), bishop [of Dorchester], **28**, **29**

Æthelbald (Adelbald, Adelbaldus), king of the West Saxons, **3**; 17, 21
—king of the Mercians, 8

Æthelberht (Aedelbert, Athelberd, Athelbert), king of the West Saxons, **3**, **4**; 18, 21
—(II), king of Kent, 6

Æthelflæd, ruler of the Mercians, 61

Æthelfrith, ealdorman, 61
—104

Æthelgar (Alfgar), bishop [of Crediton], **12**, **13**, **16**, **17**; 71
—bishop of Selsey, **28**

Æthelgeard (Athelgerd), *minister* **13**, **16**

Æthelgifu (Agelyue, Ayeleua), daughter of King Alfred, **7**; xiii, xiv n. 6; 29

Æthelheah (Adelheach, Adelheacus), bishop [of Sherborne], **7**; 30

Æthelmær (Athelmar, Athelmer), *minister*, **28**, **29**, **30**
—**21**; xv n. 11

Æthelmund (Athelmund), *dux*, **12**, **13**

Æthelred (Atheldred, Athelredus, Athered, Athred, Thelred), king of the West Saxons, **5**, **6**; 17–18, 21, 24–5, 50, 69
—king, **28**, **29**; xiv, xxvii; 111, 119–20, 125
—king of the Mercians, 8
—*filius regis*, **4**
—archbishop of Canterbury, **7**; 30
—*dux*, **30**; 125
—minister, **12**, **13**, **23**
—75

Æthelric (Athelric, Atheric), *minister*, **12**, **29**

Æthelsige (Aethelside, Athelsige), bishop of Sherborne, **28**
—*dux*, **18**, **21**, **23**
—minister, **16**, **28**

Æthelstan (Athelstan), king, **8**, **9**, **10**; xiv n. 6, xxiv, xxvi; 30, 33, 37, 41, 45, 74–5, 112, 125
—*filius regis*, **29**; xv
—'Half-king', ealdorman, 61
—*dux* **12**, **13** (*bis*), **16**, **18** (*bis*), **21**

Æthelweard (Athelward, Athelweard, Athelwerd), *dux*, **28**
—minister, **21**, **28**

Æthelwine (Ailwine, Alwine), bishop [of Wells], **30**; 125
—*dux*, **28**
—*minister*, **21**

Æthelwold (Atelwold, Athelwold), bishop [of Winchester], **25**, **26**, **27**, **28**; 102
—abbot, **30**
—*dux*, **12**, **13**; 61

Æthelwulf (Atelwlfus, Athulf), king of the West Saxons, **13**, **17–18**
—bishop of Hereford, **28**, **29**
—7

Æthulf, bishop of Elmham, 102

Agar *see* Edgar

Agebertus *see* Ecgberht

Agemund *see* Aghmundr

Aghmundr (Agemund), *minister*, **30**; 27, 58, 125–6

Agilbert, bishop of the West Saxons, 7

Ailwine *see* Æthelwine

Alcheferd *see* Ealhferth

Aldhelm, 120

Alestan *see* Ælfheah

Alfech *see* Ælfheah

Alfgar, bishop, **12**, **16** [*for* Æthelgar, bishop of Crediton]

Alfget, *minister*, **28**

Alfhelm, *dux*, **29**

Alfherth *see* Ealhferth

Alfred (Alured), king of the West Saxons, **7**; xiii, xxiii, xxvi; 6, 18, 25, 29–30, 46, 72 [*see also* Ælfred]
—of Marlborough, 18

Alfwig, *minister*, **23**

Alfwine, *minister*, **28**

Alhstan *see* Ealhstan

Alstanus *see* Ealhstan

Aluric *see* Ælfric

Alwerd *see* Ælfweard

Alwine *see* Æthelwine

Arnfoth *see* Ælfnoth

Arundell, Matthew, xvii n. 20

Arundell, Sir Thomas, xv, xvii

Arundell, Thomas, Baron Wardour, xvii n. 20

Aslac, *minister*, **30**

Asser, xiii, xxiii

Atheric *see* Æthelric

Athulf *see* Æthelwulf

Aubrey, John, xviii

Baldwin the Sheriff, 97

Bearnwine *see* Beornwyn

Bectun, abbot, **1**; 5–9

Beorhthun (Berctun), 6

Beornoth, *dux*, **28**

Beornwyn (Bearnwine), **2**; 12–13

Beorhtere, **10**

Beorhtwyn (Beorhtwine), daughter of Wulfhelm, 10; xxvii; 41, 56, 100

Beorthwold, *minister*, 28

Berhtwulf (Berthful, Berthwlfus), 7

Bierferth *see* Byrhtferth

Boui, *minister*, 30; 125

Brichnod, abbot, 30

Brichtric (Brichtrich), *minister*, 30 (*bis*)

Brihtgifu (Birthgiue), 27; xxvii

Brihthelm (Berhtelm, Bricthem), bishop [of London, Selsey or Wells], 18, 21 (*bis*), 22, 23 (*bis*)

Brihtmær (Brithtmer), abbot [of Old Minster, Winchester], 30; 125

Brihtric (Brithric), ['Grim'], *minister*, 18; 74–5

Brihtwig (Thrihwig), abbot, 30; 125

Brihtwine, bishop [of Sherborne], 30; 125

Brihtwold (Brithwold), bishop [of Ramsbury], 30; 125

Brithtmer *see* Brihtmær

Burgric (Bulgrif), bishop [of Rochester], 12, 13

Buruhwold, bishop [of Cornwall], 30; 125

Byrhtferth (Bierferth, Birhtferd, Byrtferth), *dux*, 18, 21
—*minister*, 23

Catwali, abbot, 1; 5, 7

Cenwold (Kenward), bishop [of Worcester], 12, 13, 18

Cerdic, *prefectus*, 1

Cinsige, bishop [of Lichfield], 18

Cnut (Knut), king, 30; xxvii; 26, 57, 125

Coenred (Coinredus), 1; 4–9

Coinredus *see* Coenred

Cuna (Cyma), 7

Cuthred (Kudredus), *alderman*, 7; 30

Cwoenthryth, abbess of Minster-in-Thanet, 6

Cyma *see* Cuna

Cyna the Old, 23; 96

Cyneberht (Cunibertus), abbot [of Redbridge], 1; 7

Cyneheard (Cyniheardus, Kyneheardus), bishop [of Winchester], 1; 4–9

Cynewulf (Kinewlf), king of the West Saxons, 1; 5, 9

Daniel, bishop [of Cornwall], 21

D'Ewes, Sir Simonds, xviii

Dodsworth, Roger, xviii

Dunstan, archbishop [of Canterbury], 24, 25, 26, 27, 28; 71, 102

Eadgifu (Adgiue), *regis mater*, 13, 16; xiii, xxvii; 71–2

Eadmund (Admund, Admundus, Edmund),

king, 11, 12, 13, 14, 15, 28; xiii, xxvi; 9, 26, 50–2, 56–7, 64, 96, 104, 110–12, 126
—*filius regis*, 29
—*dux*, 13 (*for minister*), 18, 23
—*minister*, 12, 13 (*dux in error*), 16, 29, 30

Eadnoth, 75

Eadred (Adred, Adredus), king, 16, 17, 18, 20; xxvii; 64, 71, 74–5, 82, 94, 96, 120
—*regis frater*, 11, 12, 13
—*filius regis*, 29
—13

Eadric (Adric), *comes*, 14; 61
—*dux*, 13, 16
—*vassallus*, 12; 51
—*minister*, 23, 29

Eadwig (Adric, Aduig, Adwi, Adwic, Adwid, Adwig, Adwith), king, 19, 21, 22, 23, 28; xxiv, xxvi; 30, 45, 64, 71–2, 74–5, 78, 87–8, 94, 96, 110–11
—*cliton*, 18
—*filius regis*, 29

Eadwulf (Adwlf, Radwlfus), *ealdorman*, 7; 30
—*homo*, 11
—13

Ealdred (Atheldred), bishop of Cornwall, 29; 119

Ealdwulf (Ealdwit), archbishop of York, 29

Ealhferth (Alcheferth, Alfherth, Alfredus, Ealferth), bishop [of Winchester], 5, 6, 7; 25, 30

Ealhhelm (Ealhdem, Elhhelm), *dux*, 12, 13, 16

Ealhstan (Adelstan, Alhstan), bishop [of Sherborne], 2, 3, 4; 12, 18, 21

Ecgberht (Agebertus, Ecgebirht), king of the West Saxons, 2; 11–13
—*filius regis*, 29

Edgar (Adgar), king, 24, 25, 26, 27; xxiii; 56, 71–2, 75, 94, 99, 102, 104
—*clito(n)*, 18, 21
—*regis frater*, 19
—*filius regis*, 29

Edward (Adward, Edwardus) the Elder, king, xiii, xxvi; 11, 112
—son of King Alfred, 7; 30
—(the Martyr), king, 29; xiv–xv; 69, 118–20
—(the Confessor), king, xv; 27, 58, 104, 125–6

Egwald, abbot [of Tisbury], 1

Eilífr (Eilaf), *dux*, 30; 125

Eiríkr (Yrc), *dux*, 30; 125

Elfstan *see* Ælfstan

Eluric *see* Ælfric

Emma, Queen, 104 (*see also* Ælfgifu)

Goda, Countess, xviii

Godwine, bishop of Rochester, 29
—abbot, 29

—*dux*, **30**; 125
—*minister*, **28**, **29**

Hædde (Hadde), abbot, **1**; 7
Hakon (Hacun, Acun), *dux*, **30**
—*minister*, **30**
Harding fitz Alnoth, 52
Harold, earl, xv, xxiii, xxvi–xxvii; 27, 58, 75, 104, 126
Hastin, *minister*, **30**
Heahmund, bishop [of Sherborne], **5**, **6**; 25
Helmstan, 111–12
Herewald, bishop [of Sherborne], **1**; 9

Ine, king of the West Saxons, 6, 8–9

Judith (Iudith), queen, **3**

Kaerl, *minister*, **30**
Kenward *see* Cenwold
Kinewlf *see* Cynewulf
Knut *see* Cnut
Kudredus *see* Cuthred

Lefsige, *dux*, **29**
Leofa, *minister*, **23**; 100 (*see also* Wulfgar Leofa)
Leofric, abbot [? of Muchelney], **29**
—*minister*, **28** (*bis*)
Leofwine, bishop [of Lindsey and Dorchester], **18**
—*dux*, **29**
—*minister*, **28**, **29**
—king's huntsman, 121
Leuthere (Leotherius), bishop [of the West Saxons], **1**; 6–9
Leuuig *see* Lyfing
Liefwine *see* Lyfing
Lowe (Law, Low), Sir John, xviii
Lyfing (Leuuig, Liefwine), archbishop [of Canterbury], **30**; 119
—bishop of Wells, **29**; 119

Mildred (Midred, Mildredus), *thegn*, 7
Mortain, Count of, xxiii; 104

Oda (Odda, Odo), archbishop [of Canterbury], **12**, **13**, **14**, **15**, **16**, **17**, **18**, **19**, **20**; 52, 71
—*dux*, **13** (*error for minister*)
—minister, **12**, **13** (*dux in error*)
Offa, king of the Mercians, 45
Orc, 125
Ordbriht (Ordbritht), bishop of Selsey, **29**
Ordeah, *minister*, **12**
Ordulf, *minister*, **28**, **29**
Osburh, wife of King Æthelwulf, 18

Oscytel (Oscytelin, Oscytil), archbishop [of York], **24**, **26**, **27**
—bishop [of Dorchester], 21
Osferth, 72
Oslac, 18
Osmund, *minister*, **3**, **4**; 17–18
Osric, *dux*, **3**, **4**; 18
—7
Osulf, bishop [of Ramsbury], **18**, **21**, **22**, **23**, **24**
Oswold, archbishop of York, **28**

Phillipps, Sir Thomas, xvii

Rawlfus *see* Eadwulf
Roger Arundel, 104

Schutz, Thomas, xviii
Scilling, *prefectus*, **1**
Seaxwulf, bishop [of Lichfield], 8
Sigeferth, bishop of Lindsey, **29**
Sigestan, *minister*, **25**; 102
Sired, *minister*, **29**
Siward (Siwerto), *minister*, **29**, **30**; 97
Spelman, Henry, xviii
Swithhun (Suidhun, Suithhun), bishop [of Winchester], **3**, **4**; 18, 21

Thelred *see* Æthelred
Theodred (Thedred), bishop [of London], **12**, **13**, **14**, **15**, **16**, **20**
Thorkell (Thurkil), *dux*, **30**; 125
Thrihwig *see* Brihtwig
Thurkil *see* Thorkell
Thurstan, 52, 88
Tidbald, abbot, **1**
Toga, *minister*, **30**
Toui, *minister*, **30**
Tumberht (Tumbert, Turebertus), abbot, 7; 30
Twynyho (Twyneyne), Margery, abbess of Shaftesbury, xvii

Uhtred (Uhterd), *dux*, **12**, **13**

Walenburh (Walenburch), **2**; 12–13
Wenflede *see* Wynflæd
Wihtsige (Wihsige, Withsige), *minister*, **19**, **20**; 68
William (the Conqueror), king, xxiii, xxvii; 27, 58, 68, 79, 82, 97, 104, 126
William of Malmesbury, xiv n. 6; 75, 120
Wimbertus *see* Wynberht
Wine, bishop, **30**; 125
Winfled *see* Wynflæd
Wintra, abbot [of Tisbury], **1**; 5, 9
Withgar, *minister*, **12**, **13**
Wlf- *see* Wulf-
Wlsige *see* Wulfsige

Wulfgar (Wlfgar, Wlgar, Wulgar), bishop of Ramsbury, **28**
—abbot, **29**
—*dux*, **12**, **13** (*bis*, second instance in error for *minister*)
—*minister*, **12**, **13** (*dux in error*), **15**, **23**, **29**; 64–5, 94, 96–7
—Leofa, **22**; 65, 94 (*see also* Leofa)
Wulfheah (Wlfheah), *minister*, **29**
Wulfhelm (Wlfhelm, Wlfhelmus), archbishop [of Canterbury], **8**, **9**, **10**; 52
—bishop [of Wells], **12**, **13**, **18**
—*minister*, **12**
—father of Beorhtwyn, **10**; 41
Wulfhere (Wlfhere), Ealdorman, **7**; 30
Wulfred, archbishop of Canterbury, 6
Wulfric (Wluric, Wuluric), *minister*, **12**, **16** (*bis*), **21**, **23**, **28**, **29**

Wulfsige (Wlfsige, Wlsige), (II) bishop [of Sherborne], **16**, **18**, **21**
—(III) bishop of Sherborne, **29**
—*minister*, **28** (*bis*)
Wulfstan (Wlfstan, Wlfstanus, Wlstan), archbishop [of York], **8**, **13**, **18**; 74
—bishop of London, **29**
Wullaf (Wllaf), *minister*, **12**, **13** (*dux in error*)
Wynflæd (Wenflede, Winfled), grandmother of King Edgar, nun, **13**, **26**; xiv, xv n. 11, xvi n. 17, xxvi–xxvii; 26–7, 56–8, 68, 71, 104, 110,.126
Wynberht (Wimbertus, Winberctus), priest, **1**; 7–8

Yrc *see* Eirikr

Zouche, Elizabeth, abbess of Shaftesbury, xv

2. INDEX OF PLACE-NAMES

Abbas Combe, Somerset, xxii, xxiv; 75–6
Abbotsbury (Abbey), Dorset, 125
Abingdon (Abbey), Berks., 6, 8, 17, 45, 65, 111
Æscantun, 12
Aldermore (Broad, Little, Long, Copse), Dorset, 14
Almer, Dorset (*Elmere*), **14**; 61–2
Alvestone, Wilts., xxvii; 120
Amesbury, Wilts. (*Ambresburch*), **8**; 33, 71, 119
Archet see Orchard
Ardington, Berks., 102
Ashdown, Berks., 61
Atworth, Wilts. (*Attenwrthe*), **29**; 121
Avon, river, Wilts. (*Auene*), **29**; 53, 121

Badbury, Wilts., 46–7
Barker's Hill *see* St Bartholomew's Hill
Barking (Minster), Essex, 5, 56
Barton in Shaftesbury, Dorset, xv n. 15
Basing, Hants., 71
Bath (Abbey), Somerset, 8
Baverstock, Wilts., 19, 21
Bedchester, Dorset, 34
Beechingstoke, Wilts (*Stoke*), **12**; xxiv; 52–3
Bersted, Sussex, 72
Berwick St John, Wilts., xxiv; 88, 90
Berwick St Leonard, Wilts., 112, 114
Biss, river, Wilts. (*Bissy, Byssi*), **29**; 121
Bittlesmore (lost) near Shaftesbury, Dorset (*Bytelesmor*), **22**; 94
Blackmoor, vale of, Dorset, xxiii, xxvi; 33

Blashenwell (Farm), Dorset (*Blachenwelle, Blechenenwelle, Blechenhamwelle*), **19**, **20**; 68, 70, 78–80, 82–3
Blynfield Farm in Cann, Dorset, 35, 97
Bognor (Little) in Fittleworth, Sussex (*Boganora*), **17**
Bognor Regis, Sussex, 72
Bottle Farm in Beechingstoke, Wilts., 53
Bottlesford in Manningford Bohun, Wilts., 53
Bow Brook, Somerset (? *Cawel*), **18**; 76
Bradford-on-Avon, Wilts. (*Bradeforda*), **29**; xiv, xviii, xxiii–xxiv, xxvii; 69, 119–22
Bridmore in Berwick St John, Wilts., 90
Brokenborough, Wilts., 87
Broughton Gifford, Wilts. (*Broctune*), **29**; 121
Bul Barrow (Bulbarrow Hill) in Woolland, Dorset, 14–15
Burton-on-Trent (Abbey), Staffs., 119
Butticanlea, **28**; xxvi; 110

Cale, river, Somerset (? *Wricawel* for *Wincawel*), **18**; 76
Camel, Somerset, 75
Canterbury, Kent, St Augustine's Abbey, 6
—Christ Church, 8, 12–13, 125
Chalfield, Wilts. (*Chaldfelde*), **29**; 121
Chalke, Wilts., 88, 90, 92
Chalke Hundred, Wilts., 88
Chapman's Pool in Worth Matravers, Dorset (*on the schort mannes pol; on seortmannes pol*), **16**, **20**; 69, 82–3
Cheam, Surrey, 61

Chebbard Farm in Dewlish, Wilts., 27
Cheselbourne, Dorset (*Cheselburne, Chiselburne*), **5, 6, 13, 30**; xv n. 15, xvi, xxi, xxiii–xxiv, xxvi–xxvii; 24–8, 39, 56–8, 61, 68, 104–5, 126–7
Chichester, Sussex, 6
Chicklade, Wilts., 112
Chilmark (Brook), Wilts. (*Cigel marc, Cigel merc*), **28**; 112, 114
Chinnock, Somerset, xxvi
Chivrick's Brook, Dorset, 65
Chiseldon, Wilts., 46–7
Cole, river, Wilts., 46
Combs Ditch, Dorset (*Cunnuces dich*), **13, 14**; 59, 62
Compton Abbas, Dorset (*Cumtune, Kuntune*), **7, 21**; xv n. 15, xxiii, xxiv; 33–4, 88–9, 91
Cookham, Berks., 8
Corfe, Dorset (*Corf*), **19, 20**; xiv n. 8; 68–70, 78–80, 82–3
Corsham, Wilts. (*Coseham*), **29**; 121
Cranborne Chase, Dorset, xxvi; 33
Crichel (Long Crichel, Moor Crichel), Dorset (*Chirchelford*), **9**; 39

Dartington, Devon (*Derentune homm*), **2**; 12
Delcombe Head in Milton Abbas, Dorset (? *delesburg*) **2**
Devil's Brook, Dorset (*Deflisc, Deuelisc, Deulisc*), **5, 6, 13, 30**; 27–8, 58, 126
Devon (*Domnonia*), **2**
Dinton, Wilts. (*Duningland, Duningheland*), **4**; xv n. 15, xxiii–xxiv; 17–18, 21–2, 102
Divelish, river, Dorset, 14
Donhead (Donhead St Andrew and Donhead St Mary), Wilts. (*Dunehefda, Dunhefda, Dunheued*), **7, 21**; xv n. 15, xxiii, xxiv; 88–90, 113
Dorcan, river, Wilts. (*Dorcyn*), 11; 46–7
Dorchester, Dorset (*Dornwerecestre*), **2**; 11–12
Duningland see Dinton
Dunworth Hundred, Wilts., 18, 88

Ealderes cumbe (*Aldderescumbe*), **27**; xxvii; 107
Easton Bassett in Berwick St John, Wilts. (*Estune*), **21**; xxiv; 88, 90–1
Elmer (Farm) in Middleton, Sussex (*Almerspol, Elmerespole*), **17**; 72
Encombe in Kingston, Dorset, xv n. 15
Exeter, Devon, 7

Farnborough, Warwicks., 61
Farnham, Dorset, xxiv
Felpham, Sussex (*Felhham*), **17**; xxii–xxiv, xxvii; 71–3
Fifehead St Quinton, Dorset, xxiv
Fonthill, Wilts. (*Funtgeal, Funtal*), **28**; 113–14

Fonthill Bishop, Wilts., 19, 113–14
Fonthill Gifford, Wilts., 19, 113–14
Fontmell Brook, Dorset, (*riuus nomine Funtamel, Funtemel, anlang Funtmeales*), **1, 10, 24**; 5, 9, 33–4, 43, 92, 98
Fontmell Down, Dorset, 34
Fontmell Magna, Dorset (*Funtemel, Funtmel*), **7, 8, 10**; xv n. 15, xxiii–xxiv, xxvi; 6, 9, 30, 33–5, 42–3, 88, 91, 98, 100, 111
Fontmell Wood, Dorset, 34
Fovant, Wilts., 19
Freshford, Somerset (*Ferseford*), **29**; 121
Frome, river, Dorset (*Frome, Frume*), **5, 6, 26**; 28, 106, 121

Gillingham, Dorset, 68, 82
Gillingham Forest, Dorset, 89, 113
Glastonbury (Abbey), Somerset, 8, 17, 71, 75
Gores in North Newnton, Wilts., 53
Grim's Ditch, Wilts. (*tha ealde dich*), **3, 4**; 19, 21
Gussage (St Andrew), Dorset (*Gersicg, Gissic*), **7**; xxiii–xxiv; 30, 88

Hamtune see Hinton
Handley *see* Sixpenny Handley
Hatherly Farm in Hilton, Dorset, 15
Hawkcombe (Lane) in Compton Abbas, Dorset (*holencumbe*), **8**; 34, 91
Hazelbury (Manor), Wilts. (*Heselberi*), **29**; 121
Henning (Hill) in Melcombe Horsey, Dorset (? *Hendene, Hendune*), **5, 6**; 28, 58
Henstridge, Somerset (*Hengstesrig*), **18**; 75–6
Hindon, Wilts., 112, 114
Hinton St Mary, Dorset (*Hamtune*), **15, 23**; xxiv; 64–5, 96–7
Hlyde see Liden Brook
Hollish (lost) in Corfe Castle, Dorset (*Alle wiscan, Alle discan, Holewisken, Olle discan*), **16, 19, 20**; 69, 79, 83
Holt, Wilts. (*Wrindesholt*), **29**; 121
Horsington, Somerset, 75
Horton, Dorset, 125
Horton, Kent, 13
Houns-Tout Cliff in Corfe Castle, Dorset, 79

Idehurst (Farm) in Kirdford, Sussex (*Hidhirst*), **17**; 72
Iwerne, river, Dorset (*Iwernbroc*), **23**; 92, 98
Iwerne Courtney, Dorset, 64, 92, 96–8
Iwerne Minster, Dorset (*Hywerna, Iwern, Ywern*), **7, 21**; xxiii–xxiv; 30, 43, 87–9, 92–3, 98

Key Brook, Dorset (*Cagbroc*), **10**; 43, 97–8
Kingston, Dorset, xvii, xxiii–xxiv, xxvii; 68–9, 79, 82

Knoyle (East and West), Wilts. (*Cnugel*), **28**; 113

Langford (Little), Wilts., 19, 21
Liden Brook, Wilts. (*Lyden, Liden*), **11**; 46
Liddington, Wilts. (*at Lidentune*), **11**; xxiii–xxiv; 46–7, 52
Limbo Farm (*Palinga schittas*) in Petworth, Sussex, **17**; 72
Longcombe (Bottom) in Fontmell Magna, Dorset (*to Langencumbes hauede*), **8**; 34
Lydden, river, Dorset, 15
Lynch Farm in Corfe Castle, Dorset, 70
Lyscombe (Bottom, Farm) in Cheselbourne, Dorset, 27, 58, 126–7

Malacombe Bottom in Tollard Royal, Wilts. (*Mapeldere cumb*), **21**; 90
Malmesbury Abbey, Wilts., 7, 9, 87, 120
Manston, Dorset, 43, 65
Manston Brook, Dorset, 43
Marden, Wilts. (*Mercdene*), **12**; 53
Margaret Marsh, Dorset, 96–7
Marnhull, Dorset, 96–7
Mapperton in Almer, Dorset (*Mapeldertune*), **14**; xxiv; 59, 61–2
Medbourne, Wilts (*Medeburne*), **11**; 47
Medeshamstede (Peterborough), Northants., 8
Melbury Abbas, Dorset (*Meleburge imare*), **21**; xv n. 15, xxiii–xxiv; 91
Melcombe Horsey, Dorset, xvi, xxiii; 104, 126
Melbury Hill (in Melbury Abbas), Dorset (*Meleberig dune*) **21**; 91
Midford, Somerset (*Mitford*), **29**; 121
Milton Abbas, Dorset, 13, 16
Minster-in-Thanet, Kent, 8
Mistleberry (Wood) in Sixpenny Handley, Dorset, 92
Monkton Farleigh, Wilts. (*Farnleghe*), **29**; 121
Morden, Dorset, 61

Nadder, river, Wilts. (*Nodre*), **3**, **4**, **28**; xxiii; 18–19, 21, 89, 112–14
Nippard (lost) in East Tisbury, Wilts. (*Nipedeforde*), **28**; 113
North Newnton, Wilts., 52–3
Nursling (Minster), Hants., 7

Oakley (Lane) in Sixpenny Handley, Dorset (*ac hylle*), **21**; 92
Ogbourne, Wilts., 61
Orchard (East and West), Dorset (*Archet*), **10**, **23**, **24**; xxvii; 34–5, 42–3, 65, 87, 97–8, 99–100

Pagham, Sussex, 72
Palinga schittas see Limbo Farm
Patney, Wilts., 52–3

Pen Hill in Sutton Waldron, Dorset (*littlen Seaxpennes suth eke*), **8**, **34**; 89 (*see also* Sixpenny)
Piddle, river, Dorset (*Pidelen stream*), **26**; 58, 104–6
Piddlehinton, Dorset, xxiii; 104
Piddletrenthide, Dorset (*Uppidele, Uppidelen*), **26**; xxiii, xxvi; 57, 104–6
Pidele, Dorset, xxiii, xxvi; 104, 126
Pimperne, river, Dorset (*Pimpern, Pimpernwelle*), **9**; 38–9
Plush in Buckland Newton, Dorset, 105
Poling, Sussex, 72
Pomeroy (Wood and Farm) in Winkfield, Wilts. (*Pumberig*), **29**; 121
Poole Harbour, Dorset, 69
Portesham, Dorset, 125
Puddletown, Dorset, xxiii
Purbeck, Dorset (*pars telluris Purbicinga*), **16**; xvii, xxiii, xxvii; 68–70, 79–80, 83

Rams Hill (Farm) in Marnhull, Dorset (*Rumanhelle*), **23**; 97
Rawlsbury Camp in Hilton, Dorset, 15
Redbridge, near Southampton, Hants., 7
Ridge, Wilts., 114
Rimpton, Somerset, 74
Rushmore, hundred-name, Dorset, 61

St Bartholomew's (*formerly* Barker's) Hill in Semley, Wilts. (*on berg hore*), **21**; 89
Sedgehill, Wilts., 111–13
Selsey, Sussex, 6, 42
Sem, river, Wilts. (*Semene*), **28**; 113
Semley, Wilts., 88–9, 112–13
Sfgcnyllebar, name of wood (? for Sedgehill *bær*), Wilts., **28**
Shaftesbury (Abbey), Dorset (*Scaftesberi, Scaftesbury, Sceaftesberi, Sceaftesburi, Sceftesbirio, Sceptoniensis, Schaftesbiri, Schaftesbiry, Schaftesbury, Sheftesbury*), **5**, **7**, **21**, **22**, **28**; archive of, xvi–xviii; cartulary of, xviii–xx; estates of, xxii–xxvii; history of, xiii–xv
Sherborne Abbey, Dorset, 17, 33
Sherrington, Wilts., 19, 21
Sixpenny Farm in Fontmell Magna, Dorset, 34
Sixpenny Handley, Dorset (*Hanlee, Heanlegen, Henlee*), **7**, **21**; xv n. 15, xxiii–xxiv; 30, 88–9, 91–2
Sixpenny Handley Hundred, Dorset, 89
Somerton, Somerset (*Sumertun*), **4**
Southampton, Hants., 12
Stirchel, river, Dorset, **8**, **10**, **21**; 34, 43, 91, 100
Stoce, Stoke see Beechingstoke

Stoke Wake, Dorset, xxiv; 11, 13–16
Stour, river, Dorset (*Sture*), **15**; 62, 65
Stour (East and West), xvi, xxiii–xxiv; 104
Stour Provost, Dorset, 97
Sturkel *see Stirchel*
Sturminster Newton, Dorset, 65
Sugar Way, Wilts., 47
Sutton Waldron, Dorset (*Suttune*), **8**; 33–4, 65, 92, 94, 100
Swallowcliffe, Wilts., 112
Swansbrook (Farm) in Winkfield, Wilts. (*Swinbroch*), **29**; 121
Swindley (Copse) in Dinton, Wilts. (*Suinlea*), **4**; 21
Swyre (Head) in Corfe Castle, Dorset (*ouer Swuran, on Swuren*), **20**; 79, 82

Tamworth, Staffs., 8
Tarrant, river, Dorset (*Terente, Terrente*), **9**, **21**; 62, 92
Tarrant Hinton, Dorset (*Tarente, Terentam, Terente, Terrente*), **7**, **9**, **21**; xxiv, xxvi; 30, 38–9, 88
Teffont Evias, Wilts., 18–19
Teffont Magna, Wilts. (*Tefunte, Teofunte, Teofunten*), **3**, **25**; 17–19, 21, 102
Tellisford, Somerset (*Tefleforde*), **29**; 121
Temple Combe, Somerset, 76
Thornton or Thorton (Farm) in Marnhull, Dorset (*Thortune, Thorntune*), **23**; 35, 43, 64–5, 96–7, 100
Tinkley (Down, Wood and Coppice) in Tollard Royal, Wilts. (*Tilluches lege*), **21**; 92
Tisbury, Wilts. (*Tissebiri, Tisseburi*), **1**, **28**; xv n. 15, xviii, xxiii–xxiv, xxvi; 5, 9–10, 19, 110–14
Tisbury (West), Wilts., 112–13

Uppidele(n), **26**; xxiii; 104–6 (*see* Piddletrenthide)

Wanborough, Wilts., 46
Wantage, Berks., 71
Wardour, Wilts., xvii; 89–90, 112–13
Wareham, Dorset, xiv; 69
Warleigh (Manor), Somerset (*Werleghe*), **29**
Warminster, Wilts., 121

Warrington Hundred, Wilts., 18
Washer's Pit in Ashmore, Dorset (*thas soces seath*), **8**; 34
Washington, Sussex, 61
Week Street, Dorset (*anlang wic herepathes*), 39
Wennland see Woolland
Were, river, Wilts. (? *wret*), **29**; 121
Westwood, Wilts., 121
Wherwell Abbey, Hants, 119
Whitemarsh (Farm) in Sedgehill, Wilts. (*on there hwiten mercs*), **28**; 113
White Sheet Hill in Ansty, Wilts., 90
Whitley, Wilts. (*Witlege*), **29**; 121
Wilsford, Wilts. (*Wiuelesford*), **12**; 53
Wilton Abbey, Wilts., xiii n. 5; 37–8, 68, 88, 107, 113
Wincanton, Somerset, 76
Winchester, Hants., New Minster, xxiii, xxvi; 104
—Nunnaminster, 120
—Old Minster, 9, 17, 30, 57, 74
Winkelbury Camp in Berwick St John, Wilts., 90
Winterborne, river, Dorset (*Winterburne*), **13**, **14**; 26, 58, 61–2
Winterborne Kingston, Dorset, 58
Winterborne Tomson, Dorset (*Winterburne*), **13**; 56–9, 61–2, 104
Winterborne Zelstone, 61–2
Wittenham *alias* Rowley (lost) in Farleigh Hungerford, Wilts. (*Wutenham*), **29**; 121
Woodborough, Wilts., 52
Woodbridge, Dorset (*Wdebricge, Wdebrige, Wdebrigthe, Wudebricge*), **8**, **24**; 33–5, 43, 100
Woodyates, Dorset (*Wdegeate, Wudegate*), **5**, **6**; 24
Woolland, Dorset (*Wennland*), **2**; 11, 13–16
Wych (*formerly* Corfe), river-name, Dorset (*Wicanford, on Wicean, of Wiche, Wichenford, Wickenford, andlang Wicumstreames, on Wicun, andlang Wicunstreames, andlang Wiken, Wikenford*), **16**, **19**, **20**; 69–70, 79–80, 82–3
Wylye, river, Wilts. (*Wilig*), **3**; 18–19

Yeovilton, Somerset, 75

3. WORDS AND PERSONAL NAMES USED IN BOUNDARY MARKS

abbod 'abbot'. *þes abbotes imare* **29**
ac, oc 'oak tree'. *anne oc* **2**; *leaxen oc* **13**; *litlen ac lee, aclee, ac hylle, anclee* **21**

ad 'beacon'. *on þat ealde ad* **21**
adrifen (pp. **adrifan**) 'driven'. *þat furch ðe is aðe riuen to Nodre* **3**

adun, adune 'down, downward'. **16, 19, 21, 24, 27, 28**

Æbba (pers. n) *abbenbeorg* **3**

** Æcci** (pers. n.) ? *acceslegle* **29**

æcer 'field, plot of land, measure of land'. *sex made eres* **5, 6**; *.xxiiii. akeres meade* **8**; *þry akeres* **10**; *on þane forðerthe acre, forerð akere* **13**; *be þane akeren heueden* **15**; *mad alleres* (for *æceras*) **21**; *twelf akeres yrðlandes* **27**; *be twelf aceron* **28**

Ælfgar (pers. n.) *alfgares imare* **28, 29** (bis)

Ælfric (pers. n.) *alfricheswelle* **20**

Ælfnoþ (pers. n.) ? *alnoþes imare* **29** (or **Æthelnoþ, Ealhnoþ**)

Ælfsige (pers. n.) *alfsiges landimare* **21**

Ælfstan (pers. n.) *alfstanes paþ* **19**

Ælfweard (pers. n.) *alfwerdes landimare* **29**

Ælfwig (pers. n.) *elfwiges imare* **29**

Ælfwine (pers. n.) *alwines hlip gate (or* **Æthelwine, Ealhwine**), *alfwines imare þe horderes, alphwines imare* **29**

æppel-treow 'apple-tree'. *on þo apeltreu, of þare apeltreu* **30**

Æþelnoþ (pers. n.) ? *alnoþes imare* **29** (or **Ælfnoþ, Ealhnoþ**)

Æþelwine (pers. n.) ? *alwines hlip gate* (or **Ælfwine, Ealhwine**), *aþelwines imare* **29**

agen þorn (? for **hæg-þorn** or **hagu-þorn**, 'hawthorn') *on agen þorn* **21**

alle (discan) see **Olla**

alor 'alder tree'. *alor riðe, anne aler riðe* **2**; *þurch þo aelres* **8**; *on þane alr* **10**; *to anne wonalre, of þane alre* **24**

andheafod 'headland of field'. *be þane onheueden* **21**

anlipig 'solitary'. *on þane anlipien þorn* **21**

anstiga 'foot-path, narrow way'. *to nearuwan anstigan, of þan anstigan* **13**

apulder 'apple-tree'. *on þa heren apeldren* **21**

Archet see index 2, Orchard

Attenwrthe see index 2, Atworth

Avene (river n.) see index 2, Avon

auon (river n.) ? *aueres broc* **19**; *auenes broc* **20**

Bacga (pers. n.) ? *bacging berghe* **9**

Bæde (pers. n.) ? *beteswirþe sled* **8** (or **Biedi**)

Bædheard (pers. n.) *badherdes slede* **11**

beag 'ring'. ? *on þat withibegh* **20** (possibly for **bedd**)

Beaghild (fem. pers. n.) *bechilde treu* **11**

beam 'tree-trunk'. *beam broc* **16, 20**

bece 'beech-tree'. *becheshlewe* **21**

bedd 'plot of ground where plants grow'. *on þat holenbedde, of þat holnebedde, ? on þat withibegh, of þanne wiþibedde* **20**; *on þat ealden reshbed, of þane bedde* **30**

beneoþan, 'beneath'. *beneþen* **10**

beorc 'birch-tree'. *berg hore* **21**

beorg, 'barrow, mound, hill'. ? *delesburg, cylberge* **2**; *on brochenenberge, abbenbeorg, leon berg* **3**; *heandene beorg, bleomannes berge, of þa iberge* **5**; *ceatwanberge, hendune beorch, blieq; mannes beorg, of þa iberge* **6**; *on dollen berch* **8**; *tatanbeorge, of þane berge, bacging berghe, on þane oþerne beoit, worres berg, of þane beorge, chelesberghe, þanen graetem beorge* **9**; *berge dune, on þere tweie iberges, of þo iberghen* **11**; *to þe beorge, of þe berge, on þo berges* **13**; *windee bergh, of þane berghe* **14**; *watdune beorch, empenbeorch, dollen beorge, pegan beorh, berendes beorh, totenberg* **21**; *on chellenberge* **26**; *on þane berghe, of þane berghe, on þane rugan bergh, of þane bergh, on se bergh, of seberghe, blacmanne bergh, of þanne berghe, shete bergh, of þane berghe, bradenbergh, bradeberghe, hiwiscbergh, of þane berghe, on þane bergh, of þane bergh* **30**

beorhlem, obscure **9** (? **beorg, leam**, dat. pl. of **leah**; see *PN Dorset*, ii. 122)

Beorht (pers. n.) *berteswelle* (bis) **30**

bere-ærn 'barn'. ? *berendes beorh* **21**

berend 'carrier'. ? *berendes beorh* **21**

Bica (pers. n.) ? *bicendich* **11** (or **bicce**); *bikenmuþe* **17**; *bican pet, biken settle* **21**

bicce, bice 'bitch'. ? *bicendich* **11** (or **Bica**)

***Biedi** (pers. n.). ? *beteswirþe sled* **8** (or **Bæde**)

birce 'birch tree'. *to burch linken* **8** (or **burh**)

bisceop 'bishop'. *opes bissopes imare* **24**

Bissy (river n.) see index 2, Biss

Blæcmann (pers. n.). *bleomannes berge* **5**; *blieq; mannes beorg* **6**; *blacmanne bergh* **30**

blæc-þorn 'blackthorn tree'. *on þe blaken þorne, of þane blake þornen* **13**

blecen (stream n.) see index 2, Blashenwell

blinc (stream n.) *blinches broc, blinchesfelde* **8**; *blinnesfeld* **23** [see index 2, Blynfield]

boga 'bow, arch, curve'. ? *of bogen wylle, on bokenwelle* **22** (or **Boga**)

Boga (pers. n.) ? *of bogen wylle, on bokenwelle* **22** (or **boga**)

Bota (pers. n.) *botenwelle* **12** [and see index 2, Bottle, Bottlesford]

brad 'broad'. *bradenbergh, bradeberghe* **30**

brand 'torch, burning'. ? *on brandes hricg* **22** (or **Brant**)

Brant (pers. n.) *on brandes hricg* **22** (or **brand**)

breþling, obscure. *of breþling made* **23** [see *PN Dorset*, iii. 178]

Brisnoþ (pers. n.) *to brisnodes landshare* **29**

broc 'brook'. *melenbroc* **2**; *holebroke, blinches broc, of þanne broke* **8**; *wið eastem þane broc, Cagbroc, anlang Cagbroces* [see index 2, Key

Brook] 10; *Stokebroc, Stocbroc* 12; *lisebroke, anlang broke* 13; *beam broc, anlang broke, on þane broc, anlang broces* 16; *aueres broc, anlang brokes* 19; *auenes broc, of þane broke, beambroc* 20; *to smale broke* 21; *Iwernbroc* (bis), *of þane broke* 23; *mane broc, wiþig broch, Cigel merc broke* 28; *inne Swinbroch* [see index 2, Swansbrook], *be broke, wigewen broke* 29; *liscbroc, be broke* 30

brocen (pp. **brecan**) 'broken'. *on brochenenberge* 3; *to brokene strate* 11

Broctune see index 2, Broughton Gifford

brycg bridge'. *oxene bricge* 15; *on þat stanene bregge, of þare brigge* 20

Bryda, (pers. n.) ? *bridinghe dich* 21

Bryni (pers. n.) ? *anlang brines fleotes* 17

burh 'fortified place'. ? *delesburg, on burg* 2; *mealeburg* 21; *on þa ealde berig, of þane bery* 30

burna 'spring, stream'. *ninge burne, hringheburne* 12; *stanburne* 21

burnstow, 'channel or bed of an intermittent stream' *to burnstowe* (bis) 5; *to burnstowe, anlang burnstowe, to burnstowe* 6; *on þa burnestowe* 9; *anlang burnstowe* 26; *on burnestowe* 30

byden 'tub, vessel'. ? *on budencumbe hracan* 21

byge 'bend'. *oþ þane bige, of þane bige* 19

byrgels 'burial-place, mound, tumulus'. *on þane haþene berielese* 26

Byssi (river n.) see index 2, Biss

Bytelesmor see index 2, Bittlesmore

Cag broc (stream n.) see index 2, Key Brook

Cawel (river n.) see index 2, Bow Brook

Cead(d)a (pers. n.) *on ceadenford* 4

cealc 'chalk'. *ða chealc seðas* 8

cealf 'calf'. *chelfgraue (bis)* 13; *cealuelege, cheluedune* 21

ceastel 'heap of stones'. *on anne castel, of ðycastele, to anne castel, of ðicastele, on anne stan castel, of ða icastele* 5; *on anne castel, of þe castele, to anne castele, of þo icastel, on anne stancastel, of þi castele* 6; ? *on þane ston istel, of þan istelle* 13

Ceatwa (pers. n.) *ceatwanberge* 6

cefer 'beetle'. ? *ouer ciuerget mor, anlang cuterget mores* 15

Ceol (pers. n.) *chelesberghe* 9

Ceola (pers. n.) ? *chellenberghe* 26 (or **ceole**)

Ceolbriht (pers. n.) *chelbrichtes dich* 15

ceole 'throat, channel, gorge'. *chellenberghe* 26 (or **Ceola**)

ceolor 'throat, gorge'. ? *to cellor, of cellor* 14

Chadfelde see index 2, Chalfield

Chirchel see index 2, Crichel

ci(e)gel, 'pole'. ? *cylberge* 2 (or **Cyla, cyll**)

Cigel marc (merc) see index 2, Chilmark

clif 'cliff, escarpment, riverbank'. *hoddes clif* 3; *on þat rede clif* 4; *on þane clif* 16; *oþe clif, be eficlif* 19

clud 'rocky outcrop'. *cludesleghe* 8

cnæp 'hill-top, hillock'. *anne cnap* 5; *anne cinep* 6; *þorndunes cnep, of þane cneppe* 30

cnoll 'hill-top, knoll'. *teppen cnolle, of þane cnolle* 11

Cnugel see index 2, Knoyle

coc 'cock'. ? *cockes þorne* 9 (or **Cocc**)

Cocc (pers. n.) ? *cockes þorne* 9 (or **coc**)

Coseham see index 2, Corsham

cran 'crane'. *cranmere* 21; *cranemere* (bis) 23

crundel 'gully, quarry, chalkpit'. *on anne crundel, wið anne crundeles, of þane crundele* 5; *on anne crundel, wið anne crundeles, of þi crundele* 6; *stanegan crundel* 9; *on þane crundel, of þane crundel, on ðone crundel, of þane crundele, on þene depe crundel* 13; *on anne crundel, of þane crundele* 14; *on þone crundel, of þane crundel* 20; *on þare crundel, on þane crundel, on þere crundel* 21; *hlosstedes crundles suð ecge, of þane crundle* 26

cu 'cow'. ? *cures rigt, cyrder it* 28

cumb 'combe, hollow among hills'. *holencumbe* [see index 2, Hawkcombe], *of þanne cumbe, Langencumbes hauede* [see index 2, Longcombe] 8; *þe estre Lyde cumbe, olencumbe, grinescumb* 11; *flescumbe* 13; *hwete cumb, anlang cumbes* 14; *on þanne cumb, anlang cumbe, on þane westrene cumbe, anlang cumbes* 16; *smalencumbe* 19; *struthgeardes cum* 20; *on land* (for *onlang*) *cumbes, gemanen cumb, cumbes hracan, Mapeldere cumb* [see index 2, Malacombe], *holencumb, budencumbe hracan* 21; *sapcumbe, gificancumbe, anlang cumbe* 28; *flexcumbes heuede, holencumbe* 30

Cunnuces dic see index 2, Combs Ditch

cwabba 'marsh, bog'. *on heahstanes quabben* 27

Cyla (pers. n.) ? *to cylberge* 2 (or **ciegel, cyll**)

cyll 'flagon, vessel, leather bottle'.? *cylberge* 2 (or **ciegel, Cyla**)

cyning 'king'. *cing hille* 21; *be kinges imare* 23; *oð kinghes imare* 24; *þe kinges imare, be kinges imare* 29

Deflisc (river n.) see index 2, Devil's brook

dell 'hollow, dell'. ? *delesburg* 2; *mesdelle* 21

denu 'valley'. *anlang standene* 14; *on lang* (for *land*) *scor dene, Terente dene* (bis), *fideriches dene, waddene* 21; *þurch ðene* (? for *dene*) *holt* 24; *gofesdene* 28

deop 'deep'. *on þene depe crundel* 13

deor 'wild animal, deer'. ? *delesburg* 2

Deuelisc, Deulisc (river n.) see index 2, Devil's Brook

dic 'ditch, dyke'. *anne walle dich, on anne dich* **2**; *on ða ealden dich* **3**; *on ða ealden dich, on dic* **4**; *to þare hwitendich, andlang dich, on ðat dich, horsedich* **9**; *anlang ðere dich, bicendich* **11**; *on þe twifelde dich, of þare dic, Cunnuces dich* [see index 2, Combs Ditch] **13**; *on þa dich, to þere alde dic, andlang diche, Cunnucesdic* [see index 2, Combs Ditch] **14**; *anlang diche, to dich, anlang dich, chelbrichtes dic* **15**; *on anne dich, at lang dich, anlang dich* (bis), *on anne dich, oþ þa dich, of þare dich* **16**; *anlang dich, to þare eald dich, of þere eald idich, on ða elden dich, of þere ealden dic, andlang dich* **18**; *on anne dich* (4 times), *anlang dic* (bis), *onlang dich, þe stod dic, þat northene stod dich, of þare diche* (bis) **19**; *on anne dich* (bis), *anlang dich* (4 times), *þæt þwers dich, of þare diche, on an dich, of þane dich, onlang diche, þa holendich, on þare dich, þa ealdene dich* **20**; *bridinghe dich, miclen diches get, esnes diges get, seuen diche suð ende, anlang diche* **21**; *wyndrede dic, of þare dich* **22**; *þe lang dic, on ða dich, swo be diche* **23**; *wlfgedyce* (bis), *be dich, of þat dich* **27**; *on þere ealde diches heued, of þare dich, on þare diches hirne* **30**

Dol(l)a (pers. n.) *dollenberch* **8**; *dollenbeorge* **21**

Dorcyn (river n.) see index 2, Dorcan

duce 'duck'. ? *duccenhulle* (bis) **18**

dun 'down'. *swindune, on heandene beorg* [see index 2, Henning Hill], *of dune* **5**; *swindone, on hendune beorch* [see index 2, Henning Hill], *of dune* **6**; *hamelendune, of dune* **8**; *dungete, of dune* **9**; *dun slede, bergedune* **11**; *of dune* **13**; *safandune* **16**; *sawendune* **19**; *up on dune, of þone dune, watdune beorch, cheluedune, Meleberig dune* [see index 2, Melbury Hill] **21**; *gretindune, þorndunes cnep* **30**

duneweard 'downward'. *duneward* **21**

ea 'river'. *on þare oþer ea* **4**

Eadhelm (pers. n.) *eadelmes melne* **10**

Eadwine (pers. n.) *adwines imare* **15**

eald 'old'. *þa ealdene hage* **2**; *ða ealden dich* **3, 4**; *þanen ealden herepaþe* **8**; *þane ealde treo stede* **12**; *þane ealde seale* **13**; *þere alde dich* **14**; *þan ealden stodfald, ða ealden hege rewe* **16**; *þere ealden hege, þere eald dich, þere eald idich, ða elden dich, þere ealden dic* **18**; *þo ealde rode, þo alde stodfald* **19**; *þane ealde weg, þa ealdene dich* **20**; *þanne ealden hole weg, þat ealde ad, þane ealdan forde* **21**; *þane ealde wdeforde* **28**; *þare ealde diches heued,*

þane ealde paþe, þa ealde berig, þat ealden reshbed **30**

Ealda (pers. n.) *eldenham* **18**

Ealdmann (pers. n.) *heldmannes wrthe* **8**; *ealdmannes wyrðe* (bis) **10**; *ealdmannes wyerðe* **23**; *eldmannes wrthe, eldemannes wyrðe* **24**

ealdorman, 'ealdorman'. *þes aldremannes imare* **29**

Ealhnoþ (pers. n.) ? *alnopes imare* **29** (or Ælfnoth, Æthelnoth)

Ealhwine (pers. n.) ? *alwines hlip gate* (or Ælfwine, Æthelwine)

ears 'arse'. *on ears mores heaued* **21**

east 'east(wards)'. *est* **2, 9, 21**; *wið eastem þane broc* **10**

eastweard 'eastwards, to the east of'. *estward* **4**; *badherdes slede eastward* **11**; *astward* **13**; *of þane ealden stodfald estward* **16**; *on litlen ac lee estward* **21**

ecg 'edge'. *hamelendune north ecge, ðies littlen Seaxpennes suð eke* **8**; *on ecge, be ecge* **20**; *opes sledes northecge* **21**; *hlosstedes crundles suð ecge, greten linkes suth ecge* **26**

efisc 'edge, escarpment'. *be euisc* **19**

elchene, obscure. *elchene seað* **21**

ellen 'elder tree'. *þone ellen stub* **21**; *on þa ellen þirnen* **30**

Elmere see index 2, Almer

elþen ? for e(a)lden, 'old'. *þa elþen stret* **14**

ende 'end'. *fildene lane uppende* **9**; *higeweges ande* **10**; *stanhecheres ande* **14**; *seuen diche suð ende* **21**

eorþburh 'earthwork'. *erðerburg* **4**

Esne (pers. n) or **esne** 'servant'. *esnes diges get* **21**

fald 'fold (for animals)'. *þan ealden stodfald* **16**; *þo ealde stodfald, of þanen falde* **19**

Farnleghe see index 2, Monkton Farleigh

fearn 'fern'. *þane fearngaren* **13**; *fernhelle* **21**

feden, obscure. *feden þorn, feden þorne* **11**

feld 'open land, clearing, unit of arable land'. *blinchesfelde* **8**; *blinnesfelde* **23** [see index 2, Blynfield]

Ferseforde see index 2, Freshford

filde, 'dweller in open country'. ? *fildene lane uppende* **9** [or **filden**, 'fielden']

feower, 'four'. *þe foer stanes* **11**

fileðe 'hay'. *filed hamme* **18**

fleax 'flax'. *flescumbe* **13**; *flexcumbes heuede* **30**

fleot 'creek. stream'. *anlang brines fleotes* **17**

flode 'stream, channel, intermittent stream or spring'. *þat michle flode* **21**; *wdesfloda* **28**

foran ongean 'opposite'. *foren ongen* **13**

ford 'ford'. *on ðone forde, funtnesforde* **3**; *ceadenford* **4**; *oð þanne ford, Chirchelford, of* *þanne forde* 9; *scealden forde* 10; *stanforde* 12; *Winterburne ford* 14; *Wican ford, scyleford, Wikenforde* 16; *tilb*[. . .]*es forde, tilbirhthes forde, of þanne forde, stanford, stanforde* 17; *Wikenforde, scylenford, scylenforde, Wichenford* 19; *Wickenford, Wikenforð* 20; *þane ealdan forde, sand ford* 21; *land scorford, of þane forde, Funtemel ford, of þanne ford* 24; *þane ealde wdeforde, suthames forde, nipedeforde* 28; *of þanne forde* 29

forierð 'projecting piece of ploughland'. *on þane forð erthe acre, of þane forerð akere* 13

forðweard 'forward, onward'. *forðward* 21

fostor-land 'demesne'. *fostodr landes* 21

fox 'fox'. *foxlee* 21

Friðuric (pers. n.) *on fideriches dene* 21

Frome (river n.) see index 2

Funt (? district n.). *funtnesforde* 3; *fintes brigce* (for *hrigce*) 28

Funtal, Funtgeal, see index 2, Fonthill

Funtemel see index 2, Fontmell

furh 'furrow, trench'. *onne þat furch* 3; *anne furch* 5, 6; *anlang þere fures* 9; *oð ða furuh, on land* (for *onlang*) *furuh* 21

fyrs 'furze'. *þane imeren fyrs garan* 30

gara 'gore, point of land, promontory, triangular portion of land left after ploughing'. *þane fearngaren, þurh þane garen* 13; *þane imeren fyrs garan, of þan garan* 30

geat 'gap, opening, gate'. *dungete* 9; *widesgete, midelgete, midelgate, hornget, horngetes hirne* 13; *horgate, horgate* 14; *ciuerget mor, anlang cuterget mores* 15; *miclen diches get, esnes diges get, tor scylget, torchil gat, on þat get* 21; *to þan lipgete, from þane gete* 24; *alwines hlip gate, fram þane hlipgate* 29 [see also **hlip-geat**]

gereþrenc, obscure. *on þa gereþrenc* 8

gifete 'plover'. *gificancumbe* 28

ginne, 'wide, spacious'. ? *to ginum* (or *ginun*) *hocum* 10

gof, obscure. *gofesdene* 28

Gosa (*pers. n.*) *gosanwelle* 11

graf 'grove, copse'. *wið slahgraues* 4; *sulan graf* 8; *chelfgraue* 13; *þurth þere groue* 18

great 'great'. *þanen graetem beorge* 9; *greten linkes suth ecge, of þan gretenlinke* 26; *gretindune, þane greate hlinc* 30

grene 'green'. *grenenhille* 14; *þone gren wai* 21; *þane grene wei, þare grene wei* 28

grin 'trap, snare'. *grinescumb* 11

Hæcga (pers. n.) ? *hacggen hamme* 2 (or **haga**)

*hægen 'enclosure'. ? *on þe hegen, be west hegen paðe, anlang hegen* 8 [see *PN Dorset*, iii, 110]. Perhaps **haga** or **hege**

hægþorn or **haguþorn** 'hawthorn'. ? *on agen þorn* 21

hæðen 'heathen'. *þane haþene berielese* 26

haga 'enclosure, hedge'. *on þane ealden hage, anlang ðies hagen* 2; *on ðon hagen* 8 (easily confused with **hægen, hege**)

haga 'haw'. ? *hacggen hamme* 2 (or **Hæcga**)

halig 'holy'. *halgan weies* (for *welles*) *lake* 8

hamel 'scarred, rugged, flat-topped'. *hamelendune north ecge* 8

hamm 'river-meadow, enclosed plot'. *hacggen hamme* 2; *snelles hamme weghe, scearpanhame* 8; *þone med ham* 9; *Archet hamm* 10; *molenhame* (bis) 14; *ludenham, ludenhame, eldenham,* ? *anlang hecgham* (possibly for **hecgan**), *filed hamme* (bis) 18; *Archetham* (bis), *Archethamme* 23; *hiclesham, suthames forde* 28

han 'stone'. *þare rede hane* 9

har 'hoar, grey'. *wið ðere heren wike* 4; *þa heren apeldren* 21; *þane haren torre* 30

heafod 'headland, projecting portion, upper end of'. *on ðes linkes hauede* 3; *anne hlincheshaeued, anne linkes heaued* 5; *anne linkes haued, anne linkes heued* 6; *Langencumbes hauede* 8; *on þa iheafde, of þane iheafde* 13; *hefdeswelle, litiges heuede* (bis), *be þane akeren heuede, efdeswelle* 15; *horspoles heaued(e)* (bis) 18; *on <laiboc> heued, ears mores heauede* 21; *sucgimade hauede, of þane hauede* 24; *þare ealde diches heued, flexcumbes heuede, be anne hefden* 30

heafod-stocc 'tree pollarded at head-height'. *heaued stokes, heued stockes* 21; *þe heued stokes, of þanne heued stocken, oþ heued stoccas* 28

heah 'high'. *heandene beorg* 5; *hendune beorch* 6 [see index 2, Henning Hill]

Heahstan (pers. n.) *heahstanes quabben* 27

hecg 'hedge'. *andlang hecgan* 10; *anlang hecgham* (? for *hecgan*) 18; *on hecgan sled* 20 (possibility of confusion with ***hægen, haga, hege**)

hege 'hedge'. *anne hege* 2; *þes heges hirne* 5; *ðes heges hirnen* 6; *to stigel hege, landshare hegen, anlang heges* 10; *þane hegen* (bis) 15; *þere ealden hege, be hegen* 18; ?*wulfgedyce* (bis), *be þe hege wege* 27 (possibility of confusion with ***hægen, haga, hecg**)

hege-ræwe 'hedge-row'. *þa hege reawe* 8; *þa hege reawe, onlang heie reawe* 14; *ða ealden hege rewe, anlang þare hege rewe* 16; *þane hege reawe* 21; *anlange hege reawe* 28

heorot 'hart'. *hert mere* 21

herepæð 'highway'. *on herepaþ* 3; *anne herepað, ouer herepaþ, herepaðe* (4 times) 5; *on þere herepaþ, ðe herepað, to herepað, of þe ereðe*

6; *to þan herepaþe, to þanen ealden herepaþe* 8; *anlang herepaþes, anlang wic herepaþes* 9; *on þere herepaðe, on þare opere herepað* 11; *anlang herepaþes, onlong þane herepaþe* 13; *on ðone herepaþ, of þen herepaþe, on þene richte herepath* 16; *to herepað, of heˊrepaþe* 18; *on þare herepaþ, of þanne herepaþ* 19; *on þere herepað* 21; *on ðes herepaþe, anlang herepaþes* 26; *on þone herepoð* 28

hereweg 'highway'. *hereweg* 21; *on þere herewai, anlang herewaies* 29

Heselberi see index 2, Hazelbury

hicel 'green woodpecker' or **Hicel** (pers. n.) *hiclesham* (bis) 28

hig 'hay'. *anlang higweges, higeweges ande* 10; *hig wege* 28

Hippa (per. n.) ? *on hippepad* 30

hiwan (gen. **higna**) 'members of a religious community'. *on þere hina imare* 23; *anlang hina imares, anlang hine imares* 24

hiwisc 'hide'. *oþer half hewisse* 8; *hiwiscbergh* 30

hlæw 'barrow, tumulus'. *becheshlewe* 21

hleow 'sheltered, sunny'. *leon berg* 3

hliep-geat 'leap-gate, low gate in hedge or fence over which animals can cross'. *to þan lipgete* 24; *alwines hlip gate, fram þane hlipgate* 29

hlinc 'linchet, ridge'. *on ðes linkes hauede* 3; *land scorhlinc, anne hlinchesheaued, on þane hlinc, of þat ihlinche, on anne linkes heaued, on hlinc reawe, on þone hlinc, of þat ihlinche, land scarlinc* 5; *landscar hlinc, anne linkeshaued, on þanne hlinc, of þanne ihlinche, anne linkes heued, on þat hlinc reawe, on þane hlinc, of þanne ihlinche, land scare hlinc* 6; *burch linken* 8; *nunnenlinc, nunnene linche* 15; *of þan linche, on anne linc reawe* 16; *on þane hlinc, anlang hlinkes* 19; *on hlinc reawe, greten linkes suth ecge, of þane gretenlinke* 26; *on þane greate hlinc, of þare linke* 30

hlinc-ræw 'row of linchets'. *on hlinc reawe* 5; *on þat hlinc reawe* 6; *on anne linc reawe* 16; *on hlinc reawe* 21

hlosstede 'place where there is a pigsty'. *hlosstedes crundles suð ecge* 26

hoc 'hook, angle, bend'. *to ginum hocum* 10

Hodd (pers. n.) *hoddesclif* 3

hol 'hollow, lying in a hollow'. *holencumbe* [see index 2, Hawkcombe], *holenwelle, on holewei, off holleweie, to holebroke* 8; *olencumb* 11; *þa holendich* 20; *þanne ealden hole weg, þane imeren hole weg, holenwylle, hollenwelle, holencumbe* 21; *holencumbe* 30

holen 'holly'. *þat holenbedde, þat holnebedde, þare holne stoke* 20

holh 'hollow'. *on ða holu* 13

holt 'wood, copse'. *þurch ðene* (? for *dene) holt* 24; *Wrindesholt* 29 [see index 2, Holt]

hor 'muddy'. *on þorþiuel, of hor þiuele* 30

hord 'hoard, treasure'. *on þane hord þiuel* 30

hordere, 'treasurer'. *on ðes horderes land* 8; *alfwines imare þe horderes* 29

horn 'horn'. *hornget, horngetes hirne* 13; *horgate* (bis) 14

hors 'horse'. *horsedich* 9; *horspoles heaued(e)* (bis) 18

hraca 'throat'. *cumbes hracan, budencumbe hracan* 21

hreod 'reed'. *ðet rede sloh* 11

hring 'ring'. *hringheburne* 12

hrisc see **risc**

hrycg, hricg 'ridge'. *hrycg leah* 4; *hrigcsweg, anlang hricg weges, of rig wei* 8; *anlang ricges, anlang hricge weges* 13;? *anlang richtes* 18; *brandes hricg, anlang hrichtes* 22; ? *cures rigt,* ? *cyrder it, anlang hrigces, anlang hrygges, fintes brigce* (for *hricge), anlang hrigces* 28

hus 'house, dwelling'. *on anne hus* 21

hwæte 'wheat'. *hwete cumb* 14

hwit 'white'. *þare hwitendich* 9; *þere hwiten mercs* 28; *þone hwitenwelle* 30

hyran 'to belong to'. *ðe ðar to herað* 3; *þe ierþ on þise land* 5; *ierð to þise land* 6; *þat hirð in to, erþe into* 8; *hereð in to* 10; *þe ierð in to* 23; *þe ieraþ in to* 29

hyrne 'angle, corner'. *on þes heges hirne* 5; *on ðes heges hirnen* 6; *of horngetes hirne, to þares tunes hirne* 13; *on þen hirnen* 16; *on þare diches hirne, of þere hirne* 30

ierð 'ploughland'. *þa gereðe* 21

ierðland, yrðland 'ploughland'. *anne ierð londe* 5; *ðan gerðe lande* 6; *twelf akeres yrðlandes* 27

ifig 'ivy(-covered)'. *be eficlif* 19

Ippa (pers. n.) ? *empenbeorch* 21

Iwerne broc (river n.), see Index 2

lacu 'stream, side-channel'. *halgan weies* (for *welles) lake, on þat lake* 8; *on þa lake, one þat lake* (bis), *on þat litlen lake, lacmere* 21; *to lace mere* 23

lad 'water-course'. *on þat hrisclad, anlang þese richtledes* 12

(ge)læte 'junction of roads'. *þare weilate* 16

laiboc, obscure. *on laiboc heuede* (reading in MS unclear)

land 'land'. *a norward þan londe* **4**; *þe ierþ in þise lande* **5**; *ierð to þise land* **6**; *þes landes imare* **12**; *þe landes imare* **15**

land-(ge)mære 'boundary'. *þa land imare* **10, 11, 13, 28**; *þe land imaren* **14, 26**; *þe land imare* **16**; *þa landimare, þat westrene landimare* **19**; *þe fiftiga hide land imare, alfsiges landimare, ðane sex hide landimare, þare .x. hide land gemare* **21**; *þe landimare* **22, 24**; *þa landimare, þe tweie hide landimare* **23**; *alfwerdes land imare, lefwines land imare* **29**

landscearu 'boundary'. *land scorhlinc, landscarlinc* **5**; *land scarhlinc, land scare hlinc* **6**; *to þrem land sharen, to land share hegen* **10**; *andlang land share* (bis) **13**; *seo westere land sceare* **16**; *on lang* (for *land*) *scordene* **21**; *land scorforde* **24**; *be is land share, brisnodes land share, be his land share* **29**

lane 'lane'. *fildene lane uppende* **9**; *on þa sticelen lane, of þare lane* **30**

lang 'long'. *Langencumbes hauede* **8** [see index 2, Longcombe]; *langhelee* (bis) **13**; *on þe lang dic* **23**; *of langan riple, and* (for *on*) *lang riple* **27**

leah, 'wood, clearing'. ? *delesburg* **2**; *Suinleah* [see index 2, Swindley], *hrycg leah* **4**; *cludesleghe, of þare lege* **8**; *langhelee* (bis) **13**; *limbenlee* **14**; *cealuelege, litlen ac lee, aclee, tilluches lege* [see index 2, Tinkley], *anclee, foxlee* **21**; *tudesleghe, of þere lege* **23**; *on deodewoldding lege, of teoþewolding lege* **27**; *rodelee, poles leage, Cnugel lege, to þere litden lege* **28**; *acceslegle* **29**

Leaxa (pers. n.) *leaxen oc* **13**

Leofa (pers. n.) *leouen imare* **24** [see index 1, Leofa and Wulfgar Leofa]

Leofric (pers. n.) *leofriches imare* **28**

Leofwine (pers. n.) *lefwines imare* (bis) **29**

linden 'growing with lime-trees'. ? *limbenlee* (bis) **14**

Lippa (pers. n.) ? *on lippen scagan* **21**

lisc broc (stream n.) *lisebroke* **13**; *liscbroc* **30** [see index 1, Lyscombe Bottom]

lorte, 'muddy place'. *lortenwille* **18**

Luda (pers. n.) ? *ludenham, of ludenhame* **18**

Ludmann (pers. n.) *ludmannes putte* **8**

Lyde see index 2, *Hlyde*, Liden Brook

lytel 'little'. *on ðies littlen Seaxpennes suð eke* **8**; *litlen wde* **9**; *þat litlen lake, litlen ac lee* **21**; *þere litden lege* **28**

Lytig (pers. n.) ? *litiges heuede* (bis) **15**

mæd 'meadow'. *þa two meades* **4**; *sex made eres, Deuelisc made* **5**; *sex made eres, Deueliscmad* **6**; *meade* **8**; *on þone med ham* **9**; *sugging made* **10**; *mad alleres* **21**; *breþling*

made **23**; *sucgimade hauede* **24**; *se made be Frome* **26**; *putel made* **27**

mæle 'spotted, multicoloured'.? *mealeburg* **21** (but possibly for *miceleburg*)

(ge)mæne 'shared'. *gemanen cumb* **21**; *mane broc* **28**

(ge)mære 'boundary'. *þes landes imare* **5, 12**; *þe landes imare, adwines imare, anlang imares* **15**; *þane imeren hole weg, Meleburge imare, ? merewege* (or **mere**) **21**; *be kinges imare, on þere hina imare, anlang mares* **23**; *anlang hina imares, anlang hine imares, anlang leouen imare, oð kinghes imare, andlang gemare, oþes bissopes imare, to wlgares imaren, of þan imaren* **24**; *þat mere sled* (or **mere**), *mearhhilde mere* (or **mere**) **26**; *wilburge imare, leofriches imare, forð be gemare, alfgares imare, be his imare* **28**; *lefwines imare, þes abbotes imare* (4 times), *alfgares imare* (bis), *forð be is imare, þes kinges imare* (bis), *þes aldremannes imare, elfwiges imare, alnoþes imare, aþelwines imare, alfwines imare, alphwines imare* **29**; *þane imeren fyrs garan* **30**

mapulder 'maple-tree'. *on þane mapelder* **15**; *Mapeldere cumb* [see index 2, Malacombe] **21**; *mapeldere hille* **28**

mearc 'boundary'. *mearcweie* **13**; *mearc wei* **28**

Mearhhild (fem. pers. n.) *mearhhilde mere* **26**

Medeðurne see index 2, Medbourne

Meleberig dune see index 2, Melbury Hill

Meleburge see index 2, Melbury Abbas

meos 'moss' or 'bog'. *mesdelle* **21**

Mercdene see index 2, Marden

mere 'mere, lake, pool'. *anlang riscemeres* **14**; *hert mere, cranmere, lacmere, merewege* (or **(ge)mære**) **21**; *lacemere, cranemere* **23**; *on þat meresled* (or **(ge)mære**), *mearhhilde mere* (or **(ge)mære**) **26**

mersc 'marsh'. *ouer þane merse* **16**; *þere hwiten mercs* **28**

micel 'great'. *þat michle flode, on miclen diches get* **21**

midde 'middle'. *on midde þane punfald* **26**

middel 'middle'. *midelgete, midelgate* **13**

middewearde 'through (over, along) the middle of'. *on delesburg middenwearde* **2**; *on þa burnestowe middewardde* **9**

midstream 'midstream'. *adune mid streame* **24**

Mitford see index 2, Midford

mor 'moor, marsh, wasteland'. *ouer ciuerget mor, anlang cuterget mores* **15**; *on anne mor, anlang mores* **19**; *rupemor, of þane more* **20**; *ears mores heauede* **21**; *bytelesmor, bitelesmore* **22**; *sidinic mor* **28**; *morhelle* **30**

muþa 'mouth' (of a stream). ? *bikenmuþe* **17** (or **(ge)myðe**)

myln 'mill'. *melenbroc* **2**; *eadelmes melne* **10**; *molenhame* (bis) **14**; *on þanen mylen stede* **21**.

myln-gear 'enclosure for catching fish (yair) located at a mill'. *in þane miliere, of þan miliere* **30**

(ge)myðe 'confluence, junction of two streams'.? *bikenmuþe* **17** (or **muþa**); *inne þa imade, of þane miþon* **28**

nearu 'narrow'. *to nearuwan anstigan* **13**
niþede see index 2, Nippard
niþer 'down(ward)'. **20, 29**
niþerweard 'downward'. *neþerward* **13**
Nodre see index 2, Nadder
norð 'north(wards)'. *norð* **4, 8, 19, 20, 28**; *north ecge* **8**; *oþes sledes northecge* **21**
norðerne 'northern'. *on þat northene stod dich* **19**
norðweard 'northward, to the north of'. *northward* **3**; *a norward þan londe* **4**; *on anne ierð londe northward* **5**; *on þan gerðe lande nordewarde* **6**; *on langhelee northward, on þe blaken þorne northward* **13**; *on mealebury norþewarde, on foxlee nortwarde, on þere crundel northward* **21**
nunne 'nun'. *nunnenlinc, nunnenelinche* **15** (possibly a misreading of *minnan hlinc*)

oc see **ac**
Offa (pers. n.) *offen weg* (bis) **21**
Olla (pers. n) ? *on alle wiscan, of alle discan, oþ olle discan* **16**; *on olle discan* **19**; *holewisken* **20** [see index 2, Hollish]
ora 'ridge, bank'. *wermes hore, berg hore* **21**
ortceard 'orchard'. *ðurh ðone ordceard, of þane ordcearde* **11**
oþer 'second, other'. *on þare oþer ea* **4**; *on þane oþerne beoit* **9**; *on þare oðere herepað* **11**; *on þane oþerne (stane)* **19**
oþer … oþer 'the one … the other'. **3**
oxa 'ox'. *oxene bricge* **15**

Pæga (pers. n.) *pegan beorh* **21**
pæð 'path'. *be weste hegen paðe* **8**; *strutheardes paþe, of þane paþe* **16**; *alfstanes paþ* **19**; *on þane ealde paþe, of þane paþe,* ? *hippepad, of þane pade* **30**
Pidele (river n.) see index 2, Piddle
Pimpern (river n.) see index 2
pirig 'pear tree'. *of seuen piþien, at seuen pirien, in to þe pyrien* **29**
pol 'pool'. *þe schort mannes pol* **16** [see index 2, Chapman's Pool]; *elmerespole, almerspol* **17**; *horspoles heauede* (bis) **18**; *seortmannes pol* **20** [see index 2, Chapman's Pool]; *poles leage* **28**; *onne þan pol, of þane pole* **30**

preost 'priest'. *prestes setel* **12**
Pumberig see index 2, Pomeroy
pundfald 'pinfold, pound'. *on midde þane punfald, of þane punfalde* **26**
pytt 'pit'. *ludmannes putte* **8**; *on þane pet, of þane pitte, on ðone pet* **11**; *on anne water pet, of þane pitte* **14**; *bican pet, þo tweie pettes, of þone petten* **30**
pyttel 'hawk'. *putel made* **27**

quabbe see **cwabba**

ræw 'row'. *þurh reowe* **2**; *on hlinc reawe* **5**; *on þat hlinc reawe* **6**; *on anne linc reawe* **16**; *on hlinc reawe* **21** [see also **hlinc-ræw**]
read 'red'. *þane reanden weg, þe reden wege* **3**; *þat rede clif* **4**; *þare rede hane* **9**; *þane red stan* **11**
riht 'direct, straight'. *þene richte herepath* **16**; *richt wege, iricht weg* **19**; *on þane richt wei* **20**
(ge)riht 'directly, straight'. *on irichte* **2, 10, 18, 19, 24**; *norð richte, uppen iricht, up iricht, of irichte, niþer irichte, uppen irichte, a irichte* **20**; *adun richt* **28**
ripel 'long strip (of woodland)'. *langen riple, and* (for *on*) *lang riple* **27**
risc, hrisc 'rush'. *on þat hrisclad, anlang þese richtledes* **12**; *anlang riscemeres* **14**; *þat ealden reshbed* **30**
rið 'small stream'. *alor riðe, anne aler riðe* **2**; *on ða riþe* **8**
rod, rodu 'linear clearing, road'. *on þo ealde rode, onlang rode* **19**; *rodelee* **28**
ruh 'rough, shaggy, uncultivated'. *ruwan þorn* **14**; *on þane rupemor* **20**; *þane rugen bergh* **30**
rum 'roomy, spacious'. *rumanhelle* **23** [see index 2, Rams Hill]

sæ 'sea'. *ut on sce, of sa* **16**; *on sa, of sa* **17**; *ut on se, of se* **19**; *of sa* **20**; *on se bergh, of seberghe* **30**
sæp 'sap, juice'. *sapcumbe* **28**
safine 'safine (a kind of juniper)'. *safandune* **16**; *sawendune* **19**
sand 'sand, gravel'. *sandhellesled* **8**; *sand ford* **21**
sceaga 'small wood, copse'. *lippen scagen* **21**
sceald 'shallow'. *scealden forde* **10**
sceamol 'shelf, ledge'. *to þane shamelen* **8**; *to þan scamelen, fram þanne scamelen* **24**
sceard 'gap'. *on þe sherd, of þene sherde, of þene shearde* **13**
scearp 'sharp, rough-surfaced'. *scearpenhame* **8**

Sc(e)ortmann (pers. n.) *scortencumb* 3; *þe schort mannes pol* 16; *seortmannes pol* 20 [see index 2, Chapman's Pool]

sceotan 'to shoot, to run (to)'. *þe schet to* 8; *ut sceoþaþ* 24; *scheth on Nodre* 28; *þe schet suthward* 29

scyl(en), obscure. *scyleford* 16; *scylenford* 19

scylf 'shelf'. *tor scylget, torchil gat* 21

sealh 'sallow, variety of willow tree'. *þane ealde seale* 13; *on þa seales, of þan sealen* 23

seaÐ 'pit, well'. *þas soces seaÐ, Ða chealc seÐas* 8; *elchene seaÐ* 21

seax 'dagger'. *on sex þorn, of sex þorne* 14

Seaxpenn see index 2, Pen Hill

self '(it)self'. *to þanen welle siluen* 8

Semene (river n.) see index 2, Sem

seofon 'seven'. *seuen willes þry* 20; *seuen diche suÐ ende* 21; *of seuen piþien, at seuen pirien* 29

setl 'dwelling'. *prestes setle* 12; *biken settle* 21

shetebergh 30 (for *ceatwanberge*)

sidinic, obscure. *sidinic mor* 28

siex 'six'. *sex made eres* 5, 6; *Ðane sex hide landimare* 21

sla 'sloe tree'. *wiÐ slahgraues* 4

slæd 'slade, valley'. *beteswirþe sled, sledwich, sledweie, sandhellesled* 8; *badherdes slede, dun slede* 11; *hecgan sled, of þane slede* 20; *oþes sledes northecge* 21; *onlang sledes* 23; *þat mere sled* 26

sloh 'slough, mire'. *Ðet rede sloh, of þane slo* 11

smæl 'narrow'. *smalencumbe* 19; *smale broke* (bis), *onne smal þornes* 21; *on Ða smale þornes* 23

Snell (pers. n.) *snelles hamme weghe* 8

Snod (pers. n.) *snodeshelle* 11

soc 'suck, sucking, ? draining'. *on þas soces seaÐ* 8 [see index 2, Washers Pit]

stan 'stone'. *anne stan castel* 5, 6; *wlleuestan, þane red stan, of þane stane, þe foer stanes* 11; *stanforde* 12; *þone ston istel* 13; *stanhecheres ande* (bis), *anlang stan dene* 14; *anne ston, of þanne stane, anne stan tor* 16; *on stanford, of stanforde* 17; *anne stanweal, stan wege* 19; *stanwei, anne stan wal, anne stan, of þane stane, þare stan* (bis) 20; *stanburne, 'stan scylien* 21; *stanweie* 28; *on þo stancysten, of þane stancyste* 30

stan-cyste ' ? heap of stones' (? corresponding to **stan-ceastel**). *on þo stancysten, of þane stancyste* 30

stanen 'made of stone'. *anne stanen wal* 19; *þat stanene bregge* 20

stanhecheres, obscure (perhaps **stan-(ge)hæg**). *stanhecheres ande* 14

stanig 'stony'. *þan stanegan crundel* 9

stan-scylig ' ? stony place'. *on stan scylien* 21

stapel (stapol) 'pole, post'. *anne stapel* 2; *wigheardes stapele* 8; *on þane stapel, of þanne stapele* 17; *wigerÐes stapel* 23

stede 'place, site'. *þane ealde treo stede* 12; *þannen mylen stede* 21

sticol 'steep'. *þa sticelen lane* 30

stigel 'stile'. *þare stigele* 8; *to stigel hege* 10; *þa stigele* 28

Stirchel, Styrd (river n.) see index 2

stoc 'place, farm'. *Stocbroc, Stokebroc* 12 [see index 2, Beechingstoke]; *stoc wey, stok wei* 18

stocc 'stump'. *þare holne stoke, of þane stocke* 20 [see also **heafod-stocc**]

stod-dic 'ditch associated with a stud'. *þe stod dic, þat northene stod dich* 19

stod-fald 'stud-fold, paddock'. *þan ealden stod-fald* 16; *þo ealde stodfald* 19

stræt 'street'. *brokene strate, anlang strate, on þat strate, of þare strate* 11; *þe elþen stret, of þare streate* 14; *onlang stret* 21

stream 'stream'. *anlang streames* 4; *anlang streames, up of streame* (bis) 5; *anlang streames* (bis), *up of streame, up on streame* 6; *anlang streames* 8, 9; *anlang streame* 12; *Cheselburne stream, of þane streame* (bis), *Deulisc stream* 13; *anlang streames* (bis) 14; *on þane stream, anlang streames* 15; *anlang streames, anlang streame* 16; *anlang streames* (bis) 18; *anlang Wicum streames, of þanne streame, anlang Wicun streames, of þat streame, on þare stream, anlang streames* (3 times), *on þare stream, anlang streames, of þane streame* 20; *andlang streames, anlang streames* 21; *anlang streames* 24; *Pidelen streame* (4 times) 26; *andlang stremes, anlang stremes* (bis) 28; *be streme, forÐ mid streme* 29; *Deueliscstream, anlang streames, bi streame* 30

Strutheard (pers. n.) *strutheardes paþe* 16; *struthgeardes cum, struthherdes wege* 20

Sture (river n.) see index 2

stybb 'stump'. *þone ellen stubb, on styb* 21; *anne þorn stub, of þane stubbe* 30

Styrd see index 2, Stirchel

sug(g)a 'swampy'. ? *sugging made* 10; *sucgimade hauede* 24

Sula (pers. n.) ? *sulan graf* 8 (or **syle**)

suÐ 'south, southward'. *suÐ* 4, 19; *be suÐe ceatwanberge* 6; *on Ðies littlen Seaxpennes suÐ eke* 8; *sudwde* 15; *seuen diche suÐ ende* 21; *hlosstedes crundeles suÐ ecge, on greten linkes suth ecge* 26; *suthames ford* 28

suÐweard 'southward, to the south of'. *suthward* 3, 9, 10; *to heldmannes wrthe suthward* 8; *on þone med ham suthwardne* 9; *on* ða holu suthward **13**; on efdeswelle suthward **15**; on deodewoldding lege supeward **27**; þe schet suthward **28**

sweora 'neck of land, col'. *on Swuren, ouer Swuran* **20** [see index 2, Swyre]

swin 'swine, pig'. *Suinleah* **4** [see index 2, Swindley]; *swindune* **5**; *swindone* **6**; *Swinbroch* **29** [see index 2, Swansbrook]

swylle 'sloppy mess, place where water flows freely'. *on swylles* **21**

syle, sylu 'boggy place'. ? *sulan graf* **8** (or **Sula**)

Tæppa (pers. n.) ? *teppen cnolle* **11** (or **tæppe**)

tæppe, 'band, ribbon, tape'. ? *teppen cnolle* **11** (or **Tæppa**)

Tata (pers. n.) *tatanbeorge* **9**

Tefleford see index 2, Tellisford

Terente, Terrente (river n.) see index 2, Tarrant

Theodwold (pers. n.) *deodewoldding lege, teopewolding lege* **27**

þorn 'thorn tree'. ? *on anne þoure, oð anne þorn*, ? *on anne þ* **2**; *cockes þorne* **9**; *to þane twam þornen, feden þorn, feden þorne* **11**; *ruwan þorn, of þane þorn, sex þorn, sex þorne, anne þorn þiuel* **14**; *of þa þornen, on anne þorne, on anne þorn* **19**; *on anne þorn, of þane þorne* **20**; *þornwelles, þane anlipien þorn, onne smal þornes, agen þorn* **21**; *ða smal þornes, on þane þorn, of þane þorne, þorndunes cnep, anne þorn stub* **30**

þoure (? for **þorn**) *on anne þoure* **2**

þri 'three'. *þry akeres, þrem landsharen* **10**

þryh 'trough'. *seuen willes þry* **20**

þung, 'poisonous plant, aconite'. *þung wylle* **21**

þweores 'traversely'. *þiyres* **9**; *þiers* **16**; *þweres ouer* **19**; *þwert ouer* **20**

þweores 'cross-wise, traverse'. *on þ þwers dich* **20**

þyfel 'thicket, bush'. *wiþig þeuel, anne þorn þiuel* **14**; *anne wiþig þefele* **16**; *þorþiuel, horþiuele, þane hordþivel, of þane þiuel* **30**

þyrne 'thorn-bush'. *þa ellen þirnen, of þere þirnen, inne þe þornen, of þare þyrnen* **30**

Tilbriht (pers. n.) *tilbirhthes ford* **17**

Tilluc (pers. n.) *tilluches lege* **21** [see index 2, Tinkley]

torr 'rocky crag'. *anne stan tor, of þan tore* **16**; *on tor scylget, on torchil gat* **21**; *þare haren torre* **30**

Tota (pers. n.) ? *totenberg* **21** (or **tote**)

tote 'lookout'. ? *totenberg* **21** (or **Tota**)

treow 'tree'. *bechilde treu* **11**; *þane ealde treo stede* **12**; *wermundes trew, wermundes tre* **28**; *on þo apeltreu, of þare apeltreu* **30**

tun 'enclosure, farmstead, village, estate'. *to*

þares tunes hirne **13**; on weritune, of wertune **14**; to þane tune **26**

twa 'two'. *þa two meades* **3**; *þane twam þornen* **10**

twegen 'two'. *þere tweie iberges* **11**; *þo tweie pettes* **30**

twelf 'twelve'. *be twelf aceron* **28**

twicen 'road-junction'. *to þere twichenen, of þere twichene* **28**

twifeald 'double'. *on þe twifelde dich* **13**

twisla 'fork in road'. *at þere weie itwislen* **21**

ufan 'above, at the top'. *at merewege uue* **21**

ufeweard 'upward, upper part of'. *berg hore uuewearde* **6**; *fideriches dene uuewearde, on waddene uuewarde* **21**

uppan 'up, upon'. *uppen irichte* (bis) **20**; *uppen morhelle, up an gretindune* **30**

wad 'woad'. ? *watdune beorch* (or **waþ**), *waddene* **21**

Wærmund (pers. n.) *wermundes trew, wermundes tre* **28**

wæter 'water'. *on anne water pet* **14**

waþ, 'hunting'. ? *watdune beorch* (or **wad**), *waddene* **21**

Wdebricge see index 2, Woodbridge

wealh 'Briton, slave'. *wealwege* **28** (or **weall**)

weall 'dyke, embankment'. *anne walle dich* **2**; *anne stanweal, of þanne walle, anne stanen wal, onlang walles* **19**; *anne walle, onlang walles, anne stan wal, of þane walle* **20**; ? *wealwege* **28** (or **wealh**)

weall-dic 'ditch with an embankment'. *anne walle dich* **2**

weg 'way'. *on þane reanden weg, on þe reden wege* **3**; *snelles hamme weghe, holewei, holleweie, sledwich, sledweie, hrigcsweg, anlang hricg weges, of rig wei, þe wines weie* **8**; *anlang higweges, of higeweges ande* **10**; *onlang weies* **11**; *anlang weies, anlang weges* **12**; *anlang hricge weges, wic weie, mearcweie, anlang weies* **13**; *anne weie, anlang weies* **14**; *on þare weilate* **16**; *stoc wei, stok wei* **18**; *richt wege, of þanne weie, stane wege, anlang weies, iricht wege, of þane iwege* **19**; *anne weg, of þane wege, stanwei, þane ealde weg, andlang weies, on þare wei, anlang weies, þane richt wei, of þane weie, struthherdes wege, of þane wege* **20**; *þanne ealden holeweg, offen weg* (bis), *þane imeren hole weg, to wege, andlang weges, þare weie itwislen, þone grene wai, merewege* **21**; *on þene weie, andlang weies* **23**; *be þe hege wege* **27**; *þane grene wei* (bis), *wealwege, hig wege, mearc wei, of þane wege, anlang weges, stanweie* **28**

well(a) (**welle, wille, wylle**) 'spring, stream'. *holenwelle, of þan welle, halgan weies* (for welles) *lake, to þanen wellen siluen* **8**; *Pimpernwelle* **9**; *gosanwelle* **11**; *botenwelle* **12**; *of hefdeswelle, on efdeswelle* **15**; *anlang welles* **16**; *lortenwille* **18**; *of þane welle* **19**; *alfricheswelle, of þane welle, on þane wal, anlang welles* (bis), *seuen willes þry* **20**; *þornwelles, holenwylle, hollenwelle, þung wylle* **21**; *bogen wylle, bokenwelle* **22**; *berteswelle* (bis), *on þone hwitenwelle, of þane welle* **30**

wer(i)tun, obscure. *on weritun, of wertun* **14**

Werleghe see index 2, Warleigh

west 'west(ward)'. *west be wintrintune, be weste hegen paðe, west anlang hegen* **8**; *be westen cockes þorne* **9**; *west* **11, 28**

westerne 'western'. *on þane westrene cumbe, seo westere landsceare* **16**; *þat westrene landimare* **19**

westwearde 'westwards'. *westward* **5, 6**

wic 'dwelling, farm, dairy-farm'. *anlang wic herepaþes* **9**; *one wic weie* **13**

Wican, Wicean, Wichen (river n.) see index 2, Wych

wice 'wych elm'. *wið ðere heren wike* **4**

wigeþen or **wigewen**, probably for **wiþigen**, 'associated with willows'. *of wigeþen* (or *wigewen*) *broke* **29**

Wigheard (pers. n.) *wigheardes stapele* **8**; *wigerðes stapel* **23**

Wilburh (fem. pers. n.) *wilburge imare* **28**

Wilig see index 2, Wylye

Wincawel, Wricawel (river n.) see index 2, Cale

windig 'windy'. ? *windee bergh* **14**

windrede, obscure. *wyndrede dic* **22**

wine 'friend'. *þe wines weie* **8**

wisce 'marshy meadow'. ? *alle wiscan, alle discan, olle discan, olle discan* **16**; *olle discan* **19**; *holewisken* **20** [see index 2, Hollish]

Witlege see index 2, Whitley

Wiuelesford see index 2, Wilsford

wiðig 'willow tree'. *wiþig þeuel* **14**; *anne wiþig þefele* **16**; *on þat withi begh, of þanne wiþibedde* **20**; *wiþig broch* **28**

wiðutan 'outside of'. *withuten accesleghe* **29**

woh 'crooked'. *anne wonalre* **24**

Worr (pers. n.) *worres berg* **9**

Wret (stream n., ? for **were**) *on wret, on[lon]ghes wret* **29** [see index 2, *Were*]

Wrindesholt see index 2, Holt

wudu 'wood, forest'. *wde* **8**; *þurch þane wde, littlen wde* **9**; *widesgate, anlang wides, anlang wdes* **13**; *wde* (bis) **14**; *sudwde* **15**; *þurch þane wde* **20**; *be wde* **23**; *þane ealde wdeforde, wdesfloda* **28**; *þanne wude* **29**

wulf 'wolf'. *wlfgedyce* (bis) **27**

Wulfgar (pers. n.) *wlgares imaren* **24**

Wulflaf (pers. n.) *wlleuestan* **11**

Wutenham see index 2, Wittenham

wyndrede, obscure. *on wyndrede dic* **22**

wyrm 'snake'. *wermes hore* **21**

wyrð 'farmstead, enclosure'. *beteswirþe sled, heldmannes wrthe, ealdmannes wyrðe* **8**; *ealdmannes wyrðe* (bis) **10**; *ealdmannes wyerðe* **23**; *eldmannes wrthe, eldemannes wyrðe* **24**

wyrtrume, wyrt-(t)ruma 'wood-bank'. *on wyrtruman* **2**; *be wintrintune, be wntrune, be wyrtrunne* **8**; *be wertrumen* **19**; *be wirtrume* (3 times) **21**; *be wirtrume* (bis), *be wirtrune* **27**

yrð, yrðland, see **ierð, ierðland**

4. LATIN GLOSSARY

The following abbreviations are used: n. = noun; v. = verb; adj. = adjective; adv. = adverb; p.p. = past participle.

accola (n.) [**30**]: inhabitant, native dweller

adiuuamen (n.) [**9**]: aid, service

adstipulatio (n.) [**14**]: assent, agreement

adstipulator (n.) [**2**]: one who agrees or assents

adtectus (p.p., adtexo) [**8**]: added

aduno (v.) [**12**]: ? to agree (verb of attestation)

agellus (n.) [**2, 16**]: land (*lit.* a small piece of land)

agius (adj., from Greek ἅγιος) [**10, 11, 13, 22, 23, 25, 30**]: holy

allubesco (v.) [**28**]: to be pleasing to

Angligena (n.) [**11, 14, 28**]: English-born man, Englishman

angustiatus (p.p., from *angustio*) [**29**]: distressed

anhelo (v.) [**21**]: to pant, gasp

antidotum (n.) [**29**]: antidote, remedy

antropos (n., from Greek ἄνθρωπος) [**9**]: man

apex (n.) [**15**]: letter, writing

appellamen (n.) [**30**]: name

appendicium (n.) [**19, 20**]: appendage, appurtenance

architectorius (adj., or possibly n.) [**10**]: creative, creating (*or perhaps simply* the Creator)

archon (n., from Greek ἄρχων) [9, 17]: ruler
attestor (v) [12]: to attest, corroborate

baratrum (n., from Greek βάραθρον) [24, 26, 27, 28]: hell
basileos, basileus, basilius, basyleos (n., from Greek βασιλεύς) [9, 11, 13, 19, 20, 24, 26, 27]: king
breuicula (n.) [8]: charter, document

calcetenus (adv.) [30]: to the full, to the end
caractus (n., for *cassatus*) [18]: a measure of land, a hide
caraxo (v., from Greek χαράσσω) [24, 26, 28]: to write
carrata, -us (n., for *cassatus*) [4, 8]: a measure of land, a hide
carta (n.) [15, 16, 18, 22, 23, 24, 25, 26, 30]: charter
carticula (n.) [27]: charter
cartula (n.) [1, 2, 3, 4, 5, 9, 28, 29, 30]: charter
cassatus (n.) [2, 3, 5, 22, 24, 25, 26, 30]: a measure of land, a hide (see also *caractus*, *carrata, -us*)
cateruatim (adv.) [9]: together, in a group
celebs (n.) [9]: virgin
celicus (adj.) [30]: heavenly
census (n.) [21]: tribute, tax
ceptra (n. pl., for *sceptra*) [12]: sceptre
cerraxo (v., from Greek χαράσσω) [30]: to write
cespes (n., for *cæspes*) [1]: sod of earth
chorus (n.) [21]: chorus, choir
Christicola (n.) [9]: Christian, worshipper of Christ
circumcingo (v.) [22, 29]: to enclose, bound
circumgiro (v.) [9, 10, 11, 12, 13, 14, 15, 16, 17, 18, 19, 20, 30]: to enclose, bound
clauiger (adj.) [22, 23, 25]: key-bearing (attribute of St Peter)
cleronomus (n., from Greek κληρονόμος) [24, 27]: heir
clipeum or *clipeus* (n.) [5]: shield, protection
clito, cliton (n., ultimately from Greek κλυτός) [18, 21]: ætheling
coarto, coarcto (v.) [19, 20]: to compel, constrain
coedificatio (n.) [10, 15, 16, 25]: construction, building up
cognosticus (n., error for *gnosticus*) [24]: wise man
collatio (n.) [15, 16]: speaking together, language
colonus (n.) [12]: inhabitant
commutatio (n.) [28]: exchange
complex (n.) [24, 26, 27]: accomplice, confederate

concurrens (n.) [8]: concurrent number, corresponding to a year-letter
condono (v.) [9]: to grant
confaueo (v.) [17]: to be favourable, protect
confugium (n.) [29]: place of refuge, a shelter
conrecito (v.) [17]: to recite, repeat
consecro (v.) [12]: to consecrate (verb of attestation)
consigillo (v.) [28, 29]: to attest
constipulatio (n., probably for *constipulator*) [17]: witness, testimony
constipulator (n.) [18]: witness
cordetenus (adv.) [22, 30]: to the heart
corrobatio (n.) [2]: confirmation, corroboration
cosmus, cousmus (n., from Greek κόσμος) [10, 24, 30]: the world, universe
cunctiparens (adj.) [10]: parent of all
curanculus (n., probably error for *curagulus*) [9]: guardian, ruler

dapsilitas (n.) [8]: bounty, generosity
debacacio (n., for *debacchatio*) [1]: fury, frenzy
deceptatio (n., for *disceptatio*) [1]: dispute
Deicola (n.) [9]: worshipper of God, Christian
deitas (n.) [11, 30]: divinity
demon (n.) [15]: evil spirit, demon
dictito (v.) [25]: to dictate, compose
discreptio (n., for *descriptio*) [9]: copy, document
discribo (v., for *describo*) [1]: to copy, draw up (a charter)
doxa (n., from Greek δόξα) [9]: glory

elemosina (n.) [29]: alms
elimentum (n., for *elementum*) [12]: created being
emolumentum, emulamentum (n.) [5, 26]: advantage, benefit
eon (n., for *aeon*) [10]: age, eternity
epacta (n.) [8]: epact
erumpna (n., for *aerumpna*) [12]: distress
erumpnosus (adj.) [29]: miserable, wretched
etara (n., from Greek ἕταρη) [9]: woman
excerpto (v.) [1]: to adapt, make an edited version of

facesco (v.) [13]: to pass away, come to an end
festus (adj.) [28]: festive, joyful
floccipendo (v.) [30]: to disregard, hold cheap
fluctiuagus (adj.) [29]: driven about by the waves
fona (n., from Greek φωνή) [13]: voice, word
fulcimentum (n.) [8]: prop, support
fylos (n., from Greek φίλος) [9]: friend

gehenna (n., here used in plural) [30]: hell

genealogia (n.) [10, 29]: kindred, family, off-spring

giro (v., see *gyro*) [24, 26, 27]: to go round, surround

gnosticus (n., ultimately from Greek γνωστι-κός) [27]: learned man

graphium (n.) [9, 12, 30]: writing, document

grauido (n.) [3]: burden

gustamen (n.) [30]: taste

habitamen (n.) [30]: dwelling, abode

heroicus (n.) [15]: lordly, noble

hida (n.) [6, 7]: hide

hierarchus (n., from Greek ἱεράρχης) [9]: leader, bishop

hirialis (adj., ? for *kirialis*, from Greek κυρος) [30]: lordly

icarisma, ikarisma (n., from Greek χάρισμα) [23, 25]: favour, bounty, grace (see also *karisma*)

ignominica (n. pl.) [22, and see 25]: shameful things, disgrace

impendo (v.) [5, 11, 30]: to grant

imperitio (n., for *impertitio*) [12]: an imparting

indeclinabiliter (adv.) [16, 19, 20, 22, 23, 25]: unalterably, unceasingly

indiculus (n.) [8]: document, charter

ingenitus (adj.) [28]: unbegotten

insulanus (n.) [28]: island-dweller

iugerum (n.) [25, 27]: a measure of land

karisma (n., from Greek χάρισμα) [21, 22]: favour, bounty, grace (see *icarisma*)

karus (n.) [22]: dear friend

kata (prep., from Greek κατα) [21]: according to, in relation to

latratus (n.) [8]: baying, howling

libellus (n.) [1, 30]: charter

litteratorius (adj.) [16]: pertaining to writing, literary

machinamentum (n.) [29]: plot, device

mancusa (n.) [16]: mancus (a gold coin or its equivalent in gold or silver, with a value of 30 silver pence)

manens (n.) [1, 2, 9]: a measure of land, a hide

mansa (n.) [10, 11, 12, 13, 14, 15, 16, 19, 20, 21, 23, 28]: unit of land, a hide

mansio (n.) [17]: a measure of land, a hide; [30]: place of abode, estate

messias (n.) [21]: Messiah

metropolitana (n.) [13]: archbishop

minoro (v.) [29]: to make smaller, diminish

monarchia (n., from Greek μοναρχία) [8, 28]: monarchy

monialis (n.) [8, 13, 26]: nun

monile (n.) [8]: necklace, collar

munia (n.pl., ? byform of *munera*) [19, 20]: ? gifts

musitacio (n., for *mussitatio*) [29]:? grumbling, muttering

nodo (v., perhaps inversion of *dono*) [9]: ? to give

numen (n.) [15]: ? patrimony

obsequiolum (n.) [18]: obedience, deference

ocellus (n.) [29]: eye

omnicreans (n.) [14, 30]: the All-Creator

onoma (n., from Greek ὄνομα) [26, 28, 29]: name

oramen (n.) [9]: prayer

paraclitus (n.) [28]: defender, protector

parasitus (n.) [30]: accomplice, adherent

pascualis (adj.) [17]: affording pasture

penninus (adj.) [14]: winged

percelebro (v.) [8]: to celebrate (divine service) in full

peripsema (n., from Greek περίψημα) [8]: offscouring, rubbish (*a word which owes its currency among draftsmen of charters to Aldhelm*)

perlustro (v.) [10]: to travel through

persisto (v.) [13, 15, 16]: to be, exist

perstrepo (v.) [8]: make a great noise, resound

perstringo (v.) [18]: to touch on, narrate

philargiria (n., from Greek φιλαργιρία) [30]: love of money

plebs (n.) [2]: people, subjects

postsessor (n.) [2]: ? possessor, ? later owner

pragma (n., from Greek πραγμα) [30]: thing

preconium (n.) [29]: announcing, proclaiming

predestino (v.) [12]: to determine (verb of attestation)

prefectus (n.) [1]: important man

prelatiuus (adj.) [10]: of the ruler

prepositus (n.) [28]: reeve

prerego (v.) [17]: to rule before or above

presul (n.) [22]: bishop

presignatus (adj.) [12]: aforementioned

prestulacio (n., for *prestolatio*) [12]: expectation

pretitulo (v.) [9]: ? to have a better title, to take precedence; [30]: to sign

preuaricatio (n.) [10, 29]: error, transgression

prima (n.) [8]: prime (first hour of the day)

primatus (n.) [10]: pre-eminence

primecherius, primicherius (n.) [17, 18]: chief, king

princeps (n.) [5]: ealdorman

principalis (adj.) [5]: pertaining to an ealdorman

principatus (n.) [16, 19, 20]: kingliness

procurator (n.) [8]: official, agent
prolongo (v.) [29]: ? to detain
propositum (n.) [12]: usage
proscribo (v.) [2]: to condemn
prothomartyr (n.) [2]: first martyr, St Stephen
protoplastus, -plaustus (n.) [10, 29, 30]: the first-created man, Adam
psalmodia (n.) [29]: psalmody, psalm-singing

quisquiliae (n.pl.) [8]: waste, rubbish (*a word which owes its currency among draftsmen of charters to Aldhelm*)

reprobus (n.) [13]: reprobate
rimo (v.) [24]: to examine, explore, investigate
roborator (n.) [25]: one who confirms or corroborates, a supporter
rotiger (adj.) [8]: revolving
roto (v.) [28]: to go round, surround
ruricula, -us (n.) [10, 21]: inhabitant of the country

sanctimonialis (n.) [7, 28, 29]: nun
sartago (n.) [15, 16, 30]: *lit.* a fryingpan; *by extension, an instrument of fiery torture, a furnace*
satago (v.) [10, 15, 16, 27, 29, 30]: to endeavour
scedula (n.) [2, 8, 29, 30]: charter
scripsiuncula (n.pl.) [2]: documentation
scriptura (n.) [1]: writing, charter
septiformis (adj.) [21]: sevenfold
serpentinus (adj.) [11]: diabolic
sigillo (v.) [21]: to confirm
sigillum (n.) [9, 10, 11, 12, 13, 14, 15, 16, 19, 20, 22, 23, 30]: mark, sign
signigrapha (n., probably for *syngrapha*) [5]: charter
signo (v.) [1]: to attest
solicola (n.) [8]: local inhabitant

soma (n., from Greek σωμα) [8]: body
sophia (n., from Greek σοφία) [24]: wisdom
stigma (n.) [28]: sign, mark
stoma (n.) (n., from Greek στόμα) [30]: mouth
subarro (v.) [13, 14]: to subscribe
subleuamen (n.) [13]: support, relief
sublimo (v.) [30]: to dignify (verb of attestation)
subtraho (v.) [1]: to withdraw, keep back
subtronizatus (p.p. *subthronizo*) [17, 30]: enthroned
supraeffatus (adj.) [1]: above-mentioned

tartarus (n., here used in plural) [12]: hell
terregenus (n.) [8]: earthborn
teter (adj., *taeter*) [15, 16, 30]: offensive, foul, loathsome
Theus (n., from Greek θεός) [10]: God
thorus (n., see *torus*) [30]: marriage-bed
titulo (v.) [9]: to inscribe
torpitudo (n.) [23]: ? weariness
totillo (v.) [8]: to totter
tripudium (n.) [9]: mark, sign; [30]: jubiliation
tropheum (n.) [10, 11, 12, 13, 21]: sign (of cross)

utensilis (n.) [24, 26, 27]: appurtenance

uassallus (n.) [12]: vassal
uendico (v.) [1]: to have a legal claim to
ueridicus (adj.) [24, 30]: truth-telling
uexillum (n.) [30]: sign
uesagii (n.pl., perhaps for *uesagia*) [19, 20]: utterances ? (19 has *uestigii*, probably in error)
uocamen (n.) [23, 25, 28]: name
uolumen (n.) [19, 20]: charter

ymera (n. from Greek ἡμέρα) [30]: day

zabulicus (adj., ultimately from Greek διάβολος) [30]: diabolic, devilish

DIPLOMATIC INDEX

I. *Verbal Invocations*

Altitrono in eternum regnante 24
Conditore creaturarum uniuersalium 29
Domino dominorum dominante in secula seculorum 22, 25
In nomine Dei et Domini nostri Iesu Christi ueri redemptoris mundi 14
In nomine Dei summi et altissimi Iesu Christi 16
In nomine Domini nostri Iesu Christi 2, 19, 20

In nomine Domini nostri Iesu Christi saluatoris 1, 23
In nomine trine et une deitatis 12
In trino superne deitatis nomine 30
O altithroni genitoris ingeniti eiusdemque natiui diuinitus 28
Rege(m) regum Dominoque dominorum regnorum regnum 9
Regnante Deo imperpetuum architectorio 11
Regnante Domino nostro Iesu Christo 15

Regnante imperpetuum Deo et Domino Iesu
  Christo **3**
Regnante imperpetuum Domino nostro Iesu
  Christo **4, 5, 6, 13**
Regnante Theo in eona eonum **10**

2. *Proems*

Apostolicis imbuti uesagiis quos quodam olim
  in tempore **19, 20**
Beantis uniuersorum uoce monemur preclara
  16
Cuncta seculorum patrimonia incertis nepotum heredibus **26**
Ea que secundum ecclesiasticam disciplinam
  1
Ea que secundum legem canonicam ac dis-
  positionem **23**
Flebilia fortiter detestanda totillantis seculi
  piacula **8**
Filiis adoptionis non iam uetuste configuratis
  28
Mundi huius labentibus properanter temporibus **15**
Neminem quippe in mortali solo quamuis uniuersam cousmi seriem **10**
Omnia que uidentur temporalia sunt et que
  non uidentur eterna sunt **5**
Omnipotens celi terreque in principio creator
  21
Omnipotens supernare temporaliumque uerus
  arbiter **12**

Omnium iura regnorum celestium atque terrestrium **27**
Regna regnorum huius presentis seculi transeant **22, 25**
Sacre autem scripture edicta fona catholicorum patrum **13**
Uniuersarum conditor gubernatorque rerum
  30
Uniuersis sophie studium intento mentis conamine **24**

3. *Dispositive Words*

(a) *Past tense*
concessi **13, 18**
donaui **14**
largitus sum **24, 27**
litteratoriis apicibus roboraui quod . . . tradidi
  16
tradendo concessi **15**

(b) *Present tense*
concedo **17, 22, 25, 28**
dono **12**
dono atque concedo **3, 4**
forgiue and selle **6**
impendo **5, 30**
offero **21, 29**
tribuendo condono **9, 10**
tribuo **8, 19, 20**

(c) *Subjunctive*
donare decreuerim **1**
impenderem **11**

4. *Royal Styles*

	(A) *Dispositive clause*	(B) *Subscription*
Ecgberht **2**	gratia Dei occidentalium Saxonum rex	rex
Æthelbald **3**	gratia Dei occidentalium Saxonum rex	rex
Æthelberht **4**	gratia Dei occidentalium <Saxonum> rex	rex
Æthelred **5**	Deo donante Saxonum rex	rex
Æthelred **6**	mid Godes giue Westsaxne king	rex
Alfred **7**	king	
Æthelstan **8**	rex Anglorum per omnipotentis dex-teram totius Britannie regni solio sub-limatus	singularis priuilegii mon-archia preditus rex
Æthelstan **9**	nodante Dei gratia basileos Anglorum et eque totius Britannie orbis De-icolarumque fylos atque curanculus	gratia Dei rex Anglorum

Æthelstan **10**	rex diuina fauente gratia totius Britannie primatum regalis regiminis obtinens	rex totius Britannie
Eadmund **11**	nutu Dei gratia basileos Anglorum	rex Anglorum
Eadmund **12**	ex regali progenie Deo annuente regenteque super Angligenas aliasque gentes in circuitu habitantes rex ordinatus	Anglicarum aliarumque nationum rex
Eadmund **13**	fauente superno numine basyleos industrius Anglorum rex ceterarumque gentium in circuitu persistentium	rex Anglorum
Eadmund **14**	omnicreantis disponente clementia Angligenarum omniumque gencium undique secus habitantium rex	rex Anglorum
Eadmund **15**	rex Anglorum ceterarumque gentium in circuitu persistentium	rex Anglorum
Eadred **16**	rex Anglorum ceterarumque gentium in circuitu persistentium gubernator et rector	rex Anglorum
Eadred **17**	rex Christo perpetualiter superne numinis intuitu subtronizato preregente et eque illo confauente totius Albionis primecherius	
Eadred **18**	diuina gratia fauente rex et primecherius totius Albionis	
Eadwig **19, 20**	basileos Anglorum huiusque insule barbarorum	rex Anglorum
Eadwig **21**	gratia Dei rex Anglorum	rex
Eadwig **22, 23**	rex Anglorum gubernator et rector	rex Anglorum
Edgar **24**	totius Britannie basilius	rex Anglorum
Edgar **25**	rex Anglorum ceterarumque gentium in circuitu persistentium gubernator et rector	rex Anglorum
Edgar **26, 27**	totius Britannie basileus	rex Anglorum
Æthelred **28**	regionis Angligenarum rex	rex Anglorum
Æthelred **29**	rex Anglorum	rex
Cnut **30**	telluris Britannie totius largiflua Dei gracia subpetente subtronizatus rex ac rector	gratia Dei prestante rex